## GMS INTENSIVE METHOD
### Glossika Mass Sentences

Features: Sound files have A/B/C formats.

| A Files | English - Target language 2x |
|---------|------------------------------|
| B Files | English - space - Target 1x |
| C Files | Target language only 1x |

 Useful for students with more time to dedicate.

GW01035568

Fe…
al…
ev…
fo…
Requires less than 20 minutes daily.

Useful for people with busy schedules and limited study time.

---
## HOW TO USE
---

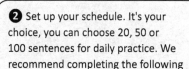

❶ To familiarise yourself with IPA and spelling, Glossika recommends using the book while listening to A or C sound files and going through all 1000 sentences on your first day. Then you can start your training.

❷ Set up your schedule. It's your choice, you can choose 20, 50 or 100 sentences for daily practice. We recommend completing the following four steps.

 Training Step **1**: Try repeating the sentences with the same speed and intonation in the A sound files.

.................................................

 Training Step **2**: Dictation: use the C sound files (and pausing) to write out each sentence (in script or IPA or your choice). Use the book to check your answers.

.................................................

 Training Step **3**: Recording: record the sentences as best you can. We recommend recording the same sentences over a 3-day period, and staggering them with new ones.

.................................................

 Training Step **4**: Use the B sound files to train your interpretation skills. Say your translation in the space provided.

❷ Set up your schedule. You can listen to a single GSR file daily or even double up. One book typically takes 3-4 months to complete.

❸ You can accompany with the GMS training when you have extra time to practice.

---
## Reminder
---

Don't forget that if you run into problems, just skip over it! Keep working through the sentences all the way to the end and don't worry about the ones you don't get. You'll probably get it right the second time round. Remember, one practice session separated by *one* sleep session yields the best results!

Features: Our sound files include an
algorithm that introduces 10 sentences
every day, with review of 40 sentences,
for a total of 1000 sentences in 104 days.

## HOW TO USE

# Glossika Mass Sentences

## French

## Fluency 2

Complete Fluency Course

Michael Campbell

Maxime Paquin

Glossika

# Glossika Mass Sentence Method

## French Fluency 2

First published : NOV 2015
via license by Nolsen Bédon, Ltd.
Taipei, Taiwan

Authors: Michael Campbell, Maxime Paquin
Chief Editor: Michael Campbell
Translator: Michael Campbell, Maxime Paquin
Recording: Michael Campbell, Maxime Paquin
Editing Team: Claudia Chen, Sheena Chen
Consultant: Percy Wong
Programming: Edward Greve
Design: Glossika team

glossika.com

# Glossika Series

The following languages are available (not all are published in English):

## Afroasiatic

AM Amharic
ARE Egyptian Arabic
HA Hausa
IV Hebrew
AR Modern Standard Arabic
ARM Moroccan Arabic

## Altaic

AZ Azerbaijani
JA Japanese
KK Kazakh
KR Korean
MN Mongolian
UZ Uzbek

## Austroasiatic

KH Khmer
VNN Vietnamese (Northern)
VNS Vietnamese (Southern)

## Austronesian

AMP Amis
TYS Atayal
BNN Bunun
ILO Ilokano
SDQ Seediq
TGL Tagalog
THW Thao

## Caucasian

## Dravidian

KAN Kannada
MAL Malayalam
TAM Tamil
TEL Telugu

## IE: Baltic

LAV Latvian
LIT Lithuanian

## IE: Celtic

CYM Welsh

## IE: Germanic

EN American English
DA Danish
NL Dutch
DE German
IS Icelandic
NO Norwegian
SV Swedish

## IE: Indo-Iranian

BEN Bengali
PRS Dari Persian
GUJ Gujarati
HI Hindi
KUR Kurmanji Kurdish
MAR Marathi
NEP Nepali
FA Persian
PAN Punjabi (India)
SIN Sinhala
KUS Sorani Kurdish
TGK Tajik
UR Urdu

## IE: Other

SQ Albanian
HY Armenian
EU Basque
EO Esperanto
EL Greek

## IE: Romance

PB Brazilian Portuguese
ES Castilian Spanish
CA Catalan
PT European Portuguese
FR French
IT Italian
ESM Mexican Spanish
RO Romanian

## IE: Slavic

BEL Belarusian
BOS Bosnian
HR Croatian
CS Czech
MK Macedonian
PL Polish
RU Russian
SRP Serbian
SK Slovak
SL Slovene
UKR Ukrainian

## Kartuli

KA Georgian

## Niger-Congo

SW Swahili
YO Yoruba

## Sino-Tibetan

MY Burmese
YUE Cantonese
ZH Chinese
HAK Hakka
ZS Mandarin Chinese (Beijing)
WUS Shanghainese
MNN Taiwanese
WUW Wenzhounese

## Tai-Kadai

LO Lao
TH Thai

## Uralic

EST Estonian
FI Finnish
HU Hungarian

# Glossika Levels

Many of our languages are offered at different levels (check for availability):

| Intro Level | Fluency Level | Expression Level |
|---|---|---|
| Pronunciation Courses | Fluency | Business Courses |
| Intro Course | Daily Life | Intensive Reading |
| | Travel | |
| | Business Intro | |

# Getting Started

## For Busy People & Casual Learners

- 20 minutes per day, 3 months per book
- Use the Glossika Spaced Repetition (GSR) MP3 files, 1 per day. The files are numbered for you.
- Keep going and don't worry if you miss something on the first day, you will hear each sentence more than a dozen times over a 5 day period.

## For Intensive Study

- 1-2 hours per day, 1 month per book

Log on to our website and download the Self Study Planner at: glossika.com/howto.

Steps:

1. Prepare (GMS-A). Follow the text as you listen to the GMS-A files (in 'GLOSSIKA-XX-GMS-A'). Listen to as many sentences as you can, and keep going even when you miss a sentence or two. Try to focus on the sounds and matching them to the text.
2. Listen (GMS-A). Try to repeat the target sentence with the speaker the second time you hear it.
3. Write (GMS-C). Write down the sentences as quickly as you can, but hit pause when you need to. Check your answers against the text.
4. Record (GMS-C). Listen to each sentence and record it yourself. Record from what you hear, not from reading the text. You can use your mobile phone or computer to do the recording. Play it back, and try to find the differences between the original and your recording.
5. Interpret (GMS-B). Try to recall the target sentence in the gap after you hear it in English. Try to say it out loud, and pause if necessary.

# Glossika Mass Sentence Method

## French

## Fluency 2

This GMS Fluency Series accompanies the GMS recordings and is a supplementary course assisting you on your path to fluency. This course fills in the fluency training that is lacking from other courses. Instead of advancing in the language via grammar, GMS builds up sentences and lets students advance via the full range of expression required to function in the target language.

GMS recordings prepare the student through translation and interpretation to become proficient in speaking and listening.

Glossika Spaced Repetition (GSR) recordings are strongly recommended for those who have trouble remembering the content. Through the hundred days of GSR training, all the text in each of our GMS publications can be mastered with ease.

# What is Glossika?

From the creation of various linguists and polyglots headed by Michael Campbell, Glossika is a comprehensive and effective system that delivers speaking and listening training to fluency.

It's wise to use Glossika training materials together with your other study materials. Don't bet everything on Glossika. Always use as many materials as you can get your hands on and do something from all of those materials daily. These are the methods used by some of the world's greatest polyglots and only ensures your success.

If you follow all the guidelines in our method you can also become proficiently literate as well. But remember it's easier to become literate in a language that you can already speak than one that you can't.

Most people will feel that since we only focus on speaking and listening, that the Glossika method is too tough. It's possible to finish one of our modules in one month, in fact this is the speed at which we've been training our students for years: 2 hours weekly for 4 weeks is all you need to complete one module. Our students are expected to do at least a half hour on their own every day through listening, dictation, and recording. If you follow the method, you will have completed 10,000 sentence repetitions by the end of the month. This is sufficient enough to start to feel your fluency come out, but you still have a long way to go.

This training model seems to fit well with students in East Asia learning tough languages like English, because they are driven by the fact that they need a better job or have some pressing issue to use their English. This drive makes them want to succeed.

Non-East Asian users of the Glossika Mass Sentence (GMS) methods are split in two groups: those who reap enormous benefit by completing the course, and others who give up because it's too tough to stick to the schedule. If you feel like our training is too overwhelming or demands too much of your time, then I suggest you get your hands on our Glossika Spaced Repetition (GSR) audio files which are designed for people like you. So if you're ambitious, use GMS. If you're too busy or can't stick to a schedule, use GSR.

# Glossika Levels

The first goal we have in mind for you is Fluency. Our definition of fluency is simple and easy to attain: speaking full sentences in one breath. Once you achieve fluency, then we work with you on expanding your expression and vocabulary to all areas of language competency. Our three levels correlate to the European standard:

- Introduction = A Levels
- Fluency = B Levels
- Expression = C Levels

The majority of foreign language learners are satisfied at a B Level and a few continue on. But the level at which you want to speak a foreign language is your choice. There is no requirement to continue to the highest level, and most people never do as a B Level becomes their comfort zone.

# Glossika Publications

Each Glossika publication comes in four formats:

- Print-On-Demand paperback text
- E-book text (available for various platforms)
- Glossika Mass Sentence audio files
- Glossika Spaced Repetition audio files

Some of our books include International Phonetic Alphabet (IPA) as well. Just check for the IPA mark on our covers.

We strive to provide as much phonetic detail as we can in our IPA transcriptions, but this is not always possible with every language.

As there are different ways to write IPA, our books will also let you know whether it's an underlying pronunciation (phonemic) with these symbols: / /, or if it's a surface pronunciation (phonetic) with these symbols: [ ].

IPA is the most scientific and precise way to represent the sounds of foreign languages. Including IPA in language training guides is taking a step away from previous decades of language publishing. We embrace the knowledge now available to everybody via online resources like Wikipedia which allow anybody to learn the IPA: something that could not be done before without attending university classes.

To get started, just point your browser to Wikipedia's IPA page to learn more about pronouncing the languages we publish.

# 4 Secrets of the Mass Sentence Method

When learning a foreign language it's best to use full sentences for a number of reasons:

1. Pronunciation—In languages like English, our words undergo a lot of pronunciation and intonation changes when words get strung together in sentences which has been well analyzed in linguistics. Likewise it is true with languages like Chinese where the pronunciations and tones from individual words change once they appear in a sentence. By following the intonation and prosody of a native speaker saying a whole sentence, it's much easier to learn rather than trying to say string each word together individually.

2. Syntax—the order of words, will be different than your own language. Human thought usually occurs in complete ideas. Every society has developed a way to express those ideas linearly by first saying what happened (the verb), or by first saying who did it (the agent), etc. Paying attention to this will accustom us to the way others speak.

3. Vocabulary—the meanings of words, never have just one meaning, and their usage is always different. You always have to learn words in context and which words they're paired with. These are called collocations. To "commit a crime" and to "commit to a relationship" use two different verbs in most other languages. Never assume that learning "commit" by itself will give you the answer. After a lifetime in lexicography, Patrick Hanks "reached the alarming conclusion that words don't have meaning," but rather that "definitions listed in dictionaries can be regarded as presenting meaning potentials rather than meanings as such." This is why collocations are so important.

4. Grammar—the changes or morphology in words are always in flux. Memorizing rules will not help you achieve fluency. You have to experience them as a native speaker says them, repeat them as a native speaker would, and through mass amount of practice come to an innate understanding of the inner workings of a language's morphology. Most native speakers can't explain their own grammar. It just happens.

# How to Use GMS and GSR

The best way to use GMS is to find a certain time of day that works best for you where you can concentrate. It doesn't have to be a lot of time, maybe just 30 minutes at most is fine. If you have more time, even better. Then schedule that time to be your study time every day.

Try to tackle anywhere from 20 to 100 sentences per day in the GMS. Do what you're comfortable with.

Review the first 50 sentences in the book to get an idea of what will be said. Then listen to the A files. If you can, try to write all the sentences down from the files as dictation without looking at the text. This will force you to differentiate all the sounds of the language. If you don't like using the A files, you can switch to the C files which only have the target language.

After dictation, check your work for any mistakes. These mistakes should tell you a lot that you will improve on the next day.

Go through the files once again, repeating all the sentences. Then record yourself saying all the sentences. Ideally, you should record these sentences four to five days in a row in order to become very familiar with them.

All of the activities above may take more than one day or one setting, so go at the pace that feels comfortable for you.

If this schedule is too difficult to adhere to, or you find that dictation and recording is too much, then take a more relaxed approach with the GSR files. The GSR files in most cases are shorter than twenty minutes, some go over due to the length of the sentences. But this is the perfect attention span that most people have anyway. By the end of the GSR files you should feel pretty tired, especially if you're trying to repeat everything.

The GSR files are numbered from Day 1 to Day 100. Just do one every day, as all the five days of review sentences are built in. It's that simple! Good luck.

# Sentence Mining

Sentence mining can be a fun activity where you find sentences that you like or feel useful in the language you're learning. We suggest keeping your list of sentences in a spreadsheet that you can re-order how you wish.

It's always a good idea to keep a list of all the sentences you're learning or mastering. They not only encompass a lot of vocabulary and their actual usage, or "collocations", but they give you a framework for speaking the language. It's also fun to keep track of your progress and see the number of sentences increasing.

Based on many tests we've conducted, we've found that students can reach a good level of fluency with only a small number of sentences. For example, with just 3000 sentences, each trained 10 times over a period of 5 days, for a total of 30,000 sentences (repetitions), can make a difference between a completely mute person who is shy and unsure how to speak and a talkative person who wants to talk about everything. More importantly, the reps empower you to become a stronger speaker.

The sentences we have included in our Glossika courses have been carefully selected to give you a wide range of expression. The sentences in our fluency modules target the kinds of conversations that you have discussing day-to-day activities, the bulk of what makes up our real-life conversations with friends and family. For some people these sentences may feel really boring, but these sentences are carefully selected to represent an array of discussing events that occur in the past, the present and the future, and whether those actions are continuous or not, even in languages where such grammar is not explicitly marked—especially in these languages as you need to know how to convey your thoughts. The sentences are transparent enough that they give you the tools to go and create dozens of more sentences based on the models we give you.

As you work your way through our Fluency Series the sentences will cover all aspects of grammar without actually teaching you grammar. You'll find most of the patterns used in all the tenses and aspects, passive and active (or ergative as is the case in some languages we're developing), indirect speech, and finally describing events as if to a policeman. The sentences also present some transformational patterns you can look out for. Sometimes we have more than one way to say something in our own language, but maybe only one in a foreign language. And the opposite is true where we may only have one way to say something whereas a foreign language may have many.

# Transformation Drills

A transformation is restating the same sentence with the same meaning, but using different words or phrasing to accomplish this. A transformation is essentially a translation, but inside the same language. A real example from Glossika's business module is:

- Could someone help me with my bags?
- Could I get a hand with these bags?

You may not necessarily say "hand" in a foreign language and that's why direct translation word-for-word can be dangerous. As you can see from these two sentences, they're translations of each other, but they express the same meaning.

To express yourself well in a foreign language, practice the art of restating everything you say in your mother language. Find more ways to say the same thing.

There are in fact two kinds of transformation drills we can do. One is transformation in our mother language and the other is transformation into our target language, known as translation.

By transforming a sentence in your own language, you'll get better at transforming it into another language and eventually being able to formulate your ideas and thoughts in that language. It's a process and it won't happen over night. Cultivate your ability day by day.

Build a bridge to your new language through translation. The better you get, the less you rely on the bridge until one day, you won't need it at all.

Translation should never be word for word or literal. You should always aim to achieve the exact same feeling in the foreign language. The only way to achieve this is by someone who can create the sentences for you who already knows both languages to such fluency that he knows the feeling created is exactly the same.

In fact, you'll encounter many instances in our GMS publications where sentences don't seem to match up. The two languages are expressed completely differently, and it seems it's wrong. Believe us, we've not only gone over and tested each sentence in real life situations, we've even refined the translations several times to the point that this is really how we speak in this given situation.

# Supplementary Substitution Drills

Substitution drills are more or less the opposite of transformation drills. Instead of restating the same thing in a different way, you're saying a different thing using the exact same way. So using the example from above we can create this substitution drill:

- Could someone help me with my bags?
- Could someone help me with making dinner?

In this case, we have replaced the noun with a gerund phrase. The sentence has a different meaning but it's using the same structure. This drill also allows the learner to recognize a pattern how to use a verb behind a preposition, especially after being exposed to several instances of this type.

We can also combine transformation and substitution drills:

- Could someone help me with my bags?
- Could someone give me a hand with making dinner?

So it is encouraged that as you get more and more experience working through the Glossika materials, that you not only write out and record more and more of your own conversations, but also do more transformation and substitution drills on top of the sentences we have included in the book.

# Memory, The Brain, and Language Acquisition

by Michael Campbell

We encounter a lot of new information every day that may or may not need to be memorized. In fact, we're doing it all the time when we make new friends, remembering faces and other information related to our friends.

After some experience with language learning you'll soon discover that languages are just like a social landscape. Except instead of interconnected friends we have interconnected words. In fact, looking at languages in this way makes it a lot more fun as you get familiar with all the data.

Since languages are natural and all humans are able to use them naturally, it only makes sense to learn languages in a natural way. In fact studies have found, and many students having achieved fluency will attest to, the fact that words are much easier to recognize in their written form if we already know them in the spoken form. Remember that you already own the words you use to speak with. The written form is just a record and it's much easier to transfer what you know into written form than trying to memorize something that is only written.

Trying to learn a language from the writing alone can be a real daunting task. Learning to read a language you already speak is not hard at all. So don't beat yourself up trying to learn how to read a complicated script like Chinese if you have no idea how to speak the language yet. It's not as simple as one word = one character. And the same holds true with English as sometimes many words make up one idea, like "get over it".

What is the relationship between memory and sleep? Our brain acquires experiences throughout the day and records them as memories. If these memories are too common, such as eating lunch, they get lost among all the others and we find it difficult to remember one specific memory from the others. More importantly such memories leave no impact or impression on us. However, a major event like a birth or an accident obviously leaves a bigger impact. We attach importance to those events.

Since our brain is constantly recording our daily life, it collects a lot of useless information. Since this information is both mundane and unimportant to us, our brain has a built-in mechanism to deal with it. In other words, our brains dump the garbage every day. Technically speaking our memories are connections between our nerve cells and these connections lose strength if they are not recalled or used again.

During our sleep cycles our brain is reviewing all the events of the day. If you do not recall those events the following day, the memory weakens. After three sleep cycles, consider a memory gone if you haven't recalled it. Some memories can be retained longer because you may have anchored it better the first time you encountered it. An anchor is connecting your memory with one of your senses or another pre-existing memory. During your language learning process, this won't happen until later in your progress. So what can you do in the beginning?

A lot of memory experts claim that making outrageous stories about certain things they're learning help create that anchor where otherwise none would exist. Some memory experts picture a house in their mind that they're very familiar with and walk around that house in a specific pre-arranged order. Then all the objects they're memorizing are placed in that house in specific locations. In order to recall them, they just walk around the house.

I personally have had no luck making outrageous stories to memorize things. I've found the house method very effective but it's different than the particular way I use it. This method is a form of "memory map", or spatial memory, and for me personally I prefer using real world maps. This probably originates from my better than average ability to remember maps, so if you can, then use it! It's not for everybody though. It really works great for learning multiple languages.

What do languages and maps have in common? Everything can be put on a map, and languages naturally are spoken in locations and spread around and change over time. These changes in pronunciations of words creates a word history, or etymology. And by understanding how pronunciations change over time and where populations migrated, it's quite easy to remember a large number of data with just a memory map. This is how I anchor new languages I'm learning. I have a much bigger challenge when I try a new language family. So I look for even deeper and longer etymologies that are shared between language families, anything to help me establish a link to some core vocabulary. Some words like "I" (think Old English "ic") and "me/mine" are essentially the same roots all over the world from Icelandic (Indo-European) to Finnish (Uralic) to Japanese (Altaic?) to Samoan (Austronesian).

I don't confuse languages because in my mind every language sounds unique and has its own accent and mannerisms. I can also use my memory map to position myself in the location where the language is spoken and imagine myself surrounded by the people of that country. This helps me adapt to their expressions and mannerisms, but more importantly, eliminates interference from other languages. And when I mentally set myself up in this way, the chance of confusing a word from another language simply doesn't happen.

When I've actually used a specific way of speaking and I've done it several days in a row, I know that the connections in my head are now strengthening and taking root. Not using them three days in a row creates a complete loss, however actively using them (not passively listening) three days in a row creates a memory that stays for a lifetime. Then you no longer need the anchors and the memory is just a part of you.

You'll have noticed that the Glossika training method gives a translation for every sentence, and in fact we use translation as one of the major anchors for you. In this way 1) the translation acts as an anchor, 2) you have intelligible input, 3) you easily start to recognize patterns. Pattern recognition is the single most important skill you need for learning a foreign language.

A lot of people think that translation should be avoided at all costs when learning a foreign language. However, based on thousands of tests I've given my students over a ten-year period, I've found that just operating in the foreign language itself creates a false sense of understanding and you have a much higher chance of hurting yourself in the long run by creating false realities.

I set up a specific test. I asked my students to translate back into their mother tongue (Chinese) what they heard me saying. These were students who could already hold conversations in English. I found the results rather shocking. Sentences with certain word combinations or phrases really caused a lot of misunderstanding, like "might as well" or "can't do it until", resulted in a lot of guesswork and rather incorrect answers.

If you assume you can think and operate in a foreign language without being able to translate what's being said, you're fooling yourself into false comprehension. Train yourself to translate everything into your foreign language. This again is an anchor that you can eventually abandon when you become very comfortable with the new language.

Finally, our brain really is a sponge. But you have to create the structure of the sponge. Memorizing vocabulary in a language that you don't know is like adding water to a sponge that has no structure: it all flows out.

In order to create a foreign language structure, or "sponge", you need to create sentences that are natural and innate. You start with sentence structures with basic, common vocabulary that's easy enough to master and start building from there. With less than 100 words, you can build thousands of sentences to fluency, slowly one by one adding more and more vocabulary. Soon, you're speaking with natural fluency and you have a working vocabulary of several thousand words.

If you ever learn new vocabulary in isolation, you have to start using it immediately in meaningful sentences. Hopefully sentences you want to use. If you can't make a sentence with it, then the vocabulary is useless.

Vocabulary shouldn't be memorized haphazardly because vocabulary itself is variable. The words we use in our language are only a tool for conveying a larger message, and every language uses different words to convey the same message. Look for the message, pay attention to the specific words used, then learn those words. Memorizing words from a wordlist will not help you with this task.

Recently a friend showed me his wordlist for learning Chinese, using a kind of spaced repetition flashcard program where he could download a "deck". I thought it was a great idea until I saw the words he was trying to learn. I tried explaining that learning these characters out of context do not have the meanings on his cards and they will mislead him into a false understanding, especially individual characters. This would only work if they were a review from a text he had read, where all the vocabulary appeared in real sentences and a story to tell, but they weren't. From a long-term point of view, I could see that it would hurt him and require twice as much time to re-learn everything. From the short-term point of view, there was definitely a feeling of progress and mastery and he was happy with that and I dropped the issue.

# French Background and Pronunciation

- **Classification:** Indo-European Language Family - Romance Branch
- **Writing:** Latin

- **Consonants:**

  /p b f v m t d s z l n ʃ ʒ j ɲ ɥ k g ʁ w/ Unvoiced stops (p, t, k) are not aspirated /pᵓ tᵓ kᵓ/ different from English.

- **Vowels:**

  /i y u e ø ə o ɛ œ ɔ ɛ̃ ɔ̃ ɑ̃ a ɑ/

- **IPA:** Phonetic transcription showing liaison

- **Intonation:** Mostly word-final and even phrase-final
- **Word Order:** Subject - Verb - Object
- **Adjective Order:** Noun - Adjective
- **Possessive Order:** Genitive - Noun
- **Adposition Order:** Preposition - Noun
- **Dependent Clause:** Dependent - Noun, Noun - Relative Clause
- **Verbs:** Tense (present, past, future), Aspect (perfect, imperfect), Mood (indicative, subjunctive)
- **Nouns:** 2 genders, definite/indefinite
- **Pronouns:** 1st/2nd/3rd, masc/feminine/neuter, singular/plural, reflexive, 6 conjugations

## Classification

French is closely related to the other Romance languages (languages of the Romans) descended from Latin. Historically all of these languages are generalisations of a dialect continuum from Italy up to France and then down to the Iberian peninsula where Catalan, Spanish and Portuguese are spoken. Today we like to give things labels such as "language" or "dialect", but the difference between them can cause disputes. Historically, there were only dialects. It wasn't until nation states sprung up and communication required a standard that languages were standardized, usually based on the "dialect" of the capital city. In some countries like Italy, when it was unified in the 19th century a national language was created with bits and pieces from various dialects spoken around the new "country". These national, standardized "languages" become a nation's identity to the rest of the world.

So as we can identify a central position among a dialectal region, perhaps a place of commerce or larger city, the speech of areas between these places of commerce become dialectal grey areas where the continuum blends slowly into the next. So from the northern region of Italy where people speak a national Italian language and a local dialect, they can just as easily switch between their local dialect and the neighboring French language, simply because their dialect is at the halfway point between the two national languages. Likewise those in southern France may also be able to communicate with Italians in the border areas. In southern France one finds the language of the "Ocs" because they say "òc" instead of "oui" for the word "yes". This language, Occitan (or Provençal) has its own dialectal regions, but it is gradually blends into the "Catalan" of Spain. Our Glossika course for "Catalan" is based on the speech of Barcelona, but you could still use it to communicate in or acquire "Occitan" in southern France. It should be seen as an intermediary language between French, Spanish and Italian.

One might wonder how dialects came about in the first place. Languages evolve naturally, and like biological evolution, the traits that are adopted by the masses are those that continue to live on from one generation to the next. No one individual can take control over the future course of a language or how it evolves. But then you may wonder, how can a national language be created and how can it be adopted by everyone in the country? The matter is not as simple as you may think. What happens in most cases (or we could say, in most countries) is a dual register. If you are from England, then you will definitely be aware of the regional dialects and how words and sometimes how grammar differs from area to area. The English language also differs between different classes of people, from the poor to the rich, historically one's speech defines a man's social status.

The Académie française, restored in its modern form by Napoleon in 1803, polices the French language as a national standard. So on the one hand we can say that no individual person or "academy" can control a language's evolution, on the other hand it is precisely for this reason that the Académie has been established, so that a standard of speech can be maintained among all the dialects within France. To this day, as in most countries, a dichotomy remains: the local dialects in all their flavours, and the national standard. It is quite possible that as a student of the language you will eventually learn how to recognize and switch between them yourself, depending on the circumstances and your audience.

Due to the dichotomy that exists in most languages (the real world spoken dialect vs. the national standard), most textbooks only teach the national standard and there are peculiarities with the colloquial language that is seldom taught. It is our goal here at Glossika to present you with the real spoken language, not in defiance of the national standard, but to allow you as the student to get as close as humanly possible to communicating comfortably in social settings in your host country. This means that in a language like French which has a lot of tricky pronunciation with liaison, that what you will learn from this course is the relaxed and comfortable liaisons rather than the official ones. This will make it possible to meet people and let them feel comfortable with your style of speech from the very beginning. Oftentimes speaking exactly like a textbook or text-to-speech algorithm will not benefit you socially as much as you would like it to.

Thus the language presented in the Glossika recordings are based on the national standard, but the liaisons are spoken in a relaxed way. We do not need to change the spelling or the text in any way to show this (unlike our Finnish, Armenian and Persian courses which require parallel texts due to the dichotomy), however our phonetic transcription is written in such a way that it matches the surface pronunciation that you will encounter in the sound files.

# Grammar

This fluency series of books does not go into grammatical detail. This is why we recommend to use this course as a supplement to other studies, but if you are using it alone, then you can get a lot of the grammatical explanation online from Wikipedia and videos that teachers have shared. Since French is a widely taught language, we will not attempt to replicate any grammatical explanations in this course. The Glossika Fluency series really focus on speaking the language in real life, so all of your effort in this course should be spent on accent and pronunciation improvement, both in speaking and listening.

Since the course is written with syntax structure in mind, it should follow a natural sequence of ever more complex sentences, of which you will find many deliberate iterations therein in order to allow to acquire a true natural and fluent grasp of the language. The goal of this definition of fluency is not a huge vocabulary, but rather complete freedom over your ability to manipulate sentences.

The most important feature of this course is our list of words and all their variable pronunciations that occur throughout the course which we will describe below in more detail.

Due to differences between your language and French, we advise you never to get stuck analyzing just one sentence. Sometimes word orders are different. Oftentimes there is not enough data in one sentence to deduce what is happening. To take this method to heart, start of by going through the whole book listening to all 1000 sentences and take some occasional notes when you notice patterns. By learning how to notice these patterns, you are building the skills you need for natural language acquisition. Don't try to memorize any single sentence or any grammatical rules. Get a feel for how the sentences flow off the tongue.

The native speaker will speak long strings of syllables in such rapid succession that you'll find it impossible to follow or imitate in the beginning. This is due to the aforementioned problem: too small of a data set to extract or deduce what you need to learn. To learn effectively, or whenever you get stuck, just sit back with your book and relax, play through all 1000 sentences in a single setting and let the repetitive parts of the phrases fill your ears and your brain. Soon you'll be on the right track to mimicking these phrases just as a child does. A child will always have a rough approximation of speech before the age of five, but has no problem in saying complete sentences. So always focus first on fluency and continue to work hard on perfecting your pronunciation, intonation, and accent.

As a foreigner, it may take you many years to master the language. We've given you about six to twelve months of training here depending on your personal schedule. Everything included here is just the basic of basics, so you really need to get to the point where all of these sentences become quite easy to manipulate and produce, and then you can spend the next five to ten years conversing in French and learning how to say more and more, learning directly inside the language without the need for translating. We've given you the tools to get to that point.

## Structure

French stress evolved out of Latin stress, so the stress patterns are almost identical to those found in Italian, Catalan, Spanish and Portuguese. But since a lot of phonological degradation has occurred in French over the centuries, the penultimate stress you find in Italian and Spanish has become final stress in both French and Catalan (Occitan). French has been moving more and more to a non-stress pattern as words get shorter and shorter getting strung together in rapid succession, and in most cases you'll find that stress on individual words has disappeared and has moved to the end of the phrase. This is usually the case in fluent speech. This has also given rise to innovations in the language, for example "pas" placed after the negated verb, because the negative participle can almost get completely lost in speech due to nasalization and shortening of words. And so in almost every instance of "pas", you'll find it with a strong stress as to make sure the phrase is understood as being negative.

Unlike Italian or Spanish, the diacritics above letters in French do not indicate stress patterns at all. These are used simply to indicate different pronunciations. For example, the letter {e} can very easily disappear or be swallowed by neighboring consonants (in which case we write as a tiny superscript schwa [ᵊ] as a possible phonetic realization). If the letter {e} is still to be pronounced, it depends on its position (is it followed by {-s} or {-t} or {-z} at the end of a word?) or it would be written with an acute accent {é}. In this case it should sound like its IPA equivalent /e/. The other two letters {è, ê} are both pronounced like the English short vowel /ɛ/. The letter {ê} in most cases gave rise from a disappearing {-s} as can be observed in "même" (Spanish: mismo) and "forêt" (English: forest) and other evolutions of the language. Likewise the letter {é} can also represent the disappearing {-s} at the beginning of words which can be observed in "étude" (Spanish: estudio, English: study).

## Names

The Glossika Fluency series is a global production with over a hundred languages in development, so we include names from all the major languages and cultures around the world. Many of these are foreign to French speakers, and probably including yourself. However, it is of particular interest to us how languages deal with foreign names, both in localizing and dealing with them grammatically. In this edition we have not attempted to write the pronunciation of names, but left the pronunciation up to the native speaker. However, note how word endings are attached to names, because as a foreigner speaking French, you will undoubtedly have to use foreign names. Also use these names to your advantage, as an anchor in each sentence to figure out how all the other parts of speech interact with the name.

The pronunciation guide used in this book (please read the following section for details) does not account for foreign words or borrowings and so we simply do not transcribe the pronunciations in this case.

# IPA

Almost all language teaching books over the last century have resorted to awkward explanations of pronunciation. You may have seen lots of strange pronunciation guides over the years in all kinds of publications. The problem with these kinds of publications is many-fold. Many times the pronunciation being taught is very specific to American pronunciation in particular, which means even if you're not American, you'll end up pronouncing the language you're learning like an American. I've seen similar devices used in British publications, but many times when I see a book explain: "pronounce it like the vowel in 'hear'" I have no idea which version of

English they're referring to. The British books often make references to Scottish speakers, which is not really common knowledge for Americans. So I think it is important to consider where your readers are coming from without making assumptions.

The second problem is why would anybody want to pronounce the language they're learning like an American? Isn't the point to learn pronunciation as closely as we can to the way native speakers speak? In any case, it pays off well to work hard at eliminating a trace of one's foreign accent when speaking other languages. It also puts your listeners at ease as they won't have to strain so hard to understand what you're saying. Here we will avoid criticizing all the problems related to the transcription of other pronunciation guides and why they may be misleading, and focus our attention instead to amazing solutions.

Over the last century our knowledge of phonetics has improved greatly. All of this knowledge seems to have been known by the elite few professors and students of Linguistics departments scattered around the globe. But with the internet comes the explosion of information that is now accessible to everybody. Not only that, but language learners, even average language learners, are a lot smarter about the process of going about learning other languages than people were just a mere twenty or thirty years ago. It is now possible for teenagers to achieve fluency in any number of languages they want from the comfort of their own home just by using the resources available on the internet. I personally attempted to do so when I was a teenager without the internet, and trying to make sense of languages with very little data or explanation was quite frustrating.

As well-informed language learners of the twenty-first century, we now have access to all the tools that make languages much easier to learn. If you can read other languages as well, there are literally thousands of blogs, discussion groups, communities and places to go on the internet to learn everything you want to know about language learning. There is still a lot of misinformation getting passed around, but the community is maturing. The days of using such hackneyed pronunciation guides are hopefully over.

All the secrets that linguists have had are now available to the general public. Linguists have been using the International Phonetic Alphabet (IPA) as a standard for recording languages, where every letter is given one and only one sound, what is called a point of articulation. This enables linguists to talk about linguistic phenomena in a scientific and precise way. Since the point of articulation can be slightly different from language to language, a single letter like /t/ does not have a very specific point, but just a general area that we can call "alveolar" the location known as the alveolar ridge behind the teeth. IPA has extra diacritics available to indicate where the /t/ is to be pronounced. In a lot of cases, this information is not necessary for talking about the language in broad terms, especially topics unrelated to pronunciation, so as long as the language has no other kind of /t/ in that same area, there's no need to indicate the precise location: this is known as phonemic.

English is a good example. For example, we don't think about it much that {t} is pronounced differently in "take", "wanted", "letter", "stuff" and "important". If you're North American, the {t} in each of these words is actually pronounced differently: aspirated, as a nasal, as a flap, unaspirated, as a glottal stop. Maybe you never even realized it. But to a foreign learner of English, hearing all these different sounds can get very confusing especially when everybody says "it's a T!" but in reality they're saying different things. It's not that Americans don't hear the different sounds, it's just that they label all of the sounds as {t} which leads them to believe that what they're actually hearing are the same. But it more difficult for the foreigners to learn when a {t} is pronounced as a glottal stop or as a flap, etc. The task for the language learner is often underestimated by teachers and native speakers.

Many letters in English have these variations which are called "allophones" and we can record them as separate letters in IPA or with diacritical marks. In order to indicate that this pronunciation is "precise" I should use square brackets: [tʰ, t̚, ɾ, ʔ]. So we can say that although English has one phonemic /t/, in reality there are many allophones. Actually every language has allophones! So what we learn as spelling, or in a book, usually is just the general phonemic guide, and it differs quite a bit from the way people actually speak with allophones. When I'm learning a foreign language I always ask what the allophones are because it helps me speak that language much clearer and much more like a native.

Why does a language learner need a "precise" pronunciation guide?

Let's take the English learner again. If that person is told to always pronounce {t} exactly the same way, then his speech will actually become very emphatic, unnatural sounding and forced. To native speakers this learner will always have a strong foreign accent, have choppy pronunciation and be difficult to understand. We should always set our goals high enough even if we can't attain them perfectly, but at least we're pushing ourselves to achieve more than we would have otherwise. So if you have an accurate transcription of native speakers which indicates all the variations that they use, you will have access to a wealth of information that no other language learner had access to before. Not only that but you have the tools available for perfecting your pronunciation.

There is no better solution than IPA itself, the secret code of the linguists. Now the IPA is available in Wikipedia with links for each letter to separate pages with recordings and a list of languages that use those sounds.

From the beginning you must take note that French has absolutely no aspirated sounds, so that the English {p, t, k} are completely different from French {p, t, k}. To summarize:

English {p, t, k} = lots of aspiration (puff of air) French {p, t, k} = no aspiration whatsoever. To the untrained English ear, they may actually sound like {b, d, g}, which means you'll need more exposure and practice.

# French Pronunciation

The IPA transcription in this book is based on a computer program written by the Glossika staff which produces pronunciation in two steps which is required for all languages: 1) phonemic, 2) phonetic. The computer program is based on the official spelling of the language alone rather than pronunciation guides. Some languages require additional steps of adding stress and tone in order to get the correct phonetic output, as in the case for French "appele" and "appeler", otherwise the unstressed {e} in the second example would get deleted.

Liaison is a big issue that any student of French is acutely aware of. Our transcription works like this:

1. If the ending of a word is not pronounced, the phonemes get deleted.
2. If the ending of a word carries over to the next word, the phoneme moves to the next word and *starts* it.
3. If a word contains the sometimes pronounced schwa, we write it as [°] or which some speakers do not pronounce. This results in consonant "clusters", but consonant clusters occur in two different ways among world languages:

A) Languages with consonant clusters that fuse together: English, Russian, German, etc. B) Languages with consonant clusters where every consonant is spoken individually with an epenthetic [°]: French, Georgian, Atayal, etc.

In other words, consonant clusters in English and French are produced differently. Where you come across [db] in "debout" does not sound like the [db] in English "bad boy", but rather spoken slightly separately as [d°b]. An English speaker would consider "bad° boy" with an epenthetic [°] an incorrect pronunciation, whereas this is not the case in French.

Last two pieces of advice: Please consult the IPA transcription whenever in doubt.

Don't forget that if you ever get frustrated, just go back through all 1000 sentences and relax while you listen. No need to force yourself to remember or repeat during this. This is just to help clear your mind of a few problematic sentences. Chances are, if you keep moving through all the sentences, those troublesome sentences will no longer be troublesome when you loop back around again.

## Vocabulary Index

1.  The vocabulary index does not include foreign names and places, or words without an IPA transcription.
2.  The index lists every variation of every French word found in this book. However, for common words, we do not list every single sentence in which they occur in order to save space. The first few sentences that we do list should be enough of a resource for you to check that special occurrence or pronunciation pattern.
3.  Words that are combined in transcription in the text are separated in the index for individual lookup.
4.  All words that have a change in liaison can be looked up in the index by observing the IPA transcription. Do you want to know when "tous" is pronounced [tu] or [tus]? Do you want to know when "allé" is pronounced [ale] or [zale] or [tale] because of the preceding liaison? Do you want to know how many different conjugations appear in our text? All of these are listed as separate entries in the index for your convenience.

We sincerely hope that our unique way of presenting the language will be useful for both students and teachers alike and will remain as a useful reference and tool for years to come.

# Vocabulary: French

## Prepositions

| | |
|---|---|
| about | sur |
| above | au-dessus |
| according to | selon |
| across | à travers |
| after | après |
| against | contre |
| among | entre |
| around | autour de |
| as | comme |
| as far as | autant que |
| as well as | aussi bien que |
| at | à |
| because of | en raison de |
| before | avant |
| behind | derrière |
| below | en dessous |
| beneath | sous |
| beside | à côté de |
| between | entre |
| beyond | au-delà |
| but | mais |
| by | par |
| close to | près de |
| despite | malgré |

| | |
|---|---|
| down | vers le bas |
| due to | à cause de |
| during | au cours de |
| except | sauf |
| except for | à l'exception de |
| far from | loin d'être |
| for | pour |
| from | à partir de |
| in | dans |
| in addition to | en plus de |
| in front of | en face de |
| in spite of | en dépit de |
| inside | à l'intérieur |
| inside of | l'intérieur de |
| instead of | au lieu de |
| into | dans |
| near | près de |
| near to | près de |
| next | prochain |
| next to | à côté de |
| of | de |
| on | sur |
| on behalf of | au nom de |
| on top of | au sommet de |
| opposite | opposé |
| out | à |
| outside | à l'extérieur |
| outside of | en dehors des |
| over | sur |

| | |
|---|---|
| per | par |
| plus | plus |
| prior to | avant |
| round | tour |
| since | depuis |
| than | que |
| through | par |
| till | jusqu'à |
| to | à |
| toward | vers |
| under | sous |
| unlike | contrairement à |
| until | jusqu'à ce que |
| up | jusqu'à |
| via | via |
| with | avec |
| within | dans |
| without | sans |

## Adjectives

| | |
|---|---|
| a few | quelques |
| bad | mauvais |
| big | grand |
| bitter | amer |
| clean | propre |
| correct | correct |
| dark | sombre |
| deep | profond |

| difficult | difficile |
|-----------|-----------|
| dirty | sale |
| dry | sec |
| easy | facile |
| empty | vide |
| expensive | cher |
| fast | rapide |
| few | peu |
| foreign | étranger |
| fresh | frais |
| full | plein |
| good | bon |
| hard | dur |
| heavy | lourd |
| inexpensive | peu coûteux |
| light | léger |
| little | peu |
| local | local |
| long | long |
| many | beaucoup |
| much | beaucoup |
| narrow | étroit |
| new | nouveau |
| noisy | bruyant |
| old | vieux |
| part | partie |
| powerful | puissant |
| quiet | calme |
| short person | salé |

| small | court |
|-------|-------|
| salty | lent |
| slow | petit |
| soft | doux |
| some | certains |
| sour | aigre |
| spicy | épicé |
| sweet | doux |
| tall | haut |
| thick | épais |
| thin | mince |
| very | très |
| weak | faible |
| wet | humide |
| whole | ensemble |
| wide | large |
| wrong | faux |
| young | jeune |

## Adverbs

| absolutely | absolument |
|------------|------------|
| ago | il y a |
| almost | presque |
| alone | seul |
| already | déjà |
| always | toujours |
| anywhere | n'importe où |
| away | loin |

| | |
|---|---|
| barely | à peine |
| carefully | soigneusement |
| everywhere | partout |
| fast | rapide |
| frequently | fréquemment |
| hard | dur |
| hardly | à peine |
| here | ici |
| home | maison |
| immediately | immédiatement |
| last night | dernière nuit |
| lately | récemment |
| later | plus tard |
| mostly | surtout |
| never | jamais |
| next week | semaine prochaine |
| now | maintenant |
| nowhere | nulle part |
| occasionally | de temps en temps |
| out | dehors |
| over there | là-bas |
| pretty | joli |
| quickly | rapidement |
| quite | tout à fait, assez |
| rarely | rarement |
| really | vraiment |
| recently | récemment |
| right now | pour le moment, en ce moment |
| seldom | rarement |

| slowly | lentement |
|---|---|
| sometimes | parfois |
| soon | bientôt |
| still | encore |
| then | puis |
| there | là |
| this morning | ce matin |
| today | aujourd'hui |
| together | ensemble |
| tomorrow | demain |
| tonight | ce soir |
| usually | habituellement |
| very | très |
| well | bien |
| yesterday | hier, la vielle |
| yet | encore |

# Glossika Mass Sentences

# GMS #1001 - 1100

**1001**

EN  Have you seen any of her paintings?

FR  As-tu vu quelques-uns de ses tableaux?
IPA  [a ty vy kɛlkᵊzœ̃ dø se tablo ‖]

**1002**

EN  I saw some of her work last week.

FR  J'ai vu quelques-unes de ses œuvres la semaine dernière.
IPA  [ʒ‿ɛ vy kɛlkᵊzyn dø se z‿œvʁ la sᵊmɛn dɛʁnjɛʁ ‖]

**1003**

EN  Brigitte works in a factory, but she's had a lot of different jobs.

FR  Brigitte travaille dans une usine, mais elle a eu des tas d'emplois différents.
IPA  [(...) tʁavaj dɑ̃ z‿yn yzin | mɛ ɛ l‿a y de ta d‿ɑ̃plwa difeʁɑ̃ ‖]

**1004**

EN  Five years ago she was a waitress in a restaurant.

FR  Il y a cinq ans, elle était serveuse dans un restaurant.
IPA  [i l‿i a sɛ̃ k‿ɑ̃ | ɛ l‿ete sɛʁvøz dɑ̃ z‿œ̃ ʁɛstoʁɑ̃ ‖]

**1005**

EN  After that, she worked on a farm, but she didn't enjoy it very much.

---

FR  Après ça, elle a travaillé dans une ferme, mais ça ne lui plaisait pas beaucoup.

IPA  [apʁɛ sa | ɛ l̩a tʁavaje dɑ̃ z̩yn fɛʁm | mɛ sa nø lɥi plɛzɛ pa boku ‖]

**1006**

EN  Do you know Jianhong's sister?

---

FR  Connais-tu la sœur de Jianhong?

IPA  [konɛ ty la sœʁ dø (...) ‖]

**1007**

EN  I've seen her a few times, but I've never spoken to her.

---

FR  Je l'ai déjà vue quelques fois, mais je ne lui ai jamais parlé.

IPA  [ʒø l̩ɛ deʒa vy kɛlk fwa | mɛ ʒø nø lɥi ɛ ʒamɛ paʁle ‖]

**1008**

EN  Have you ever spoken to her?

---

FR  Lui as-tu déjà parlé?

IPA  [lɥi a ty deʒa paʁle ‖]

**1009**

EN  I met her at a party last week. She's very nice.

FR  Je l'ai rencontrée à une fête la semaine dernière. Elle est très sympa.

IPA  [ʒø l‿ɛ ʁɑ̃kɔ̃tʁe a yn fɛt la s°men dɛʁnjɛʁ ‖ ɛ l‿e tʁɛ sɛ̃pa ‖]

**1010**

EN  Somebody cleans the office every day. > The office is cleaned every day.

FR  Quelqu'un nettoie le bureau tous les jours. Le bureau est nettoyé tous les jours.

IPA  [kɛlkɶ̃ nɛtwa lø byʁo tu le ʒuʁ ‖ lø byʁo e netwaje tu le ʒuʁ ‖]

**1011**

EN  Somebody cleaned the office yesterday. > The office was cleaned yesterday.

FR  Quelqu'un a nettoyé le bureau hier. Le bureau a été nettoyé hier.

IPA  [kɛlkɶ̃ n‿a netwaje lø byʁo jɛʁ ‖ lø byʁo a ete netwaje jɛʁ ‖]

**1012**

EN  Butter is made from milk.

FR  Le beurre est fait à partir de lait.

IPA  [lø bœʁ e fɛ a paʁtiʁ dø lɛ ‖]

**1013**

EN Oranges are imported into Canada.

FR Les oranges sont importées au Canada.
IPA [le z‿oʁɑ̃ʒ sɔ̃ ɛ̃pɔʁte o kanada ‖]

**1014**

EN How often are these rooms cleaned?

FR À quelle fréquence ces pièces sont-elles nettoyées?
IPA [a kɛl fʁekɑ̃s se pjɛs sɔ̃ t‿ɛl netwaje ‖]

**1015**

EN I'm never invited to parties.

FR Je ne suis jamais invité aux fêtes.
IPA [ʒø nø sɥi ʒamɛ z‿ɛ̃vite o fɛt ‖]

**1016**

EN This house was built one hundred (100) years ago.

FR Cette maison a été construite il y a cent ans.
IPA [sɛt mɛzɔ̃ a ete kɔ̃stʁɥit i l‿i a sɑ̃ t‿ɑ̃ ‖]

**1017**

EN These houses were built one hundred (100) years ago.

FR Ces maisons ont été construites il y a cent ans.
IPA [se mɛzɔ̃ ɔ̃ ete kɔ̃stʁɥi t‿i l‿i a sɑ̃ t‿ɑ̃ ‖]

**1018**

EN When was the telephone invented?

FR Quand le téléphone a-t-il été inventé?

IPA [kã lø telefɔn a t‿il ete ɛ̃vãte ||]

**1019**

EN We weren't invited to the party last week.

FR On n'a pas été invités (♀invitées) à la fête de la semaine dernière.

IPA [ɔ̃ n‿a pa z‿ete ɛ̃vite (♀ɛ̃vite) a la fɛt dø la sᵊmɛn dɛʁnjeʁ ||]

**1020**

EN Was anybody injured in the accident?

FR Est-ce que quelqu'un a été blessé lors de l'accident?

IPA [ɛsᵊ kø kɛlkœ̃ n‿a ete blese lɔʁ dø l‿aksidã ||]

**1021**

EN Two people were taken to the hospital.

FR Deux personnes ont été transportées à l'hôpital.

IPA [dø pɛʁsɔn ɔ̃ ete tʁãspɔʁte a l‿opital ||]

**1022**

EN I was born in Colombia in nineteen eighty-nine (1989).

---

FR Je suis né (♀née) en Colombie en mille neuf cents quatre-vingt-neuf (1989).

IPA [ʒø sɥi ne (♀ne) ɑ̃ colombie ɑ̃ mil nœf sɑ̃ katʁə vɛ̃nœf (1989) ||]

**1023**

EN Where were you born? — In Taipei.

---

FR Où es-tu né (♀née)? — À Taipei.

IPA [u ɛ ty ne (♀ne) || — a (...) ||]

**1024**

EN The telephone was invented by Bell in eighteen seventy-six (1876).

---

FR Le téléphone a été inventé par Bell en mille huit cents soixante-seize (1876).

IPA [lø telefɔn a ete ɛ̃vɑ̃te paʁ bell ɑ̃ mil ɥit sɑ̃ swasɑ̃tsɛz (1876) ||]

**1025**

EN I was bitten by dog a few days ago.

---

FR J'ai été mordu (♀mordue) par un chien il y a quelques jours.

IPA [ʒ ɛ ete mɔʁdy (♀mɔʁdy) pa ʁ œ̃ ʃjɛ̃ i lⁱi a kɛlk ʒuʁ ||]

**1026**

EN  Do you like these paintings? They were painted by a friend of mine.

FR  Aimes-tu ces tableaux? Ils ont été peints par un ami (♀une amie).

IPA  [ɛm ty se tablo || i l ɔ̃ ete pɛ̃ pa ʁ œ̃ n ami (♀yn ami) ||]

**1027**

EN  Are these rooms cleaned every day?

FR  Est-ce que ces chambres sont nettoyées tous les jours?

IPA  [ɛsˀ kø se ʃɑ̃bʁ sɔ̃ netwaje tu le ʒuʁ ||]

**1028**

EN  Glass is made from sand.

FR  Le verre est fait de sable.

IPA  [lø vɛʁ e fɛ dø sabl ||]

**1029**

EN  Stamps are sold at the post office.

FR  Les timbres sont vendus au bureau de poste.

IPA  [le tɛ̃bʁ sɔ̃ vɑ̃dy o byʁo dø pɔst ||]

**1030**

EN  This word is not used very often.

FR  Ce mot n'est pas utilisé très souvent.
IPA  [sø mo n‿e pa z‿ytilize tʁɛ suvã ‖]

**1031**

EN  Are we allowed to park here?

FR  Est-il permis de se garer ici?
IPA  [e t‿il pɛʁmi dø sø gaʁe isi ‖]

**1032**

EN  How is this word pronounced?

FR  Comment ce mot est-il prononcé?
IPA  [komã sø mo e t‿il pʁonɔ̃se ‖]

**1033**

EN  The house was painted last month.

FR  La maison a été peinte le mois dernier.
IPA  [la mɛzɔ̃ a ete pɛ̃t lø mwa dɛʁnje ‖]

**1034**

EN  My phone was stolen a few days ago.

FR  Mon téléphone a été volé il y a quelques jours.
IPA  [mɔ̃ telefɔn a ete vole i l‿i a kɛlk ʒuʁ ‖]

**1035**

EN   Three people were injured in the accident.

---

FR   Trois personnes ont été blessées dans l'accident.
IPA  [tʁwa pɛʁsɔn ɔ̃ ete blese dɑ̃ l̯aksidɑ̃ ‖]

**1036**

EN   When was this bridge built?

---

FR   Quand ce pont a-t-il été construit?
IPA  [kɑ̃ sø pɔ̃ a t̯il ete kɔ̃stʁɥi ‖]

**1037**

EN   I wasn't woken up by the noise.

---

FR   Je n'ai pas été réveillé (♀réveillée) par le bruit.
IPA  [ʒø n̯ɛ pa z̯ete ʁeveje (♀ʁeveje) paʁ lø bʁɥi ‖]

**1038**

EN   How were these windows broken?

---

FR   Comment ces fenêtres ont-elles été brisées?
IPA  [komɑ̃ se fᵊnɛtʁ ɔ̃ t̯ɛl ete bʁize ‖]

**1039**

EN   Were you invited to Adrian's party last week?

---

FR   As-tu été invité (♀invitée) à la fête d'Adrian la
     semaine dernière?
IPA  [a ty ete ɛ̃vite (♀ɛ̃vite) a la fɛt d̯(...) la sᵊmɛn
     dɛʁnjɛʁ ‖]

**1040**

EN    Football is played in most countries of the world.

FR    Le football est pratiqué dans la plupart des pays du monde.

IPA    [lø futbɔl e pʁatike dɑ̃ la plypaʁ de pei dy mɔ̃d ‖]

**1041**

EN    Why did the email get sent to the wrong address?

FR    Pourquoi le courriel a-t-il été envoyé à la mauvaise adresse?

IPA    [puʁkwa lø kuʁjɛl a t͜ il ete ɑ̃vwaje a la movɛz adʁɛs ‖]

**1042**

EN    A garage is a place where cars are repaired.

FR    Un garage est un endroit où on répare les voitures.

IPA    [œ̃ gaʁaʒ e t͜ œ̃ n͜ ɑ̃dʁwa u ɔ̃ ʁepaʁ le vwatyʁ ‖]

**1043**

EN    Where were you born?

FR    Où es-tu né (♀née)?

IPA    [u ɛ ty ne (♀ne) ‖]

**1044**

EN How many languages are spoken in Switzerland?

FR Combien de langues parle-t-on en Suisse?

IPA [kɔ̃bjɛ̃ dø lɑ̃g paʁl t‿ɔ̃ ɑ̃ sɥis ‖]

**1045**

EN Somebody broke into our house, but nothing was stolen.

FR Quelqu'un est entré par effraction dans notre maison, mais rien n'a été volé.

IPA [kɛlkœ̃ n‿e ɑ̃tʁe pa ʁ‿efʁaksjɔ̃ dɑ̃ nɔtʁ mɛzɔ̃ | mɛ ʁjɛ̃ n‿a ete vole ‖]

**1046**

EN When was the bicycle invented?

FR Quand la bicyclette a-t-elle été inventée?

IPA [kɑ̃ la bisiklɛt a t‿ɛl ete ɛ̃vɑ̃te ‖]

**1047**

EN I saw an accident yesterday. Two people were taken to the hospital.

FR J'ai vu un accident hier. Deux personnes ont été conduites à l'hôpital.

IPA [ʒ‿ɛ vy œ̃ n‿aksidɑ̃ jɛʁ ‖ dø pɛʁsɔn ɔ̃ ete kɔ̃dɥit a l‿opital ‖]

**1048**

EN Paper is made from wood.

FR Le papier est fabriqué à partir de bois.
IPA [lø papje e fabʁike a paʁtiʁ dø bwa ‖]

**1049**

EN There was a fire at the hotel last week. Two of the rooms were damaged.

FR Il y a eu un incendie à l'hôtel la semaine dernière. Deux des chambres ont été endommagées.
IPA [i l‿i a y œ̃ n‿ɛsɑ̃di a l‿otɛl la sᵊmɛn dɛʁnjɛʁ ‖ dø de ʃɑ̃bʁ ɔ̃ ete ɑ̃domaʒe ‖]

**1050**

EN Where did you get this picture? — It was given to me by a friend of mine.

FR Où as-tu trouvé cette photo? — Elle m'a été donnée par un ami.
IPA [u a ty tʁuve sɛt foto ‖ — ɛl m‿a ete done pa ʁ‿œ̃ n‿ami ‖]

**1051**

EN Many British programs are shown on American television.

FR Plusieurs émissions britanniques sont diffusées sur la télévision américaine.
IPA [plyzjœʁ‿emisjɔ̃ bʁitanik sɔ̃ difyze syʁ la televizjɔ̃ ameʁiken ‖]

**1052**

EN Did Aleksey and Anastasia go to the wedding? —
No, they weren't invited.

FR Aleksey et Anastasia sont-ils allés au mariage? >
Est-ce qu'Aleksey et Anastasia sont allés au mariage?
— Non, ils n'étaient pas invités.

IPA [(...) e (...) sɔ̃ t‿il ale o maʁjaʒ || > ɛs° k (...) e (...) sɔ̃
ale o maʁjaʒ || — nɔ̃ | il n‿etɛ pa z‿ɛ̃vite ||]

**1053**

EN How old is this movie? — It was made in nineteen
sixty-five (1965).

FR Quel âge a ce film? — Il a été réalisé en mille neuf
cents soixante-cinq (1965).

IPA [kɛ l‿aʒ a sø film || — i l‿a ete ʁealize ɑ̃ mil nœf sɑ̃
swasɑ̃tsɛ̃k (1965) ||]

**1054**

EN My car was stolen last week, but the next day it was
found by the police.

FR Ma voiture a été volée la semaine dernière, mais elle
a été retrouvée le lendemain par la police.

IPA [ma vwatyʁ a ete vole la s°mɛn dɛʁnjɛʁ | mɛ ɛ l‿a ete
ʁ°tʁuve lø lɑ̃d°mɛ̃ paʁ la polis ||]

**1055**

EN Arturo was born in Havana.

FR Arturo est né à La Havane.
IPA [(...) e ne a la avan ||]

**1056**

EN Anna was born in Rome.

FR Anna est née à Rome.
IPA [anna e ne a (...) ||]

**1057**

EN Her parents were born in Rio de Janeiro.

FR Ses parents sont nés à Rio de Janeiro.
IPA [se paʁɑ̃ sɔ̃ ne a (...) ||]

**1058**

EN I was born in London.

FR Je suis né (♀née) à Londres.
IPA [ʒø sɥi ne (♀ne) a lɔ̃dʁ° ||]

**1059**

EN My mother was born in Paris.

FR Ma mère est née à Paris.
IPA [ma mɛʁ e ne a (...) ||]

**1060**

EN Somebody is painting the door. The door is being painted.

---

FR Quelqu'un peint la porte. > On peint la porte.
IPA [kɛlkœ̃ pɛ̃ la pɔʁt || > ɔ̃ pɛ̃ la pɔʁt ||]

**1061**

EN My car is at the garage. It's being repaired.

---

FR Ma voiture est au garage. Elle se fait réparer. > Ma voiture est au garage. On la répare.
IPA [ma vwatyʁ e o gaʁaʒ || ɛl sø fɛ ʁepaʁe || > ma vwatyʁ e o gaʁaʒ || ɔ̃ la ʁepaʁ ||]

**1062**

EN Some new houses are being built across from the park.

---

FR De nouvelles maisons sont construites de l'autre côté du parc. > On construit de nouvelles maisons de l'autre côté du parc.
IPA [dø nuvɛl mɛzɔ̃ sɔ̃ kɔ̃stʁɥit dø l‿otʁ kote dy paʁk || > ɔ̃ kɔ̃stʁɥi dø nuvɛl mɛzɔ̃ dø l‿otʁ kote dy paʁk ||]

**1063**

EN The office is being cleaned right now.

---

FR Le bureau est en train d'être nettoyé. > On nettoie présentement le bureau.
IPA [lø byʁo e t‿ã tʁɛ̃ d‿ɛtʁ netwaje || > ɔ̃ nɛtwa pʁezɑ̃t°mã lø byʁo ||]

1064

EN The office is cleaned every day.

FR Le bureau est nettoyé tous les jours.
IPA [lø byʁo e netwaje tu le ʒuʁ ‖]

1065

EN In the United States, football games are usually played on the weekends, but no big games are being played next weekend.

FR Aux États-Unis, les parties de football ont généralement lieu le week-end, mais il n'y a pas de partie importante le week-end prochain.
IPA [o z‿etazuni | le paʁti dø futbɔl ɔ̃ ʒeneʁalᵊmã ljø lø wikɛnd | mɛ il n‿i a pa dø paʁti ɛ̃pɔʁtãt lø wikɛnd pʁoʃɛ̃ ‖]

1066

EN Somebody has painted the door. > The door has been painted.

FR Quelqu'un a peint la porte. La porte a été peinte.
IPA [kɛlkœ̃ n‿a pɛ̃ la pɔʁt ‖ la pɔʁt a ete pɛ̃t ‖]

**1067**

EN Somebody has stolen my key. > My key has been stolen.

---

FR Quelqu'un m'a volé ma clé. Ma clé a été volée. > On m'a volé ma clé.

IPA [kɛlkœ̃ m‿a vole ma kle || ma kle a ete vole || > ɔ̃ m‿a vole ma kle ||]

**1068**

EN Somebody has stolen my keys. > My keys have been stolen.

---

FR Quelqu'un m'a volé mes clés. Mes clés ont été volées. > On m'a volé mes clés.

IPA [kɛlkœ̃ m‿a vole me kle || me kle ɔ̃ ete vole || > ɔ̃ m‿a vole me kle ||]

**1069**

EN Nobody has invited me to the party. > I haven't been invited to the party.

---

FR Personne ne m'a invité (♀invitée) à la fête. Je n'ai pas été invité (♀invitée) à la fête.

IPA [pɛʁsɔn nø m‿a ẽvite (♀ẽvite) a la fɛt || ʒø n‿ɛ pa z‿ete ẽvite (♀ẽvite) a la fɛt ||]

**1070**

EN  Has somebody washed this shirt? > Has this shirt been washed?

FR  Est-ce que quelqu'un a lavé cette chemise? Cette chemise a-t-elle été lavée?

IPA  [ɛs° kø kɛlkœ̃ n‿a lave sɛt ʃ°miz || sɛt ʃ°miz a t‿ɛl ete lave ||]

**1071**

EN  The room isn't dirty anymore. It's been cleaned.

FR  La chambre n'est plus sale. Elle a été nettoyée.

IPA  [la ʃɑ̃bʁ n‿e plys sal || ɛ l‿a ete netwaje ||]

**1072**

EN  The room was cleaned yesterday.

FR  La chambre a été nettoyée hier.

IPA  [la ʃɑ̃bʁ a ete netwaje jɛʁ ||]

**1073**

EN  I can't find my keys. I think they've been stolen.

FR  Je ne trouve pas mes clés. Je crois qu'elles ont été volées.

IPA  [ʒø nø tʁuv pa me kle || ʒø kʁwa k‿ɛl ɔ̃ ete vole ||]

**1074**

EN My keys were stolen last week.

FR Mes clés ont été volées la semaine dernière.
IPA [me kle ɔ̃ ete vole la sᵊmɛn dɛʁnjɛʁ ||]

**1075**

EN The car's being repaired. > The car's getting repaired.

FR On répare la voiture. La voiture se fait réparer.
IPA [ɔ̃ ʁepaʁ la vwatyʁ || la vwatyʁ sø fɛ ʁepaʁe ||]

**1076**

EN A bridge is being built. > A bridge is getting built.

FR On construit un pont. Un pont se fait construire.
IPA [ɔ̃ kɔ̃stʁ yi t‿œ̃ pɔ̃ || œ̃ pɔ̃ sø fɛ kɔ̃stʁ yiʁ ||]

**1077**

EN The windows are being washed. > The windows are getting washed.

FR On nettoie les fenêtres. Les fenêtres se font nettoyer.
IPA [ɔ̃ nɛtwa le fᵊnɛtʁ || le fᵊnɛtʁ sø fɔ̃ netwaje ||]

**1078**

EN The grass is being cut. > The grass is getting cut.

FR On coupe l'herbe. L'herbe se fait couper.
IPA [ɔ̃ kup l‿ɛʁb || l‿ɛʁb sø fɛ kupe ||]

**1079**

EN The office is being cleaned. > The office is getting cleaned.

FR On nettoie le bureau. Le bureau se fait nettoyer.

IPA [ɔ̃ nɛtwa lø byʁo || lø byʁo sø fɛ netwaje ||]

**1080**

EN The shirts have been ironed. > The shirts got ironed.

FR On a repassé les chemises. Les chemises ont été repassées.

IPA [ɔ̃ n̪a ʁ°pase le ʃ°miz || le ʃ°miz ɔ̃ ete ʁ°pase ||]

**1081**

EN The window's been broken. > The window got broken.

FR On a cassé la fenêtre. La fenêtre a été cassée.

IPA [ɔ̃ n̪a kase la f°nɛtʁ || la f°nɛtʁ a ete kase ||]

**1082**

EN The roof is being repaired. > The roof is getting repaired.

FR On répare le toit. Le toit se fait réparer.

IPA [ɔ̃ ʁepaʁ lø twa || lø twa sø fɛ ʁepaʁe ||]

**1083**

EN The car's been damaged. > The car got damaged.

FR On a endommagé la voiture. La voiture a été endommagée.

IPA [ɔ̃ n a ɑ̃domaʒe la vwatyʁ || la vwatyʁ a ete ɑ̃domaʒe ||]

**1084**

EN The houses are being torn down. > The houses are getting torn down.

FR On démolit les maisons. Les maisons se font démolir.

IPA [ɔ̃ demoli le mɛzɔ̃ || le mɛzɔ̃ sø fɔ̃ demoliʁ ||]

**1085**

EN The trees have been cut down. > The trees got cut down.

FR On coupe les arbres. Les arbres se font couper.

IPA [ɔ̃ kup le z aʁbʁ || le z aʁbʁ sø fɔ̃ kupe ||]

**1086**

EN They've been invited to a party. > They got invited to a party.

FR On les a invités (♀invitées) à la fête. Ils (♀elles) ont été invités (♀invitées) à la fête.

IPA [ɔ̃ le z a ɛ̃vite (♀ɛ̃vite) a la fɛt || il (♀ɛl) ɔ̃ ete ɛ̃vite (♀ɛ̃vite) a la fɛt ||]

**1087**

EN I can't use my office right now. It's being painted.

FR Je ne peux pas utiliser mon bureau en ce moment. On refait la peinture.

IPA [ʒø nø pø pa zˌytilize mɔ̃ byʁo ɑ̃ sø momɑ̃ || ɔ̃ ʁ°fɛ la pɛ̃tyʁ ||]

**1088**

EN We didn't go to the party. We weren't invited.

FR Nous ne sommes pas allés (♀allées) à la fête. Nous n'étions pas invités (♀invitées). > On ne nous a pas invités (♀invitées).

IPA [nu nø sɔm pa zˌale (♀ale) a la fɛt || nu nˌetjɔ̃ pa zˌɛ̃vite (♀ɛ̃vite) || > ɔ̃ nø nu zˌa pa zˌɛ̃vite (♀ɛ̃vite) ||]

**1089**

EN The washing machine was broken. It's been repaired now.

FR La machine à laver était en panne. Elle est maintenant réparée.

IPA [la maʃin a lave etɛ tˌɑ̃ pan || ɛ lˌe mɛ̃t°nɑ̃ ʁepaʁe ||]

**1090**

EN The washing machine was getting repaired yesterday afternoon.

FR La machine à laver se faisait réparer hier après-midi.

IPA [la maʃin a lave sø f°zɛ ʁepaʁe jɛ apʁɛ midi ||]

**1091**

EN A factory is a place where things are made.

FR Une usine est un endroit où on fabrique des choses.

IPA [yn yzin e t‿œ̃ n‿ɑ̃dʁwa u ɔ̃ fabʁik de ʃoz ‖]

**1092**

EN How old are these houses? When were they built?

FR Quel âge ont ces maisons? Quand ont-elles été construites?

IPA [kɛ l‿aʒ ɔ̃ se mɛzɔ̃ ‖ kɑ̃ ɔ̃ t‿ɛl ete kɔ̃stʁɥit ‖]

**1093**

EN Is the computer being used at the moment? — Yes, Boris is using it.

FR Est-ce que quelqu'un utilise l'ordinateur en ce moment? — Oui, Boris l'utilise.

IPA [ɛsə kø kɛlkœ̃ n‿ytiliz l‿ɔʁdinatœʁ ɑ̃ sø momɑ̃ ‖ wi ‖ (...) l‿ytiliz ‖]

**1094**

EN I've never seen these flowers before. What are they called?

FR Je n'ai jamais vu ces fleurs auparavant. Comment les appelle-t-on?

IPA [ʒø n‿ɛ ʒamɛ vy se flœʁ opaʁavɑ̃ ‖ komɑ̃ le apɛl t‿ɔ̃ ‖]

**1095**

EN My sunglasses were stolen at the beach yesterday.

FR On m'a volé mes verres fumés à la plage hier.
IPA [ɔ̃ m‿a vole me vɛʁ fyme a la plaʒ jɛʁ ‖]

**1096**

EN The bridge is closed. It got damaged last week, and it hasn't been repaired yet.

FR Le pont est fermé. Il a été endommagé la semaine dernière, et on ne l'a pas encore réparé.
IPA [lø pɔ̃ e fɛʁme ‖ i l‿a ete ɑ̃domaʒe la sᵊmɛn dɛʁnjɛʁ | e ɔ̃ nø l‿a pa z‿ɑ̃kɔʁ ʁepaʁe ‖]

**1097**

EN It hasn't gotten repaired yet.

FR On ne l'a pas encore réparé. > Il n'a pas encore été réparé.
IPA [ɔ̃ nø l‿a pa z‿ɑ̃kɔʁ ʁepaʁe ‖ > il n‿a pa z‿ɑ̃kɔʁ ete ʁepaʁe ‖]

**1098**

EN Please be quiet. I'm working.

FR Silence, s'il vous plaît. Je travaille.
IPA [silɑ̃s | s‿il vu plɛ ‖ ʒø tʁavaj ‖]

1099

EN  It isn't raining right now.

---

FR  Il ne pleut pas en ce moment.
IPA  [il nø plø pa z‿ɑ̃ sø momɑ̃ ‖]

1100

EN  What are you doing tonight?

---

FR  Que fais-tu ce soir?
IPA  [kø fɛ ty sø swaʁ ‖]

# GMS #1101 - 1200

**1101**

EN I was working when she arrived.

FR Je travaillais lorsqu'elle est arrivée.

IPA [ʒø tʁavajɛ lɔʁsk ɛl e t‿aʁive ‖]

**1102**

EN It wasn't raining, so we didn't need an umbrella.

FR Il ne pleuvait pas, alors nous n'avions pas besoin de parapluie.

IPA [il nø pløvɛ pa | alɔʁ nu n‿avjɔ̃ pa bøzwɛ̃ dø paʁaplɥi ‖]

**1103**

EN What were you doing at three o'clock (3:00)?

FR Que faisais-tu à trois heures (3 h)?

IPA [kø fᵊzɛ ty a tʁwa z‿œʁ (3 h) ‖]

**1104**

EN These offices aren't cleaned every day.

FR Ces bureaux ne sont pas nettoyés tous les jours.

IPA [se byʁo nø sɔ̃ pa netwaje tu le ʒuʁ ‖]

**1105**

EN The office was cleaned yesterday. The office got cleaned yesterday.

FR On a nettoyé le bureau hier. Le bureau a été nettoyé hier.

IPA [ɔ̃ n‿a netwaje lø byʁo jɛʁ || lø byʁo a ete netwaje jɛʁ ||]

**1106**

EN How was the window broken? How did the window get broken?

FR Comment a-t-on cassé la fenêtre? Comment la fenêtre a-t-elle été cassée?

IPA [komã a t‿ɔ̃ kase la fᵖnɛtʁ || komã la fᵖnɛtʁ a t‿ɛl ete kase ||]

**1107**

EN I've lived in this house for ten (10) years.

FR J'ai vécu dans cette maison durant dix ans.

IPA [ʒ‿ɛ veky dã sɛt mɛzɔ̃ dyʁã di z‿ã ||]

**1108**

EN Dietrich has never ridden a horse.

FR Dietrich n'est jamais monté à cheval.

IPA [(...) n‿e ʒamɛ mɔ̃te a ʃᵖval ||]

**1109**

EN Filippa hasn't been to South America.

FR Filippa n'est jamais allée en Amérique du Sud.
IPA [(...) n̪e ʒamɛ z̪ale ɑ̃ n̪ameʁik dy syd ‖]

**1110**

EN Where have Daisuke and Aiko gone?

FR Où sont allées Daisuke et Aiko?
IPA [u sɔ̃ ale (...) e (...) ‖]

**1111**

EN I like coffee, but I don't like tea.

FR J'aime le café, mais je n'aime pas le thé.
IPA [ʒ̪ɛm lø kafe | mɛ ʒø n̪ɛm pa lø te ‖]

**1112**

EN Gabriele doesn't go out very often.

FR Gabriele ne sort pas souvent.
IPA [(...) nø sɔʁ pa suvɑ̃ ‖]

**1113**

EN What do you usually do on weekends?

FR Que fais-tu généralement les week-ends?
IPA [kø fɛ ty ʒeneʁalᵊmɑ̃ le wikɛnd ‖]

**1114**

EN Does Fyodor live alone?

FR Est-ce que Fyodor vit seul? > Fyodor vit-il seul?
IPA [ɛsˤ kø (...) vi sœl ‖ > (...) vi t̯il sœl ‖]

**1115**

EN I didn't watch TV yesterday.

FR Je n'ai pas regardé la télé hier.
IPA [ʒø n̯ɛ pa ʁˤgaʁde la tele jɛʁ ‖]

**1116**

EN It didn't rain last week.

FR Il n'a pas plu la semaine dernière.
IPA [il n̯a pa ply la sˤmɛn dɛʁnjɛʁ ‖]

**1117**

EN What time did Fabio and Donatella go out?

FR À quelle heure Fabio et Donatella sont-ils sortis?
IPA [a kɛ l̯œʁ (...) e (...) sɔ̃ t̯il sɔʁti ‖]

**1118**

EN Do you work at night?

FR Travailles-tu la nuit?
IPA [tʁavaj ty la nɥi ‖]

**1119**

EN Where are they going?

FR Où vont-ils (♀elles)?
IPA [u vɔ̃ t‿il (♀ɛl) ||]

**1120**

EN Why are you looking at me?

FR Pourquoi me regardes-tu? > Pourquoi tu me regardes?
IPA [puʁkwa mø ʁ°gaʁd ty || > puʁkwa ty mø ʁ°gaʁd ||]

**1121**

EN Does Xenia live near you?

FR Xenia habite-t-elle près de chez toi? > Xenia vit-elle près de chez toi?
IPA [(...) abit t‿ɛl pʁɛ dø ʃe twa || > (...) vi t‿ɛl pʁɛ dø ʃe twa ||]

**1122**

EN Do you like to cook?

FR Aimes-tu cuisiner?
IPA [ɛm ty kɥizine ||]

**1123**

EN Is the sun shining?

FR Le soleil brille-t-il?
IPA [lø solɛj bʁij t‿il ‖]

**1124**

EN What time do the stores close?

FR À quelle heure les magasins ferment-ils?
IPA [a kɛ l‿œʁ le magazɛ̃ fɛʁmã t‿il ‖]

**1125**

EN Is Franz working today?

FR Franz travaille-t-il aujourd'hui?
IPA [(...) tʁavaj t‿il oʒuʁdɥi ‖]

**1126**

EN What does this word mean?

FR Qu'est-ce que ça veut dire? > Qu'est-ce que ça
signifie?
IPA [kɛs° kø sa vø diʁ ‖ > kɛs° kø sa siɲifi ‖]

**1127**

EN Are you feeling all right?

FR Tu te sens bien? > Te sens-tu bien?
IPA [ty tø sãs bjɛ̃ ‖ > tø sãs ty bjɛ̃ ‖]

**1128**

EN Heidi doesn't work at night.

FR Heidi ne travaille pas la nuit.
IPA [(...) nø tʁavaj pa la nɥi ‖]

**1129**

EN I'm very tired. I don't want to go out tonight.

FR Je suis très fatigué (♀ fatiguée). Je ne veux pas sortir ce soir.
IPA [ʒø sɥi tʁɛ fatige (♀ fatige) ‖ ʒø nø vø pa sɔʁtiʁ sø swaʁ ‖]

**1130**

EN I'm very tired. I'm not going out tonight.

FR Je suis très fatigué (♀ fatiguée). Je ne sors pas ce soir.
IPA [ʒø sɥi tʁɛ fatige (♀ fatige) ‖ ʒø nø sɔʁ pa sø swaʁ ‖]

**1131**

EN Takahiro's not working this week. He's on vacation.

FR Takahiro ne travaille pas cette semaine. Il est en vacances.
IPA [(...) nø tʁavaj pa sɛt sᵊmɛn ‖ i l̩e t̪ ᾶ vakᾶs ‖]

**1132**

EN My parents are usually at home. They don't go out very often.

FR Mes parents sont généralement à la maison. Ils ne sortent pas très souvent.

IPA [me paʁɑ̃ sɔ̃ ʒeneʁalᵊmɑ̃ a la mɛzɔ̃ ‖ il nø sɔʁt pa tʁɛ suvɑ̃ ‖]

**1133**

EN Mitsuko has traveled a lot, but she doesn't speak any foreign languages.

FR Mitsuko a beaucoup voyagé, mais elle ne parle pas de langues étrangères.

IPA [(...) a boku vwajaʒe | mɛ ɛl nø paʁl pa dø lɑ̃g etʁɑ̃ʒɛʁ ‖]

**1134**

EN You can turn off the television. I'm not watching it.

FR Tu peux éteindre la télé. Je ne la regarde pas.

IPA [ty pø etɛ̃dʁ la tele ‖ ʒø nø la ʁᵊgaʁd pa ‖]

**1135**

EN Flora has invited us to her party next week, but we're not going.

FR Flora nous a invités (♀invitées) à sa fête la semaine prochaine, mais nous n'y allons pas.

IPA [(...) nu z̲a ɛ̃vite (♀ɛ̃vite) a sa fɛt la sᵊmɛn pʁoʃɛn | mɛ nu n̲i alɔ̃ pa ‖]

**1136**

EN Where were your shoes made?

FR Où tes chaussures ont-elles été fabriquées?
IPA [u te ʃosyʁ ɔ̃ t‿ɛl ete fabʁike ‖]

**1137**

EN Did you go out last night?

FR Es-tu sorti (♀ sortie) hier soir?
IPA [ɛ ty sɔʁti (♀ sɔʁti) jɛʁ swaʁ ‖]

**1138**

EN What were you doing at ten thirty (10:30)?

FR Que faisais-tu à dix heures trente (10 h 30)?
IPA [kø fᵊzɛ ty a di z‿œʁ tʁɑ̃t (10 h 30) ‖]

**1139**

EN Where was your mother born?

FR Où ta mère est-elle née?
IPA [u ta mɛʁ e t‿ɛl ne ‖]

**1140**

EN Has Marco gone home?

FR Est-ce que Marco est rentré à la maison? > Marco est-il rentré à la maison?
IPA [ɛsᵊ kø (...) e ʁɑ̃tʁe a la mɛzɔ̃ ‖ > (...) e t‿il ʁɑ̃tʁe a la mɛzɔ̃ ‖]

**1141**

EN What time did he go?

FR À quelle heure est-il parti?
IPA [a kɛ l̬œʁ e t̬il paʁti ‖]

**1142**

EN When were these houses built?

FR Quand ces maisons ont-elles été construites?
IPA [kɑ̃ se mɛzɔ̃ ɔ̃ t̬ɛl ete kɔ̃stʁɥit ‖]

**1143**

EN Has Konstantin arrived yet?

FR Konstantin est-il déjà arrivé?
IPA [(...) e t̬il deʒa aʁive ‖]

**1144**

EN Why did you go home early?

FR Pourquoi es-tu rentré (♀rentrée) tôt à la maison?
IPA [puʁkwa ɛ ty ʁɑ̃tʁe (♀ʁɑ̃tʁe) to a la mɛzɔ̃ ‖]

**1145**

EN How long have they been married?

FR Depuis quand sont-ils mariés?
IPA [dᵊpɥi kɑ̃ sɔ̃ t̬il maʁje ‖]

**1146**

EN Milena's lost her passport.

FR Milena a perdu son passeport.
IPA [(...) a pɛʁdy sɔ̃ paspɔʁ ‖]

**1147**

EN This bridge was built ten (10) years ago.

FR Ce pont a été construit il y a dix ans.
IPA [sø pɔ̃ a ete kɔ̃stʁɥi t̪i l̪i a di z̪ɑ̃ ‖]

**1148**

EN Have you finished your work yet?

FR As-tu déjà terminé ton travail?
IPA [a ty deʒa tɛʁmine tɔ̃ tʁavaj ‖]

**1149**

EN This town is always clean. The streets get cleaned every day.

FR Cette ville est toujours propre. Les rues sont nettoyées chaque jour.
IPA [sɛt vil e tuʒuʁ pʁopʁ ‖ le ʁy sɔ̃ netwaje ʃak ʒuʁ ‖]

**1150**

EN I've just made some coffee. Would you like some?

FR Je viens de faire du café. Tu en veux?
IPA [ʒø vjɛ̃ dø fɛʁ dy kafe ‖ ty ɑ̃ vø ‖]

**1151**

EN This is a very old photograph. It was taken a long time ago.

FR C'est une très vieille photo. Elle a été prise il y a longtemps.

IPA [sɛ t‿yn tʁɛ vjɛj foto ‖ ɛ l‿a ete pʁiz i l‿i a lɔ̃tɑ̃ ‖]

**1152**

EN Paolo's bought a new car.

FR Paolo a acheté une nouvelle voiture.

IPA [(...) a aʃºte yn nuvɛl vwatyʁ ‖]

**1153**

EN I'm going to take an umbrella with me. It's raining.

FR Je vais apporter un parapluie. Il pleut.

IPA [ʒø vɛ apɔʁte ʁ‿œ̃ paʁaplɥi ‖ il plø ‖]

**1154**

EN Why are you so tired? Did you go to bed late last night?

FR Pourquoi es-tu si fatigué (♀fatiguée)? T'es-tu couché (♀couchée) tard hier soir?

IPA [puʁkwa ɛ ty si fatige (♀fatige) ‖ t‿ɛ ty kuʃe (♀kuʃe) ta ʁ jɛʁ swaʁ ‖]

**1155**

EN Where are the chocolates? Have you eaten all of them?

FR Où sont les chocolats? Les as-tu tous mangés?
IPA [u sɔ̃ le ʃokola || le a ty tu mɑ̃ʒe |||]

**1156**

EN How is your new job? Are you enjoying it?

FR Comment est ton nouveau travail? Ça te plaît?
IPA [komɑ̃ t̪e tɔ̃ nuvo tʁavaj || sa tø plɛ |||]

**1157**

EN My car was badly damaged in the accident, but I was okay.

FR Ma voiture a été gravement endommagée lors de l'accident, mais je vais bien.
IPA [ma vwatyʁ a ete gʁav°mɑ̃ t̪ɑ̃domaʒe lɔʁ dø l̪aksidɑ̃ | mɛ ʒø vɛ bjɛ̃ |||]

**1158**

EN Giuliana has a car, but she doesn't drive it very often.

FR Giuliana a une voiture, mais elle ne la conduit pas très souvent.
IPA [(...) a yn vwatyʁ | mɛ ɛl nø la kɔ̃dɥi pa tʁɛ suvɑ̃ |||]

**1159**

EN Kasumi isn't at home. She's gone away for a few days.

---

FR Kasumi n'est pas à la maison. Elle est partie pour quelques jours.

IPA [(...) n̪e pa a la mɛzɔ̃ || ɛ l̪e paʁti puʁ kɛlk ʒuʁ ||]

**1160**

EN I don't understand the problem. Can you explain it again?

---

FR Je ne comprends pas le problème. Peux-tu l'expliquer une autre fois?

IPA [ʒø nø kɔ̃pʁã pa lø pʁoblɛm || pø ty l̪ɛksplike yn otʁ fwa ||]

**1161**

EN Kenichi's in his room. He's listening to music.

---

FR Kenichi est dans sa chambre. Il écoute de la musique.

IPA [(...) e dã sa ʃãbʁ || i l̪ekut dø la myzik ||]

**1162**

EN I don't know how to say this word. How is it pronounced?

---

FR Je ne sais pas comment dire ce mot. Comment est-il prononcé?

IPA [ʒø nø sɛ pa komã diʁ sø mo || komã e t̪il pʁonɔ̃se ||]

**1163**

EN How do you open this window? Can you show me?

FR Comment ouvres-tu cette fenêtre? Peux-tu me montrer?

IPA [komã uvʁ ty sɛt fⁿnɛtʁ || pø ty mø mɔ̃tʁe ||]

**1164**

EN I cleaned my room yesterday.

FR J'ai nettoyé ma chambre hier.

IPA [ʒ‿ɛ netwaje ma ʃɑ̃bʁ jɛʁ ||]

**1165**

EN Henrik studied engineering in college.

FR Henrik a étudié l'ingénierie au collège.

IPA [(...) a etydje l‿ɛ̃ʒeniʁi o kolɛʒ ||]

**1166**

EN I've cleaned my room.

FR J'ai nettoyé ma chambre.

IPA [ʒ‿ɛ netwaje ma ʃɑ̃bʁ ||]

**1167**

EN Magda has lived in Miami for thirteen (13) years.

FR Magda a vécu à Miami durant treize (13) ans.

IPA [(...) a veky a (...) dyʁã tʁɛz (13) ã ||]

**1168**

EN These rooms are cleaned every day. These rooms get cleaned every day.

---

FR Ces chambres sont nettoyées tous les jours. Ces chambres se font nettoyer tous les jours.

IPA [se ʃɑ̃bʁ sɔ̃ netwaje tu le ʒuʁ ‖ se ʃɑ̃bʁ sø fɔ̃ netwaje tu le ʒuʁ ‖]

**1169**

EN My car has been repaired.

---

FR Ma voiture a été réparée.

IPA [ma vwatyʁ a ete ʁepaʁe ‖]

**1170**

EN I made a cake yesterday.

---

FR J'ai fait un gâteau hier.

IPA [ʒ‿ɛ fɛ t‿œ̃ gato jɛʁ ‖]

**1171**

EN I've made some coffee.

---

FR J'ai fait du café.

IPA [ʒ‿ɛ fɛ dy kafe ‖]

**1172**

EN  Somebody broke this window last night.

FR  Quelqu'un a fracassé cette fenêtre la nuit dernière.

IPA  [kɛlkœ̃ n‿a fʁakase sɛt fʰnɛtʁ la nɥi dɛʁnjɛʁ ‖]

**1173**

EN  Somebody's broken this window.

FR  Quelqu'un a fracassé cette fenêtre.

IPA  [kɛlkœ̃ n‿a fʁakase sɛt fʰnɛtʁ ‖]

**1174**

EN  This window was broken last night. This window got broken last night.

FR  Cette fenêtre a été fracassée la nuit dernière.

IPA  [sɛt fʰnɛtʁ a ete fʁakase la nɥi dɛʁnjɛʁ ‖]

**1175**

EN  I washed my hands because they were dirty.

FR  Je me suis lavé les mains, parce qu'elles étaient sales.

IPA  [ʒø mø sɥi lave le mɛ̃ | paʁs k‿ɛl etɛ sal ‖]

**1176**

EN  I feel good. I slept very well last night.

FR  Je me sens bien. J'ai très bien dormi la nuit dernière.

IPA  [ʒø mø sɑ̃s bjɛ̃ ‖ ʒ‿ɛ tʁɛ bjɛ̃ dɔʁmi la nɥi dɛʁnjɛʁ ‖]

**1177**

EN We saw a really good movie yesterday.

FR Nous avons vu un très bon film hier.
IPA [nu z‿avɔ̃ vy œ̃ tʀɛ bɔ̃ film jɛʀ ‖]

**1178**

EN It rained a lot while we were on vacation.

FR Il a beaucoup plu pendant que nous étions en vacances.
IPA [i l‿a boku ply pɑ̃dɑ̃ kø nu z‿etjɔ̃ z‿ɑ̃ vakɑ̃s ‖]

**1179**

EN I've lost my bag. Have you seen it?

FR J'ai perdu mon sac. L'as-tu vu?
IPA [ʒ‿ɛ pɛʀdy mɔ̃ sak ‖ l‿a ty vy ‖]

**1180**

EN Linda's bicycle was stolen last week.

FR La bicyclette de Linda a été volée la semaine dernière.
IPA [la bisiklɛt dø (...) a ete vole la sᵊmɛn dɛʀnjɛʀ ‖]

**1181**

EN I went to bed early because I was tired.

FR Je suis allé (♀allée) au lit tôt, parce que j'étais fatigué (♀fatiguée).

IPA [ʒø sɥi ale (♀ale) o li to | paʁs kø ʒ‿ete fatige (♀fatige) ‖]

**1182**

EN The shopping mall was built about twenty (20) years ago.

FR Ce centre commercial a été construit il y a environ vingt (20) ans.

IPA [sø sɑ̃tʁ komɛʁsja l‿a ete kɔ̃stʁɥi t‿i l‿i a ɑ̃viʁɔ̃ vɛ̃ (20) ɑ̃ ‖]

**1183**

EN Pietro learned to drive when he was sixteen (16).

FR Pietro a appris à conduire à seize (16) ans.

IPA [(...) a apʁi a kɔ̃dɥiʁ a sɛz (16) ɑ̃ ‖]

**1184**

EN I've never ridden a horse.

FR Je ne suis jamais monté à cheval.

IPA [ʒø nø sɥi ʒamɛ mɔ̃te a ʃºval ‖]

---

**1185**

**EN**  Monika's a good friend of mine. I've known her for a long time.

---

**FR**  Monika est une bonne amie. Je la connais depuis longtemps.

**IPA**  [(...) e t‿yn bɔn ami ‖ ʒø la konɛ dᵊpɥi lɔ̃tɑ̃ ‖]

---

**1186**

**EN**  Yesterday I fell and hurt my leg.

---

**FR**  Hier, je suis tombé (♀tombée) et je me suis blessé (♀blessée) à la jambe.

**IPA**  [jɛʁ | ʒø sɥi tɔ̃be (♀tɔ̃be) e ʒø mø sɥi blese (♀blese) a la ʒɑ̃b ‖]

---

**1187**

**EN**  My brother ran in the Boston Marathon last year. Have you ever run in a marathon?

---

**FR**  Mon frère a couru le marathon de Boston l'an dernier. As-tu déjà couru un marathon?

**IPA**  [mɔ̃ fʁɛʁ a kuʁy lø maʁatɔ̃ dø (...) l‿ɑ̃ dɛʁnje ‖ a ty deʒa kuʁy œ̃ maʁatɔ̃ ‖]

---

**1188**

**EN**  Have you told Herman about your new job?

---

**FR**  As-tu parlé de ton nouveau travail à Herman?

**IPA**  [a ty paʁle dø tɔ̃ nuvo tʁavaj a (...) ‖]

**1189**

EN We played basketball on Sunday. We didn't play very well, but we won the game.

FR Nous avons joué au basketball ce dimanche. Nous n'avons pas très bien joué, mais nous avons gagné le match. > On a joué au basketball ce dimanche. On n'a pas très bien joué, mais on a gagné le match.

IPA [nu z̥avɔ̃ ʒwe o (...) sø dimɑ̃ʃ || nu n̥avɔ̃ pa tʁɛ bjɛ̃ ʒwe | mɛ nu z̥avɔ̃ gaɲe lø matʃ || > ɔ̃ n̥a ʒwe o (...) sø dimɑ̃ʃ || ɔ̃ n̥a pa tʁɛ bjɛ̃ ʒwe | mɛ ɔ̃ n̥a gaɲe lø matʃ ||]

**1190**

EN I know Masaru, but I've never met his wife.

FR Je connais Masaru, mais je n'ai jamais rencontré sa femme.

IPA [ʒø konɛ (...) | mɛ ʒø n̥ɛ ʒamɛ ʁɑ̃kɔ̃tʁe sa fam ||]

**1191**

EN We were woken up by loud music in the middle of the night.

FR Nous avons été réveillés (♀réveillés) par de la musique forte au milieu de la nuit.

IPA [nu z̥avɔ̃ ete ʁeveje (♀ʁeveje) paʁ dø la myzik fɔʁt o miljø dø la nɥi ||]

**1192**

EN  Kimiko jumped into the river and swam to the other side.

FR  Kimiko a sauté dans la rivière et nagé jusque de l'autre côté.

IPA  [(...) a sote dã la ʁivjɛʁ e naʒe ʒysk dø l̩otʁ kote ‖]

**1193**

EN  Did you like the movie? — Yes, I thought it was very good.

FR  As-tu aimé le film? — Oui, je l'ai trouvé bon.

IPA  [a ty eme lø film ‖ — wi | ʒø l̩ɛ tʁuve bõ ‖]

**1194**

EN  Many different languages are spoken in the Philippines.

FR  Plusieurs langues différentes sont parlées aux Philippines.

IPA  [plyzjœʁ lãg difeʁãt sõ paʁle o filipin ‖]

**1195**

EN  Our vacation cost a lot of money because we stayed in an expensive hotel.

FR  Nos vacances ont coûté très cher, parce que nous avons séjourné dans un hôtel cher.

IPA  [no vakãs õ kute tʁɛ ʃɛʁ | paʁs kø nu z̩avõ seʒuʁne dã z̩œ̃ n̩otɛl ʃɛʁ ‖]

**1196**

EN Have you ever driven a very fast car?

FR As-tu déjà conduit une voiture très rapide?
IPA [a ty deʒa kɔ̃dɥi t‿yn vwatyʁ tʁɛ ʁapid ‖]

**1197**

EN All the tickets for the concert were sold very quickly.

FR Tous les billets pour le concert ont été vendus très
rapidement.
IPA [tu le bijɛ puʁ lø kɔ̃sɛʁ ɔ̃ ete vɑ̃dy tʁɛ ʁapidᵊmɑ̃ ‖]

**1198**

EN A bird flew in through the open window while we
were having our dinner.

FR Un oiseau est entré dans une fenêtre ouverte en
volant alors que nous dînions.
IPA [œ̃ n‿wazo e ɑ̃tʁe dɑ̃ z‿yn fᵊnɛtʁ uvɛʁt ɑ̃ volɑ̃ alɔʁ kø
nu dinjɔ̃ ‖]

**1199**

EN Where are Deepak and Lakshmi? — They're playing
tennis in the park.

FR Où sont Deepak et Lakshmi? — Ils jouent au tennis
dans le parc.
IPA [u sɔ̃ (...) e (...) ‖ — il ʒu o tenis dɑ̃ lø paʁk ‖]

1200

EN   Pavel's playing tennis tomorrow.

FR   Pavel joue au tennis demain.

IPA   [(...) ʒu o tenis dᵒmɛ̃ ||]

# GMS #1201 - 1300

**1201**

EN I'm not working next week.

FR Je ne travaille pas la semaine prochaine.
IPA [ʒø nø tʁavaj pa la sᵊmɛn pʁoʃɛn ‖]

**1202**

EN Yuliana's going to the dentist on Friday.

FR Yuliana va chez le dentiste vendredi.
IPA [(...) va ʃe lø dɑ̃tist vɑ̃dʁᵊdi ‖]

**1203**

EN We're having a party next weekend.

FR Nous faisons une fête le week-end prochain.
IPA [nu fᵊzɔ̃ z‿yn fɛt lø wikɛnd pʁoʃɛ̃ ‖]

**1204**

EN Are you meeting your friends tonight?

FR Rencontres-tu tes amis (♀amies) ce soir?
IPA [ʁɑ̃kɔ̃tʁ ty te z‿ami (♀ami) sø swaʁ ‖]

---

**1205**

EN  What are you doing tomorrow night?

---

FR  Que fais-tu demain soir?
IPA [kø fɛ ty dᵊmɛ̃ swaʁ ‖]

---

**1206**

EN  I'm not going out tonight. I'm staying at home.

---

FR  Je ne sors pas ce soir. Je reste à la maison.
IPA [ʒø nø sɔʁ pa sø swaʁ ‖ ʒø ʁɛst a la mɛzɔ̃ ‖]

---

**1207**

EN  I'm staying at home this evening.

---

FR  Je reste à la maison ce soir.
IPA [ʒø ʁɛst a la mɛzɔ̃ sø swaʁ ‖]

---

**1208**

EN  Are you going out tonight?

---

FR  Sors-tu ce soir?
IPA [sɔʁ ty sø swaʁ ‖]

---

**1209**

EN  Wilma isn't coming to the party next week.

---

FR  Wilma ne vient pas à la fête la semaine prochaine.
IPA [(...) nø vjɛ̃ pa a la fɛt la sᵊmɛn pʁoʃɛn ‖]

1210

EN The plane arrives in New York at seven thirty (7:30) tomorrow morning.

FR L'avion arrive à New York à sept heures trente (7 h 30) demain matin.

IPA [l̩ avjɔ̃ aʁiv a nuw jɔʁk a sɛ t‿œʁ tʁɑ̃t (7 h 30) dᵊmɛ̃ matɛ̃ ||]

1211

EN What time does the movie end tonight?

FR À quelle heure le film finit-il ce soir?

IPA [a kɛ l̩ œʁ lø film fini t‿il sø swaʁ ||]

1212

EN I'm going to a concert tomorrow.

FR Je vais à un concert demain.

IPA [ʒø vɛ a œ̃ kɔ̃sɛʁ dᵊmɛ̃ ||]

1213

EN The concert starts at seven thirty (7:30).

FR Le concert commence à dix-neuf heures trente (19 h 30).

IPA [lø kɔ̃sɛʁ komɑ̃s a diznœ v‿œʁ tʁɑ̃t (19 h 30) ||]

**1214**

EN What time are you leaving?

FR À quelle heure pars-tu?
IPA [a kɛ l‿œʁ paʁ ty ||]

**1215**

EN What time does your plane leave?

FR À quelle heure décolle ton avion?
IPA [a kɛ l‿œʁ dekɔl tɔ̃ n‿avjɔ̃ ||]

**1216**

EN Julius is playing tennis on Saturday.

FR Julius joue au tennis samedi.
IPA [(...) ʒu o tenis samᵊdi ||]

**1217**

EN Claudio's going to the movies.

FR Claudio va au cinéma.
IPA [(...) va o sinema ||]

**1218**

EN Camila's meeting with Valerio.

FR Camila rencontre Valerio.
IPA [(...) ʁɑ̃kɔ̃tʁ (...) ||]

1219

**EN** Priscilla's having lunch with Wencai.

---

**FR** Priscilla déjeune avec Wencai.
**IPA** [(...) deʒœn avɛk (...) ‖]

1220

**EN** Vitale and Rosetta are going to a party.

---

**FR** Vitale et Rosetta vont à une fête.
**IPA** [(...) e (...) vɔ̃ a yn fɛt ‖]

1221

**EN** Are you working next week?

---

**FR** Travailles-tu la semaine prochaine?
**IPA** [tʁavaj ty la sᵊmɛn pʁoʃɛn ‖]

1222

**EN** What time are your friends coming?

---

**FR** À quelle heure viennent tes amis?
**IPA** [a kɛ l‿œʁ vjɛn te z‿ami ‖]

1223

**EN** When is Yijuan going on vacation?

---

**FR** Quand Yijuan part-elle en vacances?
**IPA** [kɑ̃ d‿(...) pa ʁ‿ɛl ɑ̃ vakɑ̃s ‖]

**1224**

EN I'm going to the movies on Monday.

---

FR Je vais au cinéma lundi.

IPA [ʒø vɛ o sinema lœ̃di ‖]

**1225**

EN Listen to this! Elisa's getting married next month!

---

FR Écoute ça! Elisa se marie le mois prochain!

IPA [ekut sa ‖ (...) sø maʁi lø mwa pʁoʃɛ̃ ‖]

**1226**

EN My parents are going on vacation next week. —
Sounds good, where are they going?

---

FR Mes parents partent en vacances la semaine
prochaine. — C'est bien! Où vont-ils?

IPA [me paʁɑ̃ paʁ t‿ɑ̃ vakɑ̃s la sᵊmɛn pʁoʃɛn ‖ — sɛ bjɛ̃
‖ u vɔ̃ t‿il ‖]

**1227**

EN Esteban's taking an English course this semester. The
course is ending on Friday.

---

FR Esteban suit un cours d'anglais ce semestre. Le cours
se termine vendredi.

IPA [(...) sɥi t‿œ̃ kuʁ d‿ɑ̃glɛ sø sᵊmɛstʁ ‖ lø kuʁ sø
tɛʁmin vɑ̃dʁᵊdi ‖]

**1228**

EN There's a party tomorrow night, but I'm not going.

FR Il y a une fête demain soir, mais je n'y vais pas.

IPA [i l̬i a yn fɛt dᵊmɛ̃ swaʁ | mɛ ʒø n̬i vɛ pa ||]

**1229**

EN I'm going out with some friends tonight. Why don't you come too?

FR Je sors avec quelques amis ce soir. Pourquoi ne te joins-tu pas à nous aussi?

IPA [ʒø sɔʁ avɛk kɛl k̬ami sø swaʁ || puʁkwa nø tø ʒwɛ̃ ty pa a nu osi ||]

**1230**

EN We're meeting at Raj's house at eight o'clock (8:00).

FR Nous nous rencontrons à la maison de Raj à vingt heures (20 h). > On se rencontre à la maison de Raj à vingt heures (20 h).

IPA [nu nu ʁãkɔ̃tʁɔ̃ a la mɛzɔ̃ dø (...) a vɛ̃ t̬œʁ (20 h) || > ɔ̃ sø ʁãkɔ̃tʁ a la mɛzɔ̃ dø (...) a vɛ̃ t̬œʁ (20 h) ||]

**1231**

EN How are you getting home after the party tomorrow? By taxi?

FR Comment rentres-tu à la maison après la fête demain? En taxi?

IPA [komã ʁãtʁ ty a la mɛzɔ̃ apʁɛ la fɛt dᵊmɛ̃ || ã taksi ||]

**1232**

EN I can go by bus. The last bus leaves at midnight.

---

FR Je peux rentrer en autobus. Le dernier bus part à minuit.

IPA [ʒø pø ʁɑ̃tʁe ʁ‿ɑ̃ n‿otobys ‖ lø dɛʁnje bys paʁ a minɥi ‖]

**1233**

EN Do you want to go to the movies tonight? — Sure, what time does the movie begin?

---

FR Veux-tu aller au cinéma ce soir? — Bien sûr! À quelle heure commence le film?

IPA [vø ty ale o sinema sø swaʁ ‖ — bjɛ̃ syʁ ‖ a kɛ l‿œʁ komɑ̃s lø film ‖]

**1234**

EN What are you doing tomorrow afternoon? — I'm working.

---

FR Que fais-tu demain après-midi? — Je travaille.

IPA [kø fɛ ty dᵊmɛ̃ apʁɛ midi ‖ — ʒø tʁavaj ‖]

**1235**

EN I'm going to watch TV tonight.

---

FR Je vais regarder la télé ce soir.

IPA [ʒø vɛ ʁᵊgaʁde la tele sø swaʁ ‖]

---

**1236**

**EN** She's going to watch TV tonight.

**FR** Elle va regarder la télé ce soir.
**IPA** [ɛl va ʁ°gaʁde la tele sø swaʁ ||]

---

**1237**

**EN** I'm going to buy some books tomorrow.

**FR** Je vais acheter quelques livres demain.
**IPA** [ʒø vɛ aʃ°te kɛlk livʁ d°mɛ̃ ||]

---

**1238**

**EN** Shakti's going to sell her car.

**FR** Shakti va vendre sa voiture.
**IPA** [(...) va vɑ̃dʁ sa vwatyʁ ||]

---

**1239**

**EN** I'm not going to have breakfast this morning. I'm not hungry.

**FR** Je ne vais pas prendre le petit déjeuner ce matin. Je n'ai pas faim.
**IPA** [ʒø nø vɛ pa pʁɑ̃dʁ lø p°ti deʒœne sø matɛ̃ || ʒø n‿ɛ pa fɛ̃ ||]

**1240**

EN What are you going to wear to the wedding next week?

---

FR Que porteras-tu au mariage la semaine prochaine?
IPA [kø pɔʁtˤʁa ty o maʁjaʒ la sˤmɛn pʁoʃɛn ‖]

**1241**

EN I'm going to wash my hands.

---

FR Je vais me laver les mains.
IPA [ʒø vɛ mø lave le mɛ̃ ‖]

**1242**

EN Are you going to invite Walter to your party?

---

FR Vas-tu inviter Walter à ta fête?
IPA [va ty ɛ̃vite (...) a ta fɛt ‖]

**1243**

EN I'm playing tennis with Satomi tomorrow.

---

FR Je joue au tennis avec Satomi demain.
IPA [ʒø ʒu o tenis avɛk (...) dˤmɛ̃ ‖]

**1244**

EN Something is going to happen.

---

FR Quelque chose va se passer.
IPA [kɛlk ʃoz va sø pase ‖]

1245

EN  Look at the sky! It's going to rain.

FR  Regarde le ciel! Il va pleuvoir.
IPA [ʁˠgaʁd lø sjɛl || il va pløvwaʁ |||]

1246

EN  It's nine o'clock (9:00) and I'm not ready. I'm going
to be late.

FR  Il est neuf heures (9 h) et je ne suis pas prêt
(♀prête). Je vais être en retard.
IPA [i lˌe nœ vˌœʁ (9 h) e ʒø nø sɥi pa pʁɛ (♀pʁɛt) || ʒø
vɛ ɛtʁ ã ʁˠtaʁ |||]

1247

EN  What are you going to wear to the party tonight?

FR  Que vas-tu porter à la fête ce soir?
IPA [kø va ty poʁte a la fɛt sø swaʁ |||]

1248

EN  It's a nice day. I don't want to take the bus. I'm going
to walk.

FR  C'est une belle journée. Je ne veux pas prendre
l'autobus. Je vais marcher.
IPA [sɛ tˌyn bɛl ʒuʁne || ʒø nø vø pa pʁãdʁ lˌotobys || ʒø
vɛ maʁʃe |||]

**1249**

EN Yevgeniy's going to St. Petersburg next week. He's going to go with some friends.

FR Yevgeniy va à Saint-Pétersbourg la semaine prochaine. Il y ira avec quelques amis.

IPA [(...) va a sɛ̃ petɛʁsbuʁg la sᵊmɛn pʁoʃɛn || i lᵊi iʁa avɛk kɛl kˌami ||]

**1250**

EN I'm hungry. I'm going to have a sandwich.

FR J'ai faim. Je vais manger un sandwich.

IPA [ʒˌɛ fɛ̃ || ʒø vɛ mɑ̃ʒe ʁˌœ̃ sɑ̃dwitʃ ||]

**1251**

EN It's Violetta's birthday next week. We're going to get her a present.

FR C'est l'anniversaire de Violetta la semaine prochaine. Nous lui offrirons un cadeau.

IPA [sɛ lˌanivɛʁsɛʁ dø (...) la sᵊmɛn pʁoʃɛn || nu lɥi ofʁiʁɔ̃ zˌœ̃ kado ||]

**1252**

EN Feliciana says she's feeling very tired. She's going to lie down for an hour.

FR Feliciana dit qu'elle se sent très fatiguée. Elle va s'étendre pour une heure.

IPA [(...) di kˌɛl sø sɑ̃ tʁɛ fatige || ɛl va sˌetɑ̃dʁ pu ʁˌyn œʁ ||]

**1253**

EN The president's speech is on television tonight. Are you going to watch it?

FR Le discours du président est à la télé ce soir. Vas-tu le regarder?

IPA [lø diskuʁ dy pʁezidɑ̃ e a la tele sø swaʁ || va ty lø ʁ°gaʁde ||]

**1254**

EN What's Gerardo going to do when he finishes school?

FR Qu'est-ce que Gerardo va faire lorsqu'il terminera l'école? > Que fera Gerardo lorsqu'il terminera l'école?

IPA [kɛs° kø (...) va fɛʁ lɔʁsk il tɛʁmin°ʁa l̩ekɔl || > kø f°ʁa (...) lɔʁsk il tɛʁmin°ʁa l̩ekɔl ||]

**1255**

EN Aliyah goes to work every day. She's always there from eight thirty (8:30) until four thirty (4:30).

FR Aliyah va au travail chaque jour. Elle y est toujours de huit heures trente (8 h 30) à seize heures trente (16 h 30).

IPA [(...) va o tʁavaj ʃak ʒuʁ || ɛ l̩ i e tuʒuʁ dø ɥi t̩œʁ tʁɑ̃t (8 h 30) a sɛz œʁ tʁɑ̃t (16 h 30) ||]

**1256**

EN It's eleven o'clock (11:00) now. Aliyah's at work.

---

FR Il est onze heures (11 h) maintenant. Aliyah est au travail.

IPA [i l̯e t ɔ̃z œʁ (11 h) mɛ̃t°nɑ̃ || (...) e o tʁavaj ||]

**1257**

EN At eleven [o'clock] (11:00) yesterday, she was at work.

---

FR À onze heures (11 h) hier, elle était au travail.

IPA [a ɔ̃z œʁ (11 h) jeʁ | ɛ l̯etɛ o tʁavaj ||]

**1258**

EN At eleven [o'clock] (11:00) tomorrow, she'll be at work.

---

FR À onze heures (11 h) demain, elle sera au travail.

IPA [a ɔ̃z œʁ (11 h) d°mɛ̃ | ɛl s°ʁa o tʁavaj ||]

**1259**

EN Yuko travels a lot. Today she's in Frankfurt. Tomorrow she'll be in Dubai. Next week she'll be in Singapore.

---

FR Yuko voyage beaucoup. Aujourd'hui, elle est à Francfort. Demain, elle sera à Dubai. La semaine prochaine, elle sera à Singapour.

IPA [(...) vwajaʒ boku || oʒuʁdɥi | ɛ l̯e a fʁɑ̃kfɔʁ || d°mɛ̃ | ɛl s°ʁa a (...) || la s°mɛn pʁoʃen | ɛl s°ʁa a singapuʁ ||]

**1260**

EN You can call me tonight. I'll be at home.

---

FR Tu peux m'appeler ce soir. Je serai à la maison.
IPA [ty pø m‿apᵊle sø swaʁ || ʒø sᵊʁɛ a la mɛzɔ̃ ||]

**1261**

EN Leave the old bread in the yard. The birds will eat it.

---

FR Laisse le vieux pain dans le jardin. Les oiseaux vont le manger.
IPA [lɛs lø vjø pɛ̃ dɑ̃ lø ʒaʁdɛ̃ || le z‿wazo vɔ̃ lø mɑ̃ʒe ||]

**1262**

EN We'll probably go out tonight.

---

FR Nous allons probablement sortir ce soir.
IPA [nu z‿alɔ̃ pʁobablᵊmɑ̃ sɔʁtiʁ sø swaʁ ||]

**1263**

EN Will you be at home tonight?

---

FR Seras-tu à la maison ce soir?
IPA [sᵊʁa ty a la mɛzɔ̃ sø swaʁ ||]

**1264**

EN I won't be here tomorrow.

---

FR Je ne serai pas ici demain.
IPA [ʒø nø sᵊʁɛ pa z‿isi dᵊmɛ̃ ||]

---

**1265**

**EN** Don't drink coffee before you go to bed; otherwise, you won't sleep.

**FR** Ne bois pas de café avant d'aller au lit, sinon tu ne dormiras pas.

**IPA** [nø bwa pa dø kafe avɑ̃ d‿ale o li | sinɔ̃ ty nø dɔʁmiʁa pa ||]

---

**1266**

**EN** I think Ayman will pass his driver's test.

**FR** Je crois qu'Ayman passera son examen de conduite.

**IPA** [ʒø kʁwa k (...) pasᵊʁa sɔ̃ n‿ɛgzamɛ̃ dø kɔ̃dɥit ||]

---

**1267**

**EN** I don't think it'll rain this afternoon.

**FR** Je ne pense pas qu'il va pleuvoir cet après-midi.

**IPA** [ʒø nø pɑ̃s pa k‿il va pløvwaʁ sɛt apʁɛ midi ||]

---

**1268**

**EN** Do you think the test will be difficult?

**FR** Penses-tu que l'examen sera difficile?

**IPA** [pɑ̃s ty kø l‿ɛgzamɛ̃ sᵊʁa difisil ||]

**1269**

EN   We're going to the movies on Saturday. Do you want to come with us?

FR   Nous allons au cinéma ce samedi. Veux-tu venir avec nous?

IPA   [nu z‿alɔ̃ o sinema sø sam°di || vø ty v°niʁ avɛk nu ||]

**1270**

EN   I'm not working tomorrow.

FR   Je ne travaille pas demain.

IPA   [ʒø nø tʁavaj pa d°mɛ̃ ||]

**1271**

EN   Are you going to take your driver's test tomorrow?

FR   Vas-tu passer ton examen de conduite demain?

IPA   [va ty pase tɔ̃ n‿ɛgzamɛ̃ dø kɔ̃dɥit d°mɛ̃ ||]

**1272**

EN   Yesterday she was in Rio de Janeiro.

FR   Hier, elle était à Rio de Janeiro.

IPA   [jeʁ | ɛ l‿ete a (...) ||]

**1273**

EN Tomorrow she'll be in Caracas.

---

FR Demain, elle sera à Caracas.
IPA [dᵊmɛ̃ | ɛl sᵊʁa a (...) ||]

**1274**

EN Last week she was in Lima.

---

FR La semaine dernière, elle était à Lima.
IPA [la sᵊmɛn dɛʁnjɛʁ | ɛ l̩etɛ a (...) ||]

**1275**

EN Next week she'll be in Bogota.

---

FR La semaine prochaine, elle sera à Bogota.
IPA [la sᵊmɛn pʁoʃɛn | ɛl sᵊʁa a (...) ||]

**1276**

EN Right now she's in Buenos Aires.

---

FR En ce moment, elle est à Buenos Aires.
IPA [ɑ̃ sø momɑ̃ | ɛ l̩e a (...) ||]

**1277**

EN Three days ago she was in Santiago.

---

FR Il y a trois jours, elle était à Santiago.
IPA [i l̩i a tʁwa ʒuʁ | ɛ l̩etɛ a (...) ||]

**1278**

EN At the end of her trip she'll be very tired.

FR À la fin de son voyage, elle sera très fatiguée.
IPA [a la fɛ̃ dø sɔ̃ vwajaʒ | ɛl sᵊʁa tʁɛ fatige ||]

**1279**

EN I'll be at the movies an hour from now.

FR Je serai au cinéma d'ici une heure.
IPA [ʒø sᵊʁɛ o sinema d̪ isi yn œʁ ||]

**1280**

EN I'll be asleep at midnight tonight.

FR Je serai endormi ce soir à minuit.
IPA [ʒø sᵊʁɛ ɑ̃dɔʁmi sø swaʁ a minɥi ||]

**1281**

EN I'll be working at three [o'clock] (3:00) tomorrow afternoon.

FR Je serai en train de travailler à quinze heures (15 h) demain après-midi.
IPA [ʒø sᵊʁɛ ɑ̃ tʁɛ̃ dø tʁavaje a kɛ̃z œʁ (15 h) dᵊmɛ̃ apʁɛ midi ||]

**1282**

EN I'll be at a new job two (2) years from now.

FR J'aurai un nouvel emploi d'ici deux ans.

IPA [ʒ‿oʁɛ œ̃ nuvɛ l‿ãplwa d‿isi dø z‿ã ‖]

**1283**

EN Are you ready yet? — Not yet. I'll be ready in five (5) minutes.

FR Es-tu prêt? — Pas encore. Je le serai dans cinq minutes.

IPA [ɛ ty pʁɛ ‖ — pa z‿ãkɔʁ ‖ ʒø lø s°ʁɛ dã sɛ̃k minyt ‖]

**1284**

EN I'm going away for a few days. I'm leaving tonight, so I won't be at home tomorrow.

FR Je vais à l'extérieur pour quelques jours. Je pars ce soir, alors je ne serai pas à la maison demain.

IPA [ʒø vɛ a l‿eksteʁjœʁ puʁ kɛlk ʒuʁ ‖ ʒø paʁ sø swaʁ | alɔʁ ʒø nø s°ʁɛ pa a la mɛzɔ̃ d°mɛ̃ ‖]

**1285**

EN It won't rain, so you don't need to take an umbrella.

FR Il ne pleuvra pas, alors tu n'as pas besoin de prendre de parapluie.

IPA [il nø pløvʁa pa | alɔʁ ty n‿a pa bøzwɛ̃ dø pʁãdʁ dø paʁaplɥi ‖]

**1286**

EN   I don't feel very well tonight.

FR   Je ne me sens pas très bien ce soir.

IPA  [ʒø nø mø sãs pa tʁɛ bjɛ̃ sø swaʁ |||]

**1287**

EN   Well, go to bed early and you'll feel better in the morning.

FR   Bien, va au lit tôt et tu te sentiras mieux demain matin. > Bien, va au lit plus tôt et tu te sentiras mieux demain matin.

IPA  [bjɛ̃ | va o li to t̪e ty tø sãtiʁa mjø dᵊmɛ̃ matɛ̃ || > bjɛ̃ | va o li plys to t̪e ty tø sãtiʁa mjø dᵊmɛ̃ matɛ̃ |||]

**1288**

EN   It's Qasim's birthday next Monday. He'll be twenty-five (25).

FR   C'est l'anniversaire de Qasim lundi prochain. Il aura vingt-cinq (25) ans.

IPA  [sɛ l̪anivɛʁsɛʁ dø (...) lœ̃di pʁoʃɛ̃ || i l̪oʁa vɛ̃tsɛ̃k (25) ã |||]

**1289**

EN I'm sorry I was late this morning. It won't happen again.

---

FR Je suis désolé d'avoir été en retard ce matin. Ça n'arrivera plus.

IPA [ʒø sɥi dezole d‿avwaʁ ete ɑ̃ ʁˠtaʁ sø matɛ̃ ‖ sa n‿aʁivˠʁa plys ‖|]

**1290**

EN I think Euna will pass her driver's test.

---

FR Je crois qu'Euna passera son examen de conduite.

IPA [ʒø kʁwa k (...) pasˠʁa sɔ̃ n‿ɛgzamɛ̃ dø kɔ̃dɥit ‖|]

**1291**

EN I don't think Jiyeong will pass his driver's test.

---

FR Je ne pense pas que Jiyeong passera son examen de conduite.

IPA [ʒø nø pɑ̃s pa kø (...) pasˠʁa sɔ̃ n‿ɛgzamɛ̃ dø kɔ̃dɥit ‖|]

**1292**

EN I think we'll win the game.

---

FR Je pense que nous allons gagner la partie.

IPA [ʒø pɑ̃s kø nu z‿alɔ̃ gaɲe la paʁti ‖|]

**1293**

EN I won't be here tomorrow. > I don't think I'll be here tomorrow.

FR Je ne serai pas ici demain. Je ne pense pas que je serai ici demain.

IPA [ʒø nø sᵊʁɛ pa z‿isi dᵊmɛ̃ || ʒø nø pãs pa kø ʒø sᵊʁɛ isi dᵊmɛ̃ ||]

**1294**

EN I think Iris will like her present.

FR Je crois qu'Iris va aimer son cadeau.

IPA [ʒø kʁwa k (...) va eme sɔ̃ kado ||]

**1295**

EN They won't get married. > I don't think they'll get married.

FR Ils ne se marieront pas. Je ne pense pas qu'ils vont se marier.

IPA [il nø sø maʁiʁɔ̃ pa || ʒø nø pãs pa k‿il vɔ̃ sø maʁje ||]

**1296**

EN You won't like the movie. > I don't think you'll like the movie.

FR Tu n'aimeras pas le film. Je ne pense pas que tu vas aimer le film.

IPA [ty n‿emᵊʁa pa lø film || ʒø nø pãs pa kø ty va eme lø film ||]

**1297**

EN   We're going to the theater tonight. We've got tickets.

---

FR   Nous allons au théâtre ce soir. Nous avons des billets.
IPA  [nu z‿alɔ̃ o teatʁ sø swaʁ || nu z‿avɔ̃ de bijɛ ||]

**1298**

EN   What are you doing tomorrow night? — Nothing, I'm free.

---

FR   Que fais-tu demain? — Rien, je suis libre.
IPA  [kø fɛ ty dᵊmɛ̃ || — ʁjɛ̃ | ʒø sɥi libʁ ||]

**1299**

EN   They're leaving tomorrow morning. Their train is at eight forty (8:40).

---

FR   Ils (♀elles) partent demain matin. Leur train est à huit heures quarante (8 h 40).
IPA  [il (♀ɛl) paʁt dᵊmɛ̃ matɛ̃ || lœʁ tʁɛ̃ e a ɥi t‿œʁ kaʁɑ̃t (8 h 40) ||]

**1300**

EN   Why are you putting on your coat? — I'm going out.

---

FR   Pourquoi mets-tu ton manteau? — Je sors.
IPA  [puʁkwa mɛ ty tɔ̃ mɑ̃to || — ʒø sɔʁ ||]

# GMS #1301 - 1400

### 1301

**EN** Do you think Jorge will call us tonight?

**FR** Penses-tu que Jorge va nous appeler ce soir?
**IPA** [pãs ty kø (...) va nu z‿apᵊle sø swaʁ ‖]

### 1302

**EN** Farid can't meet us on Saturday. He's working.

**FR** Farid ne peut pas nous rencontrer ce samedi. Il travaille.
**IPA** [(...) nø pø pa nu ʁãkɔ̃tʁe sø samᵊdi ‖ il tʁavaj ‖]

### 1303

**EN** Let's fly to Barcelona instead of driving. It won't take as long.

**FR** Allons à Barcelone en avion plutôt qu'en voiture. Ça ne prendra pas autant de temps.
**IPA** [alɔ̃ a baʁsᵊlon ã n‿avjɔ̃ plyto k‿ã vwatyʁ ‖ sa nø pʁãdʁa pa z‿otã dø tã ‖]

### 1304

**EN** What are your plans for the weekend?

**FR** Quels sont tes plans ce week-end?
**IPA** [kɛl sɔ̃ te plã sø wikɛnd ‖]

**1305**

EN Some friends are coming to stay with us.

FR Quelques amis viennent séjourner chez nous.

IPA [kɛl k‿ami vjɛn seʒuʁne ʃe nu ‖]

**1306**

EN My suitcase is very heavy. — I'll carry it for you.

FR Ma valise est très lourde. — Je vais la transporter pour toi.

IPA [ma valiz e tʁɛ luʁd ‖ — ʒø vɛ la tʁɑ̃spɔʁte puʁ twa ‖]

**1307**

EN I'll call you tomorrow, okay?

FR Je vais t'appeler demain, d'accord?

IPA [ʒø vɛ t‿apˈle dˈmɛ̃ | dˈakɔʁ ‖]

**1308**

EN I'm tired. I think I'll go to bed early tonight.

FR Je suis fatigué (♀ fatiguée). Je pense que je vais aller au lit tôt ce soir.

IPA [ʒø sɥi tʁɛ fatige (fatige) ‖ ʒø pɑ̃s kø ʒø vɛ ale o li to sø swaʁ ‖]

1309

EN It's a nice day. I think I'll sit outside.

FR C'est une belle journée. Je pense que je vais m'asseoir dehors.

IPA [sɛ t‿yn bɛl ʒuʁne ‖ ʒø pãs kø ʒø vɛ m‿aswaʁ døɔʁ ‖]

1310

EN It's raining. I don't think I'll go out.

FR Il pleut. Je ne pense pas sortir.

IPA [il plø ‖ ʒø nø pãs pa sɔʁtiʁ ‖]

1311

EN I'm working tomorrow.

FR Je travaille demain.

IPA [ʒø tʁavaj dᵊmɛ̃ ‖]

1312

EN There's a good program on TV tonight. I'm going to watch it.

FR Il y a une bonne émission à la télé ce soir. Je vais la regarder.

IPA [i l‿i a yn bɔn emisjɔ̃ a la tele sø swaʁ ‖ ʒø vɛ la ʁᵊgaʁde ‖]

**1313**

EN What are you doing this weekend?

FR Que fais-tu ce week-end?
IPA [kø fɛ ty sø wikɛnd ‖]

**1314**

EN It's very warm in this room. Shall I open a window?

FR Il fait très chaud dans cette pièce. Puis-je ouvrir une fenêtre?
IPA [il fɛ tʁɛ ʃo dɑ̃ sɛt pjɛs ‖ pɥi ʒø uvʁi ʁ‿yn fᵊnɛtʁ ‖]

**1315**

EN Shall I call you tonight?

FR Je t'appelle ce soir?
IPA [ʒø t‿apɛl sø swaʁ ‖]

**1316**

EN It's a nice day. Shall we go for a walk?

FR C'est une belle journée. On va se promener?
IPA [sɛ t‿yn bɛl ʒuʁne ‖ ɔ̃ va sø pʁɔmne ‖]

**1317**

EN What shall we have for dinner?

FR Qu'est-ce qu'on pourrait manger pour dîner?
IPA [kɛsᵊ k‿ɔ̃ puʁɛ mɑ̃ʒe puʁ dine ‖]

**1318**

EN  Should I call you tonight?

FR  Devrais-je t'appeler ce soir?
IPA  [dᵊvʁɛ ʒø t‿apᵊle sø swaʁ ‖]

**1319**

EN  It's a nice day. Should we go for a walk?

FR  C'est une belle journée. On va se promener?
IPA  [sɛ t‿yn bɛl ʒuʁne ‖ ɔ̃ va sø pʁɔmne ‖]

**1320**

EN  What should we have for dinner?

FR  Qu'est-ce qu'on pourrait manger pour dîner?
IPA  [kɛsᵊ k‿ɔ̃ puʁɛ mɑ̃ʒe puʁ dine ‖]

**1321**

EN  Enjoy your vacation. — I'll send you a postcard.

FR  Profite de tes vacances. — Je t'enverrai une carte
postale.
IPA  [pʁofit dø te vakɑ̃s ‖ — ʒø t‿ɑ̃veʁe yn kaʁt pɔstal ‖]

**1322**

EN  I don't want this banana. — I'm hungry. I'll have it.

---

FR  Je ne veux pas cette banane. — J'ai faim. Je vais la prendre.

IPA  [ʒø nø vø pa sɛt banan || — ʒ‿ɛ fɛ̃ || ʒø vɛ la pʁɑ̃dʁ ||]

**1323**

EN  Do you want a chair? — No, it's okay. I'll sit on the floor.

---

FR  Veux-tu une chaise? — Non, ça va. Je vais m'asseoir par terre.

IPA  [vø ty yn ʃɛz || — nɔ̃ | sa va || ʒø vɛ m‿aswaʁ paʁ tɛʁ ||]

**1324**

EN  Did you call Gamila? — Oh no, I forgot. I'll call her now.

---

FR  As-tu appelé Gamila? — Oh! Non, j'ai oublié. Je vais l'appeler maintenant.

IPA  [a ty apᵊle (...) || — o || nɔ̃ | ʒ‿ɛ ublije || ʒø vɛ l‿apᵊle mɛ̃tᵊnɑ̃ ||]

**1325**

EN Are you coming with me? — No, I don't think so. I'm staying here.

FR Viens-tu avec moi? — Non, je ne pense pas. Je reste ici.

IPA [vjɛ̃ ty avɛk mwa ‖ — nɔ̃ | ʒø nø pɑ̃s pa ‖ ʒø ʁɛst isi ‖]

**1326**

EN How do you use this camera? — Give it to me and I'll show you.

FR Comment utilises-tu cette caméra? — Donne-la-moi et je te montrerai.

IPA [komɑ̃ ytiliz ty sɛt kameʁa ‖ — dɔn la mwa e ʒø tø mɔ̃tʁˤʁɛ ‖]

**1327**

EN It's cold today. I don't think I'll go out.

FR Il fait froid aujourd'hui. Je ne pense pas sortir.

IPA [il fɛ fʁwa oʒuʁdɥi ‖ ʒø nø pɑ̃s pa soʁtiʁ ‖]

**1328**

EN I'm hungry. I think I'll buy something to eat.

FR J'ai faim. Je pense que je vais acheter quelque chose à manger.

IPA [ʒ ɛ fɛ̃ ‖ ʒø pɑ̃s kø ʒø vɛ aʃˤte kɛlk ʃoz a mɑ̃ʒe ‖]

---

**1329**

**EN** I feel very tired. I don't think I'll play tennis today.

---

**FR** Je me sens très fatigué (♀fatiguée). Je ne pense pas jouer au tennis aujourd'hui.

**IPA** [ʒø mø sɑ̃s tʁɛ fatige (♀fatige) || ʒø nø pɑ̃s pa ʒwe o tenis oʒuʁdɥi ||]

---

**1330**

**EN** I like this hat. I think I'll buy it.

---

**FR** J'aime ce chapeau. Je pense que je vais l'acheter. > Je pense l'acheter.

**IPA** [ʒˌɛm sø ʃapo || ʒø pɑ̃s kø ʒø vɛ lˌaʃ°te || > ʒø pɑ̃s lˌaʃ°te ||]

---

**1331**

**EN** This camera is too expensive. I don't think I'll buy it.

---

**FR** Cette caméra est trop chère. Je ne pense pas que je vais l'acheter. > Je ne pense pas l'acheter.

**IPA** [sɛt kameʁa e tʁo ʃɛʁ || ʒø nø pɑ̃s pa kø ʒø vɛ lˌaʃ°te || > ʒø nø pɑ̃s pa lˌaʃ°te ||]

---

**1332**

**EN** I haven't done the shopping yet. I'll do it later.

---

**FR** Je n'ai pas encore fait les courses. Je les ferai plus tard.

**IPA** [ʒø nˌɛ pa zˌɑ̃kɔʁ fɛ le kuʁs || ʒø le fˀʁɛ plys taʁ ||]

**1333**

EN  I like sports. I watch a lot of sports on TV.

FR  J'aime le sport. Je regarde beaucoup de sports à la télé.

IPA  [ʒ‿ɛm lø spɔʁ || ʒø ʁ°gaʁd boku dø spɔʁ a la tele ||]

**1334**

EN  I need some exercise. I think I'll go for a walk.

FR  J'ai besoin de faire de l'exercice. Je pense que je vais aller marcher.

IPA  [ʒ‿ɛ bøzwɛ̃ dø fɛʁ dø l‿egzɛʁsis || ʒø pãs kø ʒø vɛ ale maʁʃe ||]

**1335**

EN  Yoshi's going to buy a new car. He told me last week.

FR  Yoshi va s'acheter une nouvelle voiture. Il me l'a dit la semaine dernière.

IPA  [(...) va s‿aʃ°te yn nuvɛl vwatyʁ || il mø l‿a di la s°men dɛʁnjɛʁ ||]

**1336**

EN  This letter is for Sachiko. — Okay, I'll give it to her.

FR  Cette lettre est pour Sachiko. — D'accord, je vais lui donner.

IPA  [sɛt lɛtʁ e puʁ (...) || — d‿akɔʁ | ʒø vɛ lɥi done ||]

---

**1337**

EN Are you doing anything this evening?

---

FR Fais-tu quelque chose ce soir? > Tu fais quelque chose ce soir?

IPA [fɛ ty kɛlk ʃoz sø swaʁ || > ty fɛ kɛlk ʃoz sø swaʁ ||]

---

**1338**

EN Yes, I'm going out with some friends.

---

FR Oui, je sors avec quelques amis (♀amies).

IPA [wi | ʒø sɔʁ avɛk kɛl k‿ami (♀ami) ||]

---

**1339**

EN I can't go out with you tomorrow night, as I'm working.

---

FR Je ne peux pas sortir avec toi demain soir, je travaille.

IPA [ʒø nø pø pa sɔʁtiʁ avɛk twa d°mɛ̃ swaʁ | ʒø tʁavaj ||]

---

**1340**

EN It's dark in this room. Should I turn on the light?

---

FR C'est sombre dans cette pièce. J'allume?

IPA [sɛ sõbʁ dɑ̃ sɛt pjɛs || ʒ‿alym ||]

**1341**

EN Shall I wait here? — No, come with me.

FR Je t'attends ici? — Non, viens avec moi.
IPA [ʒø t‿atɑ̃ isi ‖ — nɔ̃ | vjɛ̃ avɛk mwa ‖]

**1342**

EN Should I go to the store? — No, I'll go.

FR Je vais à la boutique? — Non, je vais y aller.
IPA [ʒø vɛ a la butik ‖ — nɔ̃ | ʒø vɛ z‿i ale ‖]

**1343**

EN Should we have a party? — Yes, who shall we invite?

FR On organise une fête? — D'accord, qui devrait-on inviter?
IPA [ɔ̃ n‿ɔʁganiz yn fɛt ‖ — d‿akɔʁ | ki dəvʁɛ t‿ɔ̃ ɛ̃vite ‖]

**1344**

EN I'm not sure where to go on vacation. I might go to Costa Rica.

FR Je ne suis pas sûr où j'irai en vacances. J'irai peut-être au Costa Rica.
IPA [ʒø nø sɥi pa syʁ u ʒ‿iʁe ɑ̃ vakɑ̃s ‖ ʒ‿iʁe pøtɛtʁ o (...) ‖]

**1345**

EN It looks like it might rain.

FR Il semble qu'il va pleuvoir.
IPA [il sɑ̃bl k‿il va pløvwaʁ ‖]

**1346**

EN I might go to the movies tonight, but I'm not sure.

FR Je vais peut-être aller au cinéma ce soir, mais je ne
suis pas sûr (♀ sûre).
IPA [ʒø vɛ pøtɛtʁ ale o sinema sø swaʁ | mɛ ʒø nø sɥi pa
syʁ (♀ syʁ) ‖]

**1347**

EN When's Faruq going to call you? — I don't know. He
might call this afternoon.

FR Quand Faruq t'appellera-t-il? — Je ne sais pas. Il va
peut-être appeler cet après-midi.
IPA [kɑ̃ (...) t‿apɛlˠʁa t‿il ‖ — ʒø nø sɛ pa ‖ il va pøtɛtʁ
apˠle sɛt apʁɛ midi ‖]

**1348**

EN Take an umbrella with you. It might rain.

FR Prends un parapluie. Il va peut-être pleuvoir.
IPA [pʁɑ̃ z‿œ̃ paʁaplɥi ‖ il va pøtɛtʁ pløvwaʁ ‖]

**1349**

EN  Buy a lottery ticket. You might be lucky.

FR  Achète un billet de loterie. Peut-être seras-tu chanceux.

IPA  [aʃɛt œ̃ bijɛ də lɔtᵊʁi || pøtɛtʁ sᵊʁa ty ʃɑ̃sø ||]

**1350**

EN  Are you going out tonight? — I might.

FR  Sors-tu ce soir? — Peut-être.

IPA  [sɔʁ ty sø swaʁ || — pø ɛtʁ ||]

**1351**

EN  I'm playing tennis tomorrow. > I might play tennis tomorrow.

FR  Je joue au tennis demain. Je vais peut-être jouer au tennis demain.

IPA  [ʒø ʒu o tenis dᵊmɛ̃ || ʒø vɛ pøtɛtʁ ʒwe o tenis dᵊmɛ̃ ||]

**1352**

EN  Hadiya's going to call later.

FR  Hadiya va appeler plus tard.

IPA  [(...) va apᵊle plys taʁ ||]

---

**1353**

EN Hadiya might call later.

---

FR Hadiya va peut-être appeler plus tard.
IPA [(...) va pøtɛtʁ apᵊle plys taʁ ||]

---

**1354**

EN I might not go to work tomorrow.

---

FR Je ne vais peut-être pas aller travailler demain.
IPA [ʒø nø vɛ pøtɛtʁ pa z‿ale tʁavaje dᵊmɛ̃ ||]

---

**1355**

EN Shumei might not come to the party.

---

FR Shumei ne viendra peut-être pas à la fête.
IPA [(...) nø vjɛ̃dʁa pøtɛtʁ pa a la fɛt ||]

---

**1356**

EN I may go to the movies tonight.

---

FR Je vais peut-être aller au cinéma ce soir.
IPA [ʒø vɛ pøtɛtʁ ale o sinema sø swaʁ ||]

---

**1357**

EN Jianhao may not come to the party.

---

FR Jianhao ne viendra peut-être pas à la fête.
IPA [(...) nø vjɛ̃dʁa pøtɛtʁ pa a la fɛt ||]

**1358**

EN May I ask a question?

FR Je peux poser une question?
IPA [ʒø pø poze ʁ‿yn kɛstjɔ̃ ‖]

**1359**

EN May I sit here? — Sure.

FR Puis-je m'asseoir ici? > Je peux m'asseoir ici? — Bien sûr.
IPA [pɥi ʒø m‿aswaʁ isi ‖ > ʒø pø m‿aswaʁ isi ‖ — bjɛ̃ syʁ ‖]

**1360**

EN It's possible that I'll go to the movies. > I might go to the movies.

FR Il est possible que j'aille au cinéma. Je vais peut-être aller au cinéma.
IPA [i l‿e posibl kø ʒ‿aj o sinema ‖ ʒø vɛ pøtɛtʁ ale o sinema ‖]

**1361**

EN It's possible that I'll see you tomorrow. > I might see you tomorrow.

FR Il est possible que je te voie demain. Je vais peut-être te voir demain.
IPA [i l‿e posibl kø ʒø tø vwa dᵊmɛ̃ ‖ ʒø vɛ pøtɛtʁ tø vwaʁ dᵊmɛ̃ ‖]

---

**1362**

**EN** It's possible that Hakim will forget to call. > He might forget to call.

---

**FR** Il est possible qu'Hakim oublie d'appeler. Il va peut-être oublier d'appeler.

**IPA** [i l̩e posibl k (...) ubli d̯apᵊle || il va pøtɛtʁ ublije d̯apᵊle ||]

---

**1363**

**EN** It's possible that it'll snow today. > It might snow today.

---

**FR** Il est possible qu'il neige aujourd'hui. Il va peut-être neiger aujourd'hui.

**IPA** [i l̩e posibl k̩il nɛʒ oʒuʁdɥi || il va pøtɛtʁ neʒe oʒuʁdɥi ||]

---

**1364**

**EN** It's possible that I'll be late tonight. > I might be late tonight.

---

**FR** Il est possible que je sois en retard ce soir. Je vais peut-être être en retard ce soir.

**IPA** [i l̩e posibl kø ʒø swa z̯ɑ̃ ʁᵊtaʁ sø swaʁ || ʒø ve pøtɛtʁ ɛtʁ ɑ̃ ʁᵊtaʁ sø swaʁ ||]

**1365**

EN It's possible that Jamila won't be here next week. > She might not be here next week.

---

FR Il est possible que Jamila ne soit pas ici la semaine prochaine. Elle ne sera peut-être pas ici la semaine prochaine.

IPA [i l‿e posibl kø (...) nø swa pa z‿isi la s°mɛn pʁoʃɛn ‖ ɛl nø s°ʁa pøtɛtʁ pa z‿isi la s°mɛn pʁoʃɛn ‖]

**1366**

EN It's possible that I won't have time to go out. > I might not have time to go out.

---

FR Il est possible que je n'aie pas le temps de sortir. Je ne vais peut-être pas avoir le temps de sortir.

IPA [i l‿e posibl kø ʒø n‿ɛ pa lø tɑ̃ dø sɔʁtiʁ ‖ ʒø nø vɛ pøtɛtʁ pa z‿avwaʁ lø tɑ̃ dø sɔʁtiʁ ‖]

**1367**

EN Where are you going for your vacation? — I'm not sure. I might go to Italy.

---

FR Où vas-tu pour tes vacances? — Je ne suis pas sûr (♀ sûre). J'irai peut-être en Italie.

IPA [u va ty puʁ te vakɑ̃s ‖ — ʒø nø sɥi pa syʁ (♀ syʁ) ‖ ʒ‿iʁe pøtɛtʁ ɑ̃ italie ‖]

**1368**

**EN** What are you doing this weekend? — I don't know. I might go hiking.

**FR** Que fais-tu ce week-end? — Je ne sais pas. J'irai peut-être faire de la randonnée.

**IPA** [kø fɛ ty sø wikɛnd || — ʒø nø sɛ pa || ʒ‿iʁɛ pøtɛtʁ fɛʁ dø la ʁɑ̃done ||]

**1369**

**EN** When will you see Pablo again? — I'm not sure. I might see him this summer.

**FR** Quand reverras-tu Pablo? — Je ne suis pas sûr (♀ sûre). Je vais peut-être le voir cet été.

**IPA** [kɑ̃ ʁˀvɛʁa ty (...) || — ʒø nø sɥi pa syʁ (♀ syʁ) || ʒø vɛ pøtɛtʁ lø vwaʁ sɛ t‿ete ||]

**1370**

**EN** What are you going to have for dinner? — I don't know. I might have Italian food.

**FR** Que mangeras-tu pour dîner? — Je ne sais pas. Je vais peut-être manger des mets italiens.

**IPA** [kø mɑ̃ʒˀʁa ty puʁ dine || — ʒø nø sɛ pa || ʒø vɛ pøtɛtʁ mɑ̃ʒe de mɛ italjɛ̃ ||]

**1371**

EN How are you going to get home tonight? — I'm not sure. I might take the bus.

FR Comment rentreras-tu à la maison ce soir? — Je ne suis pas sûr (♀ sûre). Je vais peut-être prendre le bus.

IPA [komã ʁãtʁəˈʁa ty a la mezɔ̃ sø swaʁ ‖ — ʒø nø sɥi pa syʁ (♀ syʁ) ‖ ʒø ve pøtɛtʁ pʁɑ̃dʁ lø bys ‖]

**1372**

EN I hear you won some money. What are you going to do with it? — I haven't decided yet. I might open a restaurant.

FR J'ai entendu dire que tu avais gagné de l'argent. Qu'en feras-tu? — Je n'ai pas encore décidé. Je vais peut-être ouvrir un restaurant.

IPA [ʒ‿ɛ ɑ̃tɑ̃dy diʁ kø ty avɛ gaɲe dø l‿aʁʒɑ̃ ‖ k‿ɑ̃ fʁa ty ‖ — ʒø n‿ɛ pa z‿ɑ̃kɔʁ deside ‖ ʒø ve pøtɛtʁ uvʁi ʁ‿œ̃ ʁestoʁɑ̃ ‖]

**1373**

EN He's playing tennis tomorrow afternoon.

FR Il joue au tennis demain après-midi.

IPA [il ʒu o tenis d‿mɛ̃ apʁɛ midi ‖]

**1374**

EN He might go out tomorrow evening.

FR Il va peut-être sortir demain soir.

IPA [il va pøtɛtʁ sɔʁtiʁ d‿mɛ̃ swaʁ ‖]

---

**1375**

EN He might get up early.

---

FR Il va peut-être se lever tôt.
IPA [il va pøtɛtʁ sø lˠve to ‖]

---

**1376**

EN He won't be working tomorrow.

---

FR Il ne travaillera pas demain.
IPA [il nø tʁavajˠʁa pa dˠmɛ̃ ‖]

---

**1377**

EN He might be at home tomorrow morning.

---

FR Il sera peut-être à la maison demain matin.
IPA [il sˠʁa pøtɛtʁ a la mɛzɔ̃ dˠmɛ̃ matɛ̃ ‖]

---

**1378**

EN He might watch television.

---

FR Il regardera peut-être la télévision.
IPA [il ʁˠgaʁdˠʁa pøtɛtʁ la televizjɔ̃ ‖]

---

**1379**

EN He's going out in the afternoon for sure.

---

FR Il sortira assurément dans l'après-midi.
IPA [il sɔʁtiʁa asyʁemɑ̃ dɑ̃ l apʁɛ midi ‖]

1380

**EN** He might go shopping, but he's not sure.

**FR** Il va peut-être aller faire du shopping, mais il n'est pas sûr.

**IPA** [il va pøtɛtʁ ale fɛʁ dy ʃɔpiŋ | mɛ il n̪e pa syʁ ||]

1381

**EN** I can play the piano. My brother can play the piano, too.

**FR** Je peux jouer du piano. Mon frère peut jouer du piano aussi.

**IPA** [ʒø pø ʒwe dy pjano || mɔ̃ fʁɛʁ pø ʒwe dy pjano osi ||]

1382

**EN** Marisol can speak Italian and Spanish, but she can't speak French.

**FR** Marisol peut parler italien et espagnol, mais elle ne peut pas parler français.

**IPA** [(...) pø paʁle ʁ‿italjɛ̃ e ɛspaɲɔl | mɛ ɛl nø pø pa paʁle fʁɑ̃sɛ ||]

---

**1383**

**EN**  Can you swim? — Yes, but I'm not a very good swimmer.

---

**FR**  Peux-tu nager? — Oui, mais je ne suis pas un très bon nageur (♀une très bonne nageuse).

**IPA**  [pø ty naʒe || — wi | mɛ ʒø nø sɥi pa z‿œ̃ tʁɛ bɔ̃ naʒœʁ (♀yn tʁɛ bɔn naʒøz) ||]

---

**1384**

**EN**  Can you change a twenty-dollar bill? — I'm sorry, I can't.

---

**FR**  Peux-tu me donner de la monnaie pour un billet de vingt (20)? — Non, désolé, je ne peux pas.

**IPA**  [pø ty mø done dø la monɛ pu ʁ‿œ̃ bijɛ dø vɛ̃ (20) || — nɔ̃ | dezole | ʒø nø pø pa ||]

---

**1385**

**EN**  I'm having a party next week, but Hyeonyeong and Maengsuk can't come.

---

**FR**  Je fais une fête la semaine prochaine, mais Hyeonyeong et Maengsuk ne peuvent pas venir.

**IPA**  [ʒø fɛ z‿yn fɛt la sᵊmɛn pʁɔʃɛn | mɛ (...) e (...) nø pœv pa vᵊniʁ ||]

---

**1386**

**EN**  When I was young, I could run very fast.

---

**FR**  Quand j'étais jeune, je pouvais courir très vite.

**IPA**  [kɑ̃ ʒ‿ete ʒœn | ʒø puvɛ kuʁiʁ tʁɛ vit ||]

1387

EN Before Nuria came to the United States, she couldn't understand much English. Now she can understand everything.

FR Avant que Nuria ne vienne aux États-Unis, elle ne pouvait pas comprendre beaucoup d'anglais. Maintenant, elle comprend tout.

IPA [avã kø (...) nø vjɛn o z‿etazuni | ɛl nø puvɛ pa kɔ̃pʁɑ̃dʁ boku d‿ɑ̃glɛ || mɛ̃t°nã | ɛl kɔ̃pʁɑ̃ tu ||]

1388

EN I was tired last night, but I couldn't sleep.

FR J'étais fatigué (♀fatiguée) la nuit dernière, mais je ne pouvais pas dormir.

IPA [ʒ‿etɛ fatige (♀fatige) la nɥi dɛʁnjɛʁ | mɛ ʒø nø puvɛ pa dɔʁmiʁ ||]

1389

EN I had a party last week, but Imran and Latifa couldn't come.

FR J'ai fait une fête la semaine dernière, mais Imran et Latifa ne pouvaient pas venir.

IPA [ʒ‿ɛ fɛ t‿yn fɛt la s°mɛn dɛʁnjɛʁ | mɛ (...) e (...) nø puvɛ pa v°niʁ ||]

**1390**

EN  Can you open the door, please? > Could you open the door, please?

---

FR  Peux-tu ouvrir la porte, s'il te plaît? Pourrais-tu ouvrir la porte, s'il te plaît?

IPA  [pø ty uvʁiʁ la pɔʁt | s‿il tø plɛ || puʁɛ ty uvʁiʁ la pɔʁt | s‿il tø plɛ ||]

**1391**

EN  Can you wait a minute, please? > Could you wait a moment, please?

---

FR  Peux-tu attendre une minute, s'il te plaît? Pourrais-tu attendre une minute, s'il te plaît?

IPA  [pø ty atɑ̃dʁ yn minyt | s‿il tø plɛ || puʁɛ ty atɑ̃dʁ yn minyt | s‿il tø plɛ ||]

**1392**

EN  Can I have change for a dollar, please? > Could I have change for a dollar, please.

---

FR  Puis-je avoir de la monnaie pour un euro, s'il vous plaît? Pourrais-je avoir de la monnaie pour un euro, s'il vous plaît?

IPA  [pɥi ʒø avwaʁ dø la monɛ pu ʁ‿œ̃ n‿øʁo | s‿il vu plɛ || puʁɛ ʒø avwaʁ dø la monɛ pu ʁ‿œ̃ n‿øʁo | s‿il vu plɛ ||]

**1393**

EN Silvio, can I borrow your umbrella? > Silvio, could I borrow your umbrella?

---

FR Silvio, puis-je t'emprunter ton parapluie? Silvio, pourrais-je t'emprunter ton parapluie?

IPA [(...) | pɥi ʒø t‿ɑ̃pʁœ̃te tɔ̃ paʁaplɥi || (...) | puʁɛ ʒø t‿ɑ̃pʁœ̃te tɔ̃ paʁaplɥi ||]

**1394**

EN Hello, can I speak to Tomas, please? > Hello, could I speak to Tomas please?

---

FR Allô, puis-je parler à Tomas, s'il vous plaît? Allô, pourrais-je parler à Tomas, s'il vous plaît?

IPA [alo | pɥi ʒø paʁle a (...) | s‿il vu plɛ || alo | puʁɛ ʒø paʁle a (...) | s‿il vu plɛ ||]

**1395**

EN Can you swim?

---

FR Peux-tu nager?

IPA [pø ty naʒe ||]

**1396**

EN Can you ski?

---

FR Peux-tu skier?

IPA [pø ty skje ||]

**1397**

EN Can you play chess?

FR Peux-tu jouer aux échecs?
IPA [pø ty ʒwe o z‿eʃɛk ‖]

**1398**

EN Can you run ten (10) kilometers?

FR Peux-tu courir dix (10) kilomètres?
IPA [pø ty kuʁiʁ dis (10) kilomɛtʁ ‖]

**1399**

EN Can you drive a car?

FR Peux-tu conduire une voiture?
IPA [pø ty kɔ̃dɥiʁ yn vwatyʁ ‖]

**1400**

EN Can you drive a motorcycle?

FR Peux-tu conduire une moto?
IPA [pø ty kɔ̃dɥiʁ yn moto ‖]

# GMS #1401 - 1500

---

**1401**

**EN** Can you ride a horse?

---

**FR** Peux-tu monter à cheval?
**IPA** [pø ty mõte a ʃºval ‖]

---

**1402**

**EN** I'm sorry, but we can't come to your party next weekend.

---

**FR** Je suis désolé (♀désolée), mais nous ne pouvons pas venir à ta fête le week-end prochain.
**IPA** [ʒø sɥi dezole (♀dezole) | mɛ nu nø puvõ pa vºniʁ a ta fɛt lø wikɛnd pʁoʃẽ ‖]

---

**1403**

**EN** I like this hotel room. You can see the mountains from the window.

---

**FR** J'aime cette chambre d'hôtel. On peut voir les montagnes de cette fenêtre.
**IPA** [ʒ͜ɛm sɛt ʃãbʁ d͜otɛl ‖ õ pø vwaʁ le mõtaɲ dø sɛt fºnɛtʁ ‖]

**1404**

EN You're speaking very quietly. I can't hear you.

FR Tu parles très doucement. Je ne t'entends pas.

IPA [ty paʁl tʁɛ dusᵒmã || ʒø nø t‿ãtã pa ||]

**1405**

EN Have you seen my suitcase? I can't find it.

FR As-tu vu ma valise? Je ne la trouve pas.

IPA [a ty vy ma valiz || ʒø nø la tʁuv pa ||]

**1406**

EN Olga got the job because she can speak five (5) languages.

FR Olga a eu l'emploi parce qu'elle peut parler cinq langues.

IPA [(...) a y l‿ãplwa paʁs k‿ɛl pø paʁle sɛ̃k lãg ||]

**1407**

EN I was tired, but I couldn't sleep.

FR J'étais fatigué (♀fatiguée), mais je ne pouvais pas dormir.

IPA [ʒ‿etɛ fatige (♀fatige) | mɛ ʒø nø puvɛ pa dɔʁmiʁ ||]

---

**1408**

EN I wasn't hungry yesterday. I couldn't finish dinner.

---

FR Je n'avais pas faim hier. Je n'ai pas pu terminer mon dîner.

IPA [ʒø n̪ave pa fɛ̃ jɛʁ || ʒø n̪ɛ pa py tɛʁmine mɔ̃ dine ||]

---

**1409**

EN Rashid doesn't know what to do. He can't decide.

---

FR Rashid ne sait pas quoi faire. Il n'arrive pas à se décider.

IPA [(...) nø sɛ pa kwa fɛʁ || il n̪aʁiv pa a sø deside ||]

---

**1410**

EN I wanted to speak to Shakira yesterday, but I couldn't find her.

---

FR Je voulais parler à Shakira hier, mais je n'ai pas réussi à la trouver.

IPA [ʒø vule paʁle a (...) jɛʁ | mɛ ʒø n̪ɛ pa ʁeysi a la tʁuve ||]

---

**1411**

EN Vikram can't go to the concert next weekend. He has to work.

---

FR Vikram ne peut pas aller au concert le week-end prochain. Il doit travailler.

IPA [(...) nø pø pa z̪ale o kɔ̃sɛʁ lø wikɛnd pʁoʃɛ̃ || il dwa tʁavaje ||]

**1412**

EN Lakshmi couldn't go to the meeting last week. She was sick.

FR Lakshmi ne pouvait pas aller à la réunion la semaine dernière. Elle était malade.

IPA [(...) nø puvɛ pa z‿ale a la ʁeynjɔ̃ la sᵊmɛn dɛʁnjɛʁ ‖ ɛ l‿etɛ malad ‖]

**1413**

EN You worked ten (10) hours today. You must be tired.

FR Tu as travaillé dix heures aujourd'hui. Tu dois être fatigué (♀ fatiguée).

IPA [ty a tʁavaje di z‿œʁ oʒuʁdɥi ‖ ty dwa ɛtʁ fatige (♀ fatige) ‖]

**1414**

EN My brother has worked at your company for years. You must know him.

FR Mon frère a travaillé pour ton entreprise pendant des années. Tu dois le connaître.

IPA [mɔ̃ fʁɛʁ a tʁavaje puʁ tɔ̃ n‿ãtʁᵊpʁiz pãdã de z‿ane ‖ ty dwa lø konɛtʁ ‖]

**1415**

EN My friends have the same postal code as you. They must live near you.

FR Mes amis ont le même code postal que toi. Ils doivent habiter près de chez toi.

IPA [me z‿ami ɔ̃ lø mɛm kɔd pɔstal kø twa || il dwav abite pʁɛ dø ʃe twa ||]

**1416**

EN This isn't the Wilsons? I'm sorry. I must have the wrong number.

FR Ce n'est pas la maison des Wilson? Je suis désolé. Je dois avoir le mauvais numéro.

IPA [sø n‿e pa la mɛzɔ̃ de (...) || ʒø sɥi dezole || ʒø dwa avwaʁ lø movɛ nymeʁo ||]

**1417**

EN The phone rang eight (8) times and Samiya didn't answer. She must not be at home.

FR Le téléphone a sonné huit fois et Samiya n'a pas répondu. Elle doit ne pas être là.

IPA [lø telefɔn a sone ɥit fwa e (...) n‿a pa ʁepɔ̃dy || ɛl dwa nø pa z‿ɛtʁ la ||]

**1418**

EN Xavier takes the bus everywhere. He must not have a car.

---

FR Xavier prend l'autobus pour aller partout. Il doit ne pas avoir de voiture.

IPA [(...) pʁɑ̃ l̩otobys pu ʁ‿ale paʁtu || il dwa nø pa z‿avwaʁ dø vwatyʁ ||]

**1419**

EN The Silvas are always home on Fridays. They must not work then.

---

FR Les Silva sont toujours à la maison les vendredis. Ils doivent ne pas travailler le vendredi.

IPA [le silva sɔ̃ tuʒuʁ a la mɛzɔ̃ le vɑ̃dʁ°di || il dwav nø pa tʁavaje lø vɑ̃dʁ°di ||]

**1420**

EN You must be careful with this knife. It's very sharp.

---

FR Tu dois être prudent (♀prudente) avec ce couteau. Il est très aiguisé.

IPA [ty dwa ɛtʁ pʁydɑ̃ (♀pʁydɑ̃t) avɛk sø kuto || i l̩e tʁɛ z‿egize ||]

**1421**

EN Workers must wear safety glasses at this machine.

---

FR Les ouvriers doivent porter des lunettes à cette machine.

IPA [le z‿uvʁije dwav poʁte de lynɛt a sɛt maʃin ||]

**1422**

EN In the United States, you must be eighteen (18) to vote.

FR Aux États-Unis, on doit avoir dix-huit (18) ans pour voter.

IPA [o z‿etazuni | ɔ̃ dwa avwaʁ dizɥit (18) ɑ̃ puʁ vote ||]

**1423**

EN They were in a dangerous situation. They had to be careful.

FR Ils (♀elles) étaient dans une situation dangereuse. Ils (♀elles) devaient être prudents (♀prudentes).

IPA [il (♀ɛl) etɛ dɑ̃ z‿yn sitɥasjɔ̃ dɑ̃ʒ°ʁøz || il (♀ɛl) d°vɛ etʁ pʁydɑ̃ (♀pʁydɑ̃t) ||]

**1424**

EN We had to wear safety glasses when we visited the factory last week.

FR Nous devions porter des lunettes de sécurité lorsque nous avons visité l'usine la semaine dernière.

IPA [nu d°vjɔ̃ poʁte de lynɛt dø sekyʁite lɔʁsk° nu z‿avɔ̃ vizite l‿yzin la s°mɛn dɛʁnjɛʁ ||]

**1425**

EN Bicyclists must not ride on the sidewalk.

FR Les cyclistes ne doivent pas rouler sur le trottoir.

IPA [le siklist nø dwav pa ʁule syʁ lø tʁotwaʁ ||]

**1426**

EN You must not be late for school again.

FR Tu ne dois plus être en retard à l'école.
IPA [ty nø dwa ply s‿etʁ ɑ̃ ʁ°taʁ a l‿ekɔl ‖]

**1427**

EN It's evening, and you haven't eaten anything all day.
You must be hungry.

FR C'est le soir et tu n'as rien mangé de la journée. Tu
dois avoir faim.
IPA [sɛ lø swaʁ e ty n‿a ʁjɛ̃ mɑ̃ʒe dø la ʒuʁne ‖ ty dwa
avwaʁ fɛ̃ ‖]

**1428**

EN It's the most popular restaurant in town, so the food
must be good.

FR C'est le restaurant le plus populaire en ville, alors la
nourriture doit être bonne.
IPA [sɛ lø ʁestoʁɑ̃ lø plys popylɛʁ ɑ̃ vil | aloʁ la nuʁityʁ
dwa etʁ bɔn ‖]

**1429**

EN I got the job. — You did? You must be excited.

FR J'ai eu l'emploi. — Ah oui? Tu dois être excité
(♀ excitée).
IPA [ʒ‿ɛ y l‿ɑ̃plwa ‖ — a wi ‖ ty dwa etʁ ɛksite
(♀ ɛksite) ‖]

**1430**

EN The phone's ringing. I know it's not for me. It must be for you.

FR Le téléphone sonne. Je sais que ce n'est pas pour moi. Ça doit être pour toi.

IPA [lø telefɔn sɔn ‖ ʒø sɛ kø sø n̩e pa puʁ mwa ‖ sa dwa etʁ puʁ twa ‖]

**1431**

EN My keys aren't in the living room, so they must be in the kitchen.

FR Mes clés ne sont pas dans le salon, alors elles doivent être dans la cuisine.

IPA [me kle nø sɔ̃ pa dɑ̃ lø salɔ̃ | alɔ ʁ̩el dwav etʁ dɑ̃ la kɥizin ‖]

**1432**

EN Renata wears something blue every day. She must like the color blue.

FR Renata porte quelque chose de bleu tous les jours. Elle doit aimer la couleur bleue.

IPA [(...) pɔʁt kɛlk ʃoz dø blø tu le ʒuʁ ‖ ɛl dwa eme la kulœʁ blø ‖]

**1433**

EN The Garcias have six (6) children and three (3) dogs. They must have a big house.

---

FR Les Garcia ont six enfants et trois chiens. Ils doivent avoir une grande maison.

IPA [le (...) ɔ̃ si z‿ɑ̃fɑ̃ e tʁwa ʃjɛ̃ || il dwav avwa ʁ‿yn gʁɑ̃d mɛzɔ̃ |||]

**1434**

EN Mrs. Chen bought three (3) liters of milk at the store. Her children drink a lot of milk.

---

FR Madame Chen a acheté trois litres de lait au magasin. Ses enfants boivent beaucoup de lait.

IPA [madam (...) a aʃᵊte tʁwa litʁ dø lɛ o magazɛ̃ || se z‿ɑ̃fɑ̃ bwav boku dø lɛ |||]

**1435**

EN I know Ms. Thompson has a job, but she's always home during the day. She must work at night.

---

FR Je sais que Madame Thompson a un emploi, mais elle est toujours à la maison durant la journée. Elle doit travailler le soir.

IPA [ʒø sɛ kø madam (...) a œ̃ n‿ɑ̃plwa | mɛ ɛ l‿e tuʒuʁ a la mɛzɔ̃ dyʁɑ̃ la ʒuʁne || ɛl dwa tʁavaje lø swaʁ |||]

**1436**

EN This isn't the Karlsons? I must have the wrong number.

---

FR Ce n'est pas la maison des Karlson? Je dois avoir le mauvais numéro.

IPA [sø n̥e pa la mɛzɔ̃ de (...) || ʒø dwa avwaʁ lø movɛ nymeʁo ||]

**1437**

EN Omar is very thin. He must not eat very much.

---

FR Omar est très mince. Il ne doit pas manger beaucoup.

IPA [(...) e tʁɛ mɛ̃s || il nø dwa pa mɑ̃ʒe boku ||]

**1438**

EN I never see my neighbor in the morning. He must leave for work very early.

---

FR Je ne vois jamais mon voisin le matin. Il doit partir pour le travail très tôt.

IPA [ʒø nø vwa ʒamɛ mɔ̃ vwazɛ̃ lø matɛ̃ || il dwa paʁtiʁ puʁ lø tʁavaj tʁɛ to ||]

**1439**

EN I always have to repeat things when I talk to Tomoko. She must not hear very well.

---

FR Je dois toujours répéter des choses quand je parle à Tomoko. Elle ne doit pas entendre très bien.

IPA [ʒø dwa tuʒuʁ ʁepete de ʃoz kɑ̃ ʒø paʁl a (...) || ɛl nø dwa pa z̥ɑ̃tɑ̃dʁ tʁɛ bjɛ̃ ||]

**1440**

EN  Ludwig wears the same clothes every day. He must not have many clothes.

---

FR  Ludwig porte les mêmes vêtements chaque jour. Il ne doit pas avoir beaucoup de vêtements.

IPA  [(...) pɔʁt le mɛm vɛtᵒmã ʃak ʒuʁ || il nø dwa pa z‿avwaʁ boku dø vɛtᵒmã ||]

**1441**

EN  You have a cold and a fever? Poor thing! You must feel awful.

---

FR  Tu as un rhume et de la fièvre? Pauvre toi! Tu dois te sentir terriblement mal.

IPA  [ty a z‿œ̃ ʁym e dø la fjɛvʁ || povʁ twa || ty dwa tø sãtiʁ teʁiblᵒmã mal ||]

**1442**

EN  In most of the United States, you must be at least sixteen (16) to get a driver's license.

---

FR  Dans la plupart des endroits aux États-Unis, on doit avoir au moins seize (16) ans pour obtenir un permis de conduire.

IPA  [dã la plypaʁ de z‿ãdʁwa o z‿etazuni | ɔ̃ dwa avwaʁ o mwɛ̃ sez (16) ã pu ʁ‿ɔptᵒni ʁ‿œ̃ peʁmi dø kɔ̃dɥiʁ ||]

1443

EN For this job, you must know both Spanish and German.

FR Pour cet emploi, tu dois connaître l'espagnol et l'allemand.

IPA [puʁ sɛ t‿ɑ̃plwa | ty dwa konɛtʁ l‿ɛspaɲɔl e l‿al°mɑ̃ ‖]

1444

EN People in the front seat of a car must wear a seat belt.

FR Les passagers avant d'une voiture doivent porter une ceinture de sécurité.

IPA [le pasaʒe z‿avɑ̃ d‿yn vwatyʁ dwav poʁte ʁ‿yn sɛ̃tyʁ dø sekyʁite ‖]

1445

EN High school students who want to go to college must get good grades.

FR Les lycéens qui veulent aller au collège doivent avoir de bonnes notes.

IPA [le liseɛ̃ ki vœl ale o kolɛʒ dwav avwaʁ dø bɔn nɔt ‖]

**1446**

EN This highway is closed. Drivers must take another road.

FR Cette autoroute est fermée. Les conducteurs doivent prendre une autre route.

IPA [sɛt otoʁut e fɛʁme || le kɔ̃dyktœʁ dwav pʁɑ̃dʁ yn otʁ ʁut ||]

**1447**

EN A tennis player must be very good to play professionally.

FR Un joueur de tennis doit être très bon pour jouer professionnellement.

IPA [œ̃ ʒwœʁ dø tenis dwa ɛtʁ tʁɛ bɔ̃ puʁ ʒwe pʁofɛsjonɛlˠmɑ̃ ||]

**1448**

EN We mustn't forget to send Rita a birthday card.

FR Nous ne devons pas oublier d'envoyer une carte d'anniversaire à Rita. > On ne doit pas oublier d'envoyer une carte d'anniversaire à Rita.

IPA [nu nø dˠvɔ̃ pa zˎublije dˎɑ̃vwaje yn kaʁt dˎanivɛʁsɛʁ a (...) || > ɔ̃ nø dwa pa zˎublije dˎɑ̃vwaje yn kaʁt dˎanivɛʁsɛʁ a (...) ||]

**1449**

EN I must hurry, or I'll be late.

---

FR Je dois me dépêcher, sinon je serai en retard.
IPA [ʒø dwa mø depeʃe | sinɔ̃ ʒø s°ʁɛ ɑ̃ ʁ°taʁ ‖]

**1450**

EN Why were you so late? — I had to wait half an hour for the bus.

---

FR Pourquoi étais-tu si en retard? — J'ai dû attendre une demi-heure pour l'autobus.
IPA [puʁkwa etɛ ty si ɑ̃ ʁ°taʁ ‖ — ʒ‿ɛ dy atɑ̃dʁ yn d°miœʁ puʁ l‿otobys ‖]

**1451**

EN Keep these papers in a safe place. You must not lose them.

---

FR Garde ces papiers dans un endroit sûr. Tu ne dois pas les perdre.
IPA [gaʁd se papje dɑ̃ z‿œ̃ n‿ɑ̃dʁwa syʁ ‖ ty nø dwa pa le pɛʁdʁ ‖]

**1452**

EN Bicyclists must follow the same traffic rules as drivers.

---

FR Les cyclistes doivent suivre les mêmes règles de circulation que les automobilistes.
IPA [le siklist dwav sɥivʁ le mɛm ʁɛgl dø siʁkylasjɔ̃ kø le z‿otomobilist ‖]

---

**1453**

EN We must not forget to turn off the lights when we leave.

---

FR On ne doit pas oublier d'éteindre les lumières lorsqu'on partira.

IPA [ɔ̃ nø dwa pa z‿ublije d‿etɛ̃dʁ le lymjɛʁ lɔʁsk ɔ̃ paʁtiʁa ‖]

---

**1454**

EN I don't usually work on Saturdays, but last Saturday I had to work.

---

FR Je ne travaille généralement pas les samedis, mais j'ai dû travailler samedi dernier.

IPA [ʒø nø tʁavaj ʒeneʁal°mã pa le sam°di | mɛ ʒ‿ɛ dy tʁavaje sam°di dɛʁnje ‖]

---

**1455**

EN Yeonhwa doesn't study enough. She should study harder.

---

FR Yeonhwa n'étudie pas assez. Elle devrait étudier plus assidûment.

IPA [(...) n‿etydi pa z‿ase ‖ ɛl d°vʁɛ etydje ply s‿asidymã ‖]

---

**1456**

EN It's a good movie. You should go and see it.

---

FR C'est un bon film. Tu devrais aller le voir.

IPA [sɛ t‿œ̃ bɔ̃ film ‖ ty d°vʁɛ ale lø vwaʁ ‖]

---

**1457**

EN  When you play tennis, you should always watch the ball.

---

FR  Quand tu joues au tennis, tu devrais toujours regarder la balle.

IPA  [kɑ̃ ty ʒu o tenis | ty dᵊvʁɛ tuʒuʁ ʁᵊgaʁde la bal ‖]

---

**1458**

EN  Should I invite Sara to dinner?

---

FR  Devrais-je inviter Sara pour dîner?

IPA  [dᵊvʁɛ ʒø ɛ̃vite (...) puʁ dine ‖]

---

**1459**

EN  Should we make something special for dinner?

---

FR  Devrait-on faire quelque chose de spécial pour dîner?

IPA  [dᵊvʁɛ t̪ɔ̃ feʁ kɛlk ʃoz dø spesjal puʁ dine ‖]

---

**1460**

EN  Leopold shouldn't go to bed so late.

---

FR  Leopold ne devrait pas aller au lit si tard.

IPA  [leopold nø dᵊvʁɛ pa z̪ale o li si taʁ ‖]

**1461**

EN You watch TV all the time. You shouldn't watch TV so much.

FR Tu regardes la télé tout le temps. Tu ne devrais pas regarder la télé autant.

IPA [ty ʁ°gaʁd la tele tu lø tã || ty nø d°vʁɛ pa ʁ°gaʁde la tele otã ||]

**1462**

EN I think Zahida should buy some new clothes.

FR Je pense que Zahida devrait acheter de nouveaux vêtements.

IPA [ʒø pãs kø (...) d°vʁɛ aʃ°te dø nuvo vɛt°mã ||]

**1463**

EN It's late. I think I should go home now.

FR Il est tard. Je pense que je devrais aller à la maison maintenant.

IPA [i l‿e taʁ || ʒø pãs kø ʒø d°vʁɛ ale a la mɛzɔ̃ mɛ̃t°nã ||]

**1464**

EN Shall I buy this coat? — Yes, I think you should.

FR Devrais-je acheter ce manteau? — Oui, je pense que tu devrais.

IPA [d°vʁɛ ʒø aʃ°te sø mãto || — wi | ʒø pãs kø ty d°vʁɛ ||]

**1465**

EN I don't think you should work so hard.

FR Je pense que tu ne devrais pas travailler autant.
IPA [ʒø pãs kø ty nø dᵊvʁɛ pa tʁavaje otã ‖]

**1466**

EN I don't think we should go yet. It's too early.

FR Je pense que nous ne devrions pas y aller tout de suite. Il est trop tôt.
IPA [ʒø pãs kø nu nø dᵊvʁijõ pa z̩ i ale tu dø sɥit ‖ i l̩e tʁo to ‖]

**1467**

EN Do you think I should buy this hat?

FR Penses-tu que je devrais acheter ce chapeau?
IPA [pãs ty kø ʒø dᵊvʁɛ aʃᵊte sø ʃapo ‖]

**1468**

EN What time do you think we should go home?

FR À quelle heure penses-tu que nous devrions rentrer à la maison?
IPA [a kɛ l̩œʁ pãs ty kø nu dᵊvʁijõ ʁãtʁe a la mɛzõ ‖]

**1469**

EN  I should study tonight, but I think I'll go to the movies.

FR  Je devrais étudier ce soir, mais je pense que je vais aller au cinéma.

IPA  [ʒø dˬvʁɛ etydje sø swaʁ | mɛ ʒø pãs kø ʒø vɛ ale o sinema ‖]

**1470**

EN  I have to study tonight. I can't go to the movies.

FR  Je dois étudier ce soir. Je ne peux pas aller au cinéma.

IPA  [ʒø dwa etydje sø swaʁ ‖ ʒø nø pø pa z̩ale o sinema ‖]

**1471**

EN  I ought to study tonight, but I think I'll go to the movies.

FR  Je devrais étudier ce soir, mais je pense que je vais aller au cinéma.

IPA  [ʒø dˬvʁɛ etydje sø swaʁ | mɛ ʒø pãs kø ʒø vɛ ale o sinema ‖]

**1472**

EN  I think Mahmud ought to buy some new clothes.

FR  Je pense que Mahmud devrait acheter de nouveaux vêtements.

IPA  [ʒø pãs kø (...) dˬvʁɛ aʃˬte dø nuvo vɛtˬmã ‖]

**1473**

EN It's late, and you're very tired. You should go to bed.

FR Il est tard et tu es très fatigué ( ♀ fatiguée). Tu devrais aller au lit.

IPA [i l̯e ta ʁ̯e ty ɛ tʁɛ fatige ( ♀ fatige) || ty dᵊvʁɛ ale o li ||]

**1474**

EN You should eat plenty of fruit and vegetables.

FR Tu devrais manger beaucoup de fruits et de légumes.

IPA [ty dᵊvʁɛ mãʒe boku dø fʁɥi e dø legym ||]

**1475**

EN If you have time, you should visit the Science Museum. It's very interesting.

FR Si tu avais le temps, tu devrais visiter le Musée des sciences. C'est très intéressant.

IPA [si ty avɛ lø tã | ty dᵊvʁɛ vizite lø myze de sjãs || sɛ tʁɛ z̯ẽteʁesã ||]

**1476**

EN When you're driving, you should wear a seat belt.

FR Lorsque tu conduis, tu devrais porter une ceinture de sécurité.

IPA [lɔʁskᵊ ty kõdɥi | ty dᵊvʁɛ poʁte ʁ̯yn sẽtyʁ dø sekyʁite ||]

**1477**

EN It's a very good book. You should read it.

FR C'est un très bon livre. Tu devrais le lire.
IPA [sε t‿œ̃ tʁε bɔ̃ livʁ || ty dᵊvʁε lø liʁ ||]

**1478**

EN She shouldn't watch TV so much.

FR Elle ne devrait pas regarder la télé autant.
IPA [εl nø dᵊvʁε pa ʁᵊgaʁde la tele otɑ̃ ||]

**1479**

EN He shouldn't eat too much.

FR Il ne devrait pas manger autant.
IPA [il nø dᵊvʁε pa mɑ̃ʒe otɑ̃ ||]

**1480**

EN You shouldn't work so hard.

FR Tu ne devrais pas travailler autant.
IPA [ty nø dᵊvʁε pa tʁavaje otɑ̃ ||]

**1481**

EN I shouldn't drive so fast.

FR Je ne devrais pas conduire si vite.
IPA [ʒø nø dᵊvʁε pa kɔ̃dɥiʁ si vit ||]

1482

EN You're trying on a jacket: "Do you think I should buy this jacket?"

FR Tu essaies un veston : « Penses-tu que je devrais acheter ce veston? »

IPA [ty ɛsɛ z‿œ̃ vɛstɔ̃ | pɑ̃s ty kø ʒø dᵊvʁɛ aʃᵊte sø vɛstɔ̃ ||]

1483

EN You can't drive: "Do you think I should learn how to drive?"

FR Tu ne sais pas conduire : « Penses-tu que je devrais apprendre à conduire? »

IPA [ty nø sɛ pa kɔ̃dɥiʁ | pɑ̃s ty kø ʒø dᵊvʁɛ apʁɑ̃dʁ a kɔ̃dɥiʁ ||]

1484

EN You don't like your job: "Do you think I should get another job?"

FR Tu n'aimes pas ton travail : « Penses-tu que je devrais me trouver un nouvel emploi? »

IPA [ty n‿ɛm pa tɔ̃ tʁavaj | pɑ̃s ty kø ʒø dᵊvʁɛ mø tʁuve ʁ‿œ̃ nuvɛ l‿ɑ̃plwa ||]

**1485**

EN You're going to have a party: "Do you think I should invite Oskar?"

---

FR Tu organises une fête : « Penses-tu que je devrais inviter Oskar? »

IPA [ty ɔʁgani z‿yn fɛt | pɑ̃s ty kø ʒø dᵊvʁɛ ɛ̃vite (...) ‖]

**1486**

EN We have to get up early tomorrow. I think we should go home now.

---

FR Nous devons nous lever tôt demain. Je pense que nous devrions rentrer maintenant. > On doit se lever tôt demain. Je pense qu'on devrait rentrer maintenant.

IPA [nu dᵊvɔ̃ nu lᵊve to dᵊmɛ̃ ‖ ʒø pɑ̃s kø nu dᵊvʁijɔ̃ ʁɑ̃tʁe mɛ̃tᵊnɑ̃ ‖ > ɔ̃ dwa sø lᵊve to dᵊmɛ̃ ‖ ʒø pɑ̃s k‿ɔ̃ dᵊvʁɛ ʁɑ̃tʁe mɛ̃tᵊnɑ̃ ‖]

**1487**

EN That coat is too big for you. I don't think you should buy it.

---

FR Ce manteau est trop grand pour toi. Je pense que tu ne devrais pas l'acheter.

IPA [sø mɑ̃to e tʁo gʁɑ̃ puʁ twa ‖ ʒø pɑ̃s kø ty nø dᵊvʁɛ pa l‿aʃᵊte ‖]

**1488**

EN  You don't need your car. You should sell it.

FR  Tu n'as pas besoin de ta voiture. Tu devrais la vendre.

IPA  [ty n‿a pa bøzwɛ̃ dø ta vwatyʁ ‖ ty dᵊvʁɛ la vɑ̃dʁ ‖]

**1489**

EN  Valentina needs a change. I think she should take a trip.

FR  Valentina a besoin de changement. Je pense qu'elle devrait partir en voyage.

IPA  [(...) a bøzwɛ̃ dø ʃɑ̃ʒᵊmɑ̃ ‖ ʒø pɑ̃s k‿ɛl dᵊvʁɛ paʁti ʁ‿ɑ̃ vwajaʒ ‖]

**1490**

EN  Nur and Zaina are too young. I don't think they should get married.

FR  Nur et Zaina sont trop jeunes. Je ne crois pas qu'ils devraient se marier.

IPA  [(...) e (...) sɔ̃ tʁo ʒœn ‖ ʒø nø kʁwa pa k‿il dᵊvʁɛ sø maʁje ‖]

**1491**

EN  You're still sick. I don't think you should go to work.

FR  Tu es encore malade. Je pense que tu ne devrais pas aller au travail.

IPA  [ty ɛ ɑ̃kɔʁ malad ‖ ʒø pɑ̃s kø ty nø dᵊvʁɛ pa z‿ale o tʁavaj ‖]

**1492**

EN Simon isn't feeling well today. I think he should go see the doctor.

FR Simon ne se sent pas bien aujourd'hui. Je pense qu'il devrait aller voir un médecin.

IPA [(...) nø sø sã pa bjɛ̃ n‿oʒuʁdɥi ‖ ʒø pãs k‿il dˠvʁɛ ale vwa ʁ‿œ̃ mɛdsɛ̃ ‖]

**1493**

EN The hotel is too expensive for us. I don't think we should stay there.

FR L'hôtel est trop cher pour nous. Je pense que nous ne devrions pas séjourner ici.

IPA [l‿otɛl e tʁo ʃɛʁ puʁ nu ‖ ʒø pãs kø nu nø dˠvʁijõ pa seʒuʁne isi ‖]

**1494**

EN I think everybody should learn another language.

FR Je pense que tout le monde devrait apprendre une autre langue.

IPA [ʒø pãs kø tu lø mõd dˠvʁɛ apʁãdʁ yn otʁ lãg ‖]

**1495**

EN I think everybody should travel to another country.

FR Je pense que tout le monde devrait visiter un autre pays.

IPA [ʒø pãs kø tu lø mõd dˠvʁɛ vizite ʁ‿œ̃ n‿otʁ pei ‖]

**1496**

EN  I don't think people should smoke.

FR  Je pense que les gens ne devraient pas fumer.

IPA  [ʒø pãs kø le ʒã nø dᵊvʁɛ pa fyme ‖]

**1497**

EN  I think I should save more money.

FR  Je pense que je devrais économiser plus d'argent.

IPA  [ʒø pãs kø ʒø dᵊvʁɛ ekonomize plys d̯aʁʒã ‖]

**1498**

EN  I'll be late for work tomorrow. I have to go to the dentist.

FR  Je serai en retard au travail demain. Je dois aller chez le dentiste.

IPA  [ʒø sᵊʁɛ ã ʁᵊtaʁ o tʁavaj dᵊmɛ̃ ‖ ʒø dwa ale ʃe lø dãtist ‖]

**1499**

EN  Yolanda starts work at seven [o'clock] (7:00), so she has to get up at six [o'clock] (6:00).

FR  Yolanda commence à travailler à sept heures (7 h), alors elle doit se lever à six heures (6 h).

IPA  [(...) komãs a tʁavaje a sɛ t̯œʁ (7 h) | alɔ ʁ‿ɛl dwa sø lᵊve a si z̯œʁ (6 h) ‖]

**1500**

**EN** You have to pass a test before you can get a driver's license.

---

**FR** Tu dois passer un examen avant de pouvoir obtenir ton permis de conduire.

**IPA** [ty dwa pase ʁ‿œ̃ n‿ɛgzamɛ̃ avɑ̃ də puvwaʁ ɔptᵊniʁ tɔ̃ pɛʁmi də kɔ̃dɥiʁ ‖]

# GMS #1501 - 1600

**1501**

**EN** You must pass a test before you can get a driver's license.

**FR** Tu dois passer un examen avant de pouvoir obtenir ton permis de conduire.

**IPA** [ty dwa pase ʁ‿œ̃ n‿ɛgzamɛ̃ avɑ̃ də puvwaʁ ɔptᵊniʁ tɔ̃ peʁmi də kɔ̃dɥiʁ ‖]

**1502**

**EN** I was late for work yesterday. I had to go to the dentist.

**FR** J'étais en retard au travail hier. Je devais aller chez le dentiste.

**IPA** [ʒ‿etɛ ɑ̃ ʁᵊtaʁ o tʁavaj jeʁ ‖ ʒø dᵊvɛ ale ʃe lø dɑ̃tist ‖]

**1503**

**EN** We had to walk home last night. There were no buses.

**FR** Nous avons dû rentrer à pied hier soir. Il n'y avait pas d'autobus.

**IPA** [nu z‿avɔ̃ dy ʁɑ̃tʁe a pje jeʁ swaʁ ‖ il n‿i avɛ pa d‿otobys ‖]

**1504**

EN What time do you have to go to the dentist tomorrow?

FR À quelle heure dois-tu aller chez le dentiste demain?
IPA [a kɛ l‿œʁ dwa ty ale ʃe lø dɑ̃tist dᵊmɛ̃ ‖]

**1505**

EN Does Amanda have to work on Saturdays?

FR Amanda doit-elle travailler les samedis?
IPA [(...) dwa t‿ɛl tʁavaje le samᵊdi ‖]

**1506**

EN Why did they have to leave the party early?

FR Pourquoi ont-ils (♀elles) dû partir tôt de la fête?
IPA [puʁkwa ɔ̃ t‿il (♀ɛl) dy paʁtiʁ to dø la fɛt ‖]

**1507**

EN I'm not working tomorrow, so I don't have to get up early.

FR Je ne travaille pas demain, alors je ne dois pas me lever tôt.
IPA [ʒø nø tʁavaj pa dᵊmɛ̃ | alɔʁ ʒø nø dwa pa mø lᵊve to ‖]

**1508**

EN Alan doesn't have to work very hard. Actually, he's got an easy job.

FR Alan n'a pas besoin de travailler très fort. En fait, il a un travail facile.

IPA [(...) n‿a pa bøzwɛ̃ də tʁavaje tʁɛ fɔʁ ‖ ɑ̃ fɛ | i l‿a œ̃ tʁavaj fasil ‖]

**1509**

EN We didn't have to wait very long for the bus; it came in a few minutes.

FR Nous n'avons pas eu besoin d'attendre l'autobus très longtemps, il est arrivé en quelques minutes.

IPA [nu n‿avɔ̃ pa z‿y bøzwɛ̃ d‿atɑ̃dʁ l‿otobys tʁɛ lɔ̃tɑ̃ | i l‿e t‿aʁive ɑ̃ kɛlk minyt ‖]

**1510**

EN In many countries, men must do military service.

FR Dans plusieurs pays, les hommes doivent participer au service militaire.

IPA [dɑ̃ plyzjœʁ pei | le ɔm dwav paʁtisipe o sɛʁvis militeʁ ‖]

**1511**

EN My eyes are not very good. I have to wear glasses.

FR Mes yeux ne sont pas très bons. Je dois porter des lunettes.

IPA [me z‿jø nø sɔ̃ pa tʁɛ bɔ̃ ‖ ʒø dwa poʁte de lynet ‖]

**1512**

EN At the end of the course all the students had to take a test.

FR À la fin du cours, tous les étudiants devaient faire un examen.

IPA [a la fɛ̃ dy kuʁ | tu le z‿etydjã dᵒvɛ fɛʁ œ̃ n‿ɛgzamɛ̃ ||]

**1513**

EN Layla is studying literature. She has to read a lot of books.

FR Layla étudie la littérature. Elle doit lire beaucoup de livres.

IPA [(...) etydi la liteʁatyʁ || ɛl dwa liʁ boku dø livʁ ||]

**1514**

EN Hassan doesn't understand much English. You have to speak very slowly to him.

FR Hassan ne comprend pas beaucoup d'anglais. Tu dois lui parler très lentement.

IPA [(...) nø kɔ̃pʁã pa boku d‿ãglɛ || ty dwa lɥi paʁle tʁɛ lãtᵒmã ||]

**1515**

EN Barbara isn't at home much. She has to travel a lot for her job.

FR Barbara n'est pas souvent à la maison. Elle doit voyager pour son travail.

IPA [(...) n̩e pa suvã a la mɛzɔ̃ || ɛl dwa vwajaʒe puʁ sɔ̃ tʁavaj ||]

**1516**

EN In tennis you have to hit the ball over the net.

FR Au tennis, tu dois frapper la balle au-dessus du filet.

IPA [o tenis | ty dwa fʁape la bal odᵒsy dy filɛ ||]

**1517**

EN We had to walk home last night. There were no buses.

FR Nous avons dû rentrer à pied hier soir. Il n'y avait pas d'autobus.

IPA [nu z̩avɔ̃ dy ʁɑ̃tʁe a pje jɛʁ swaʁ || il n̩i avɛ pa d̩otobys ||]

**1518**

EN It's late. I have to go now. I'll see you tomorrow.

FR Il est tard. Je dois y aller maintenant. On se voit demain.

IPA [i l̩e taʁ || ʒø dwa z̩i ale mɛ̃tᵒnã || ɔ̃ sø vwa dᵒmɛ̃ ||]

**1519**

EN I went to the store after work yesterday. I had to buy some food.

FR Je suis allé à la boutique après le travail hier. Je devais acheter de la nourriture.

IPA [ʒø sɥi ale a la butik apʁɛ lø tʁavaj jɛʁ || ʒø dᵊvɛ aʃᵊte dø la nuʁityʁ ||]

**1520**

EN This train doesn't go all the way downtown. You have to change at the next station.

FR Ce train ne se rend pas jusqu'au centre-ville. Tu dois changer à la prochaine station.

IPA [sø tʁɛ̃ nø sø ʁɑ̃ pa ʒysko sɑ̃tʁᵊvil || ty dwa ʃɑ̃ʒe a la pʁoʃen stasjɔ̃ ||]

**1521**

EN We took a test yesterday. We had to answer six (6) questions out of ten (10).

FR Nous avons fait un examen hier. Nous devions répondre à six questions sur dix.

IPA [nu z‿avɔ̃ fɛ t‿œ̃ n‿egzamɛ̃ jɛʁ || nu dᵊvjɔ̃ ʁepɔ̃dʁ a sis kɛstjɔ̃ syʁ dis ||]

**1522**

EN I'm going to bed. I have to get up early tomorrow.

FR Je vais au lit. Je dois me lever tôt demain.

IPA [ʒø vɛ o li || ʒø dwa mø lᵊve to dᵊmɛ̃ ||]

**1523**

EN  Ravi and his cousin Tara can't go out with us tonight.
They have to take care of Tara's little brother.

FR  Ravi et sa cousine Tara ne peuvent pas venir avec
nous ce soir. Ils doivent s'occuper du petit frère de
Tara.

IPA  [(...) e sa kuzin (...) nø pœv pa vᵊniʁ avɛk nu sø swaʁ
|| il dwav s‿okype dy pᵊti fʁɛʁ dø (...) ||]

**1524**

EN  I have to get up early tomorrow. — What time do
you have to get up?

FR  Je dois me lever tôt demain. À quelle heure dois-tu te
lever?

IPA  [ʒø dwa mø lᵊve to dᵊmɛ̃ || a kɛ l‿œʁ dwa ty tø lᵊve
||]

**1525**

EN  Chris had to wait a long time. — How long did he
have to wait?

FR  Chris a dû attendre longtemps. Combien de temps
a-t-il dû attendre?

IPA  [(...) a dy atɑ̃dʁ lɔ̃tɑ̃ || kɔ̃bjɛ̃ dø tɑ̃ a t‿il dy atɑ̃dʁ ||]

**1526**

EN Claire has to go somewhere. — Where does she have to go?

---

FR Claire doit aller quelque part. Où doit-elle aller?

IPA [(...) dwa ale kɛlk paʁ || u dwa t‿ɛl ale |||]

**1527**

EN We had to pay a lot of money. — How much money did you have to pay?

---

FR Nous avons dû payer cher. Combien avez-vous dû payer?

IPA [nu z‿avɔ̃ dy peje ʃɛʁ || kɔ̃bjɛ̃ ave vu dy peje |||]

**1528**

EN I have to do some work. — What exactly do you have to do?

---

FR J'ai du travail à faire. Que dois-tu faire exactement?

IPA [ʒ‿ɛ dy tʁavaj a fɛʁ || kø dwa ty fɛʁ ɛgzaktᵊmã |||]

**1529**

EN They had to leave early. — Why did they have to leave early?

---

FR Ils (♀elles) ont dû partir tôt. Pourquoi ont-ils (♀elles) dû partir tôt?

IPA [il (♀ɛl) ɔ̃ dy paʁtiʁ to || puʁkwa ɔ̃ t‿il (♀ɛl) dy paʁtiʁ to |||]

---

**1530**

EN  Minoru has to go to Moscow. — When does he have to go?

---

FR  Minoru doit aller à Moscou. Quand doit-il y aller?

IPA  [(...) dwa ale a moscou || kɑ̃ dwa t‿il i ale ||]

---

**1531**

EN  Why are you going out? You don't have to go out.

---

FR  Pourquoi sors-tu? Tu n'as pas besoin de sortir.

IPA  [puʁkwa sɔʁ ty || ty n‿a pa bøzwɛ̃ dø sɔʁtiʁ ||]

---

**1532**

EN  Why is Megumi waiting? She doesn't have to wait.

---

FR  Pourquoi est-ce que Megumi attend? Elle n'a pas besoin d'attendre.

IPA  [puʁkwa ɛs° kø (...) atɑ̃ || ɛl n‿a pa bøzwɛ̃ d‿atɑ̃dʁ ||]

---

**1533**

EN  Why did you get up early? You didn't have to get up so early.

---

FR  Pourquoi t'es-tu levé (♀levée) tôt? Tu n'avais pas besoin de te lever si tôt.

IPA  [puʁkwa t‿ɛ ty lᵊve (♀lᵊve) to || ty n‿avɛ pa bøzwɛ̃ dø tø lᵊve si to ||]

**1534**

EN  Why is David working so hard? He doesn't have to work so hard.

FR  Pourquoi David travaille-t-il autant? Il n'a pas besoin de travailler autant.

IPA  [puʁkwa (...) tʁavaj t̪‿il otɑ̃ ‖ il n‿a pa bøzwɛ̃ də tʁavaje otɑ̃ ‖|]

**1535**

EN  Why do you want to leave now? We don't have to leave now.

FR  Pourquoi veux-tu partir maintenant? Nous n'avons pas besoin de partir maintenant.

IPA  [puʁkwa vø ty paʁtiʁ mɛ̃t°nɑ̃ ‖ nu n‿avɔ̃ pa bøzwɛ̃ də paʁtiʁ mɛ̃t°nɑ̃ ‖|]

**1536**

EN  Why did they tell me something I already know? They didn't have to tell me that.

FR  Pourquoi m'ont-ils (♀elles) dit quelque chose que je sais déjà? Ils (♀elles) n'avaient pas besoin de me dire ça.

IPA  [puʁkwa m‿ɔ̃ t‿il (♀ɛl) di kɛlk ʃoz kø ʒø sɛ deʒa ‖ il (♀ɛl) n‿avɛ pa bøzwɛ̃ də mø diʁ sa ‖|]

**1537**

EN I have to drive fifty (50) miles to work every day. > I have to drive eighty (80) kilometers to work every day.

---

FR Je dois conduire cinquante milles chaque jour pour me rendre au travail. > Je dois conduire quatre-vingts kilomètres chaque jour pour me rendre au travail.

IPA [ʒø dwa kɔ̃dɥiʁ sɛ̃kɑ̃t mil ʃak ʒuʁ puʁ mø ʁɑ̃dʁ o tʁavaj ‖ > ʒø dwa kɔ̃dɥiʁ katʁ°vɛ̃ kilometʁ ʃak ʒuʁ puʁ mø ʁɑ̃dʁ o tʁavaj ‖]

**1538**

EN I have to take the subway to class every day.

---

FR Je dois prendre le métro chaque jour pour aller en classe.

IPA [ʒø dwa pʁɑ̃dʁ lø metʁo ʃak ʒuʁ pu ʁ‿ale ʁ‿ɑ̃ klas ‖]

**1539**

EN I had to have dinner with my family yesterday.

---

FR J'ai dû dîner avec ma famille hier.

IPA [ʒ‿ɛ dy dine avɛk ma famij jɛʁ ‖]

**1540**

EN I had to visit my grandfather in the hospital last week.

---

FR J'ai dû visiter mon grand-père à l'hôpital la semaine dernière.

IPA [ʒ‿ɛ dy vizite mɔ̃ gʁɑ̃pɛʁ a l‿opital la sᵊmɛn dɛʁnjɛʁ ‖]

**1541**

EN I had to take a lot of classes when I was younger.

---

FR J'ai dû suivre de nombreux cours quand j'étais jeune.

IPA [ʒ‿ɛ dy sɥivʁ də nɔ̃bʁø kuʁ kɑ̃ ʒ‿ete ʒœn ‖]

**1542**

EN Would you like some coffee?

---

FR Voudrais-tu du café?

IPA [vudʁɛ ty dy kafe ‖]

**1543**

EN Would you like a piece of candy?

---

FR Voudrais-tu une friandise? > Voudrais-tu un bonbon?

IPA [vudʁɛ ty yn fʁijɑ̃diz ‖ > vudʁɛ ty œ̃ bɔ̃bɔ̃ ‖]

**1544**

EN   Which would you like, tea or coffee?

FR   Que préférerais-tu, du thé ou du café?

IPA   [kø pʁefeʁ°ʁɛ ty | dy te u dy kafe ‖]

**1545**

EN   Would you like to go for a walk?

FR   Voudrais-tu aller te promener?

IPA   [vudʁɛ ty ale tø pʁɔmne ‖]

**1546**

EN   Would you like to have dinner with us on Sunday?

FR   Voudrais-tu dîner avec nous dimanche?

IPA   [vudʁɛ ty dine avɛk nu dimãʃ ‖]

**1547**

EN   I'd love to have dinner on Sunday.

FR   J'adorerais aller dîner dimanche.

IPA   [ʒ‿adɔʁ°ʁɛ ale dine dimãʃ ‖]

**1548**

EN   What would you like to do tonight?

FR   Qu'aimerais-tu faire ce soir?

IPA   [k‿ɛm°ʁɛ ty fɛʁ sø swaʁ ‖]

**1549**

EN I'm thirsty. I'd like a drink.

FR J'ai soif. J'aimerais boire quelque chose.

IPA [ʒ‿ɛ swaf ‖ ʒ‿ɛmˀʁɛ bwaʁ kɛlk ʃoz ‖]

**1550**

EN I'd like some information about hotels, please.

FR J'aimerais avoir de l'information à propos des hôtels, s'il vous plaît.

IPA [ʒ‿ɛmˀʁɛ avwaʁ də l‿ɛ̃fɔʁmasjɔ̃ a pʁopo de otɛl ‖ s‿il vu plɛ ‖]

**1551**

EN I'm feeling tired. I'd like to stay home tonight.

FR Je me sens fatigué (♀fatiguée). J'aimerais rester à la maison ce soir.

IPA [ʒø mø sãs fatige (♀fatige) ‖ ʒ‿ɛmˀʁɛ ʁeste a la mɛzɔ̃ sø swaʁ ‖]

**1552**

EN Would you like to go to the movies tonight?

FR Aimerais-tu aller au cinéma ce soir?

IPA [ɛmˀʁɛ ty ale o sinema sø swaʁ ‖]

178

**1553**

EN Do you like to go to the movies? — Yes, I go to the movies a lot.

FR Aimes-tu aller au cinéma? — Oui, je vais souvent au cinéma.

IPA [ɛm ty ale o sinema || — wi | ʒø vɛ suvɑ̃ o sinema |||]

**1554**

EN I'd like an orange juice, please. > Can I have an orange juice?

FR J'aimerais un jus d'orange, s'il vous plaît. Puis-je avoir un jus d'orange?

IPA [ʒ‿ɛm°ʁɛ œ̃ ʒy d‿oʁɑ̃ʒ | s‿il vu plɛ || pɥi ʒø avwa ʁ‿œ̃ ʒy d‿oʁɑ̃ʒ |||]

**1555**

EN I like orange juice.

FR J'aime le jus d'orange.

IPA [ʒ‿ɛm lø ʒy d‿oʁɑ̃ʒ |||]

**1556**

EN What would you like to do next weekend?

FR Qu'aimerais-tu faire le week-end prochain?

IPA [k‿ɛm°ʁɛ ty fɛʁ lø wikɛnd pʁoʃɛ̃ |||]

**1557**

EN What do you like to do on weekends?

---

FR Qu'aimes-tu faire les week-ends?

IPA [kˌɛm ty fɛʁ le wikɛnd ‖]

**1558**

EN You want to go to the movies tonight. Perhaps Emily will go with you.

---

FR Tu veux aller au cinéma ce soir. Peut-être qu'Emily y ira avec toi.

IPA [ty vø ale o sinema sø swaʁ ‖ pøtɛtʁ k (...) i iʁa avɛk twa ‖]

**1559**

EN Would you like to go to the movies with me tonight?

---

FR Aimerais-tu aller au cinéma avec moi ce soir?

IPA [ɛmᵊʁɛ ty ale o sinema avɛk mwa sø swaʁ ‖]

**1560**

EN You want to play tennis tomorrow. Perhaps Wenjie will play, too.

---

FR Tu veux jouer au tennis demain. Peut-être que Wenjie jouera aussi.

IPA [ty vø ʒwe o tenis dᵊmɛ̃ ‖ pøtɛtʁ kø (...) ʒuʁa osi ‖]

**1561**

EN Would you like to play tennis with me tomorrow?

FR Aimerais-tu jouer au tennis demain avec moi?

IPA [ɛmˠʁɛ ty ʒwe o tenis dˠmɛ̃ n‿avɛk mwa ‖]

**1562**

EN You have an extra ticket for a concert next week. Perhaps Helen will come.

FR Tu as un billet supplémentaire pour le concert de la semaine prochaine. Peut-être qu'Helen y ira.

IPA [ty a z‿œ̃ bijɛ syplemɑ̃tɛʁ puʁ lø kɔ̃sɛʁ dø la sˠmɛn pʁoʃɛn ‖ pøtɛtʁ k (...) i iʁa ‖]

**1563**

EN Would you like to go to a concert with me next week?

FR Aimerais-tu aller à un concert avec moi la semaine prochaine?

IPA [ɛmˠʁɛ ty ale a œ̃ kɔ̃sɛʁ avɛk mwa la sˠmɛn pʁoʃɛn ‖]

**1564**

EN It's raining, and Yaqin's going out. She doesn't have an umbrella, but you have one.

FR Il pleut et Yaqin sort. Elle n'a pas de parapluie, mais tu en as un.

IPA [il plø e (...) sɔʁ ‖ ɛl n‿a pa dø paʁaplɥi | mɛ ty ɑ̃ n‿a z‿œ̃ ‖]

**1565**

EN   Would you like to borrow my umbrella?

FR   Voudrais-tu emprunter mon parapluie?
IPA  [vudʁɛ ty ɑ̃pʁœ̃te mɔ̃ paʁaplɥi ‖]

**1566**

EN   What would you like to drink?

FR   Qu'aimerais-tu boire?
IPA  [kˌɛmˀʁɛ ty bwaʁ ‖]

**1567**

EN   Would you like to go out for a walk?

FR   Voudrais-tu aller te promener?
IPA  [vudʁɛ ty ale tø pʁɔmne ‖]

**1568**

EN   I like onions, but I don't eat them very often.

FR   J'aime les oignons, mais je n'en mange pas très
     souvent.
IPA  [ʒˌɛm le zˌɔɲɔ̃ | mɛ ʒø nˌɑ̃ mɑ̃ʒ pa tʁɛ suvɑ̃ ‖]

**1569**

EN   What time would you like to have dinner tonight?

FR   À quelle heure voudrais-tu dîner ce soir?
IPA  [a kɛ lˌœʁ vudʁɛ ty dine sø swaʁ ‖]

**1570**

EN Would you like something to eat?

FR Voudrais-tu quelque chose à manger?
IPA [vudʁɛ ty kɛlk ʃoz a mɑ̃ʒe ‖]

**1571**

EN Do you like your new job?

FR Aimes-tu ton nouvel emploi?
IPA [ɛm ty tɔ̃ nuvɛ l‿ɑ̃plwa ‖]

**1572**

EN I'm tired. I'd like to go to bed now.

FR Je suis fatigué (♀ fatiguée). J'aimerais aller au lit
maintenant. > Je suis fatigué (♀ fatiguée). J'aimerais
aller me coucher maintenant.
IPA [ʒø sɥi fatige (♀ fatige) ‖ ʒ‿ɛmᵊʁɛ ale o li mɛ̃tᵊnɑ̃ ‖
> ʒø sɥi fatige (♀ fatige) ‖ ʒ‿ɛmᵊʁɛ ale mø kuʃe
mɛ̃tᵊnɑ̃ ‖]

**1573**

EN I'd like some dumplings, please.

FR Je voudrais quelques boulettes, s'il vous plaît.
IPA [ʒø vudʁɛ kɛlk bulɛt | s‿il vu plɛ ‖]

**1574**

EN　What kind of music do you like?

FR　Quel genre de musique aimes-tu?

IPA　[kɛl ʒɑ̃ʁ də myzik ɛm ty ||]

**1575**

EN　Heuiyeon likes to sit on the floor. She doesn't want to sit on a chair.

FR　Heuiyeon aime s'asseoir par terre. Elle n'aime pas s'asseoir sur une chaise.

IPA　[(...) ɛm s‿aswaʁ paʁ tɛʁ || ɛl n‿ɛm pa s‿aswaʁ sy ʁ‿yn ʃɛz ||]

**1576**

EN　I'd rather sit on the floor. > I would prefer to sit on the floor.

FR　Je préférerais m'asseoir par terre.

IPA　[ʒø pʁefeʁ°ʁɛ m‿aswaʁ paʁ tɛʁ ||]

**1577**

EN　I don't really want to go out. I'd rather stay at home.

FR　Je n'ai pas vraiment envie de sortir. Je préférerais rester à la maison.

IPA　[ʒø n‿ɛ pa vʁɛmɑ̃ t‿ɑ̃vi də sɔʁtiʁ || ʒø pʁefeʁ°ʁɛ ʁeste a la mɛzɔ̃ ||]

**1578**

EN  Should we go now? — No, not yet. I'd rather wait until later.

FR  Devrions-nous partir maintenant? — Non, pas tout de suite. Je préférerais attendre encore un peu.

IPA  [dᵊvʁijɔ̃ nu paʁtiʁ mɛ̃tᵊnã ‖ nɔ̃ | pa tu dø sɥit ‖ ʒø pʁefeʁᵊʁɛ atɑ̃dʁ ɑ̃kɔʁ œ̃ pø ‖]

**1579**

EN  I'd like to go now, but Gary would rather wait until later.

FR  J'aimerais y aller maintenant, mais Gary préférerait attendre encore un peu.

IPA  [ʒ‿emᵊʁɛ i ale mɛ̃tᵊnã | mɛ (...) pʁefeʁᵊʁɛ atɑ̃dʁ ɑ̃kɔʁ œ̃ pø ‖]

**1580**

EN  I don't like to be late. I'd rather be early.

FR  Je n'aime pas être en retard. Je préfère être à l'heure.

IPA  [ʒø n‿em pa z‿etʁ ã ʁᵊtaʁ ‖ ʒø pʁefeʁ etʁ a l‿œʁ ‖]

**1581**

EN  I'm feeling tired. I'd rather not go out tonight.

FR  Je me sens fatigué (♀fatiguée). Je préférerais ne pas sortir ce soir.

IPA  [ʒø mø sãs fatige (♀fatige) ‖ ʒø pʁefeʁᵊʁɛ nø pa sɔʁtiʁ sø swaʁ ‖]

**1582**

EN Jisang is feeling tired. He'd rather not go out tonight.

---

FR Jisang se sent fatigué. Il préférerait ne pas sortir ce soir.

IPA [(...) sø sã fatige || il pʁefeʁ°ʁɛ nø pa sɔʁtiʁ sø swaʁ ||]

**1583**

EN We're not hungry. We'd rather not eat yet.

---

FR Nous n'avons pas faim. Nous préférerions ne pas manger tout de suite.

IPA [nu n‿avõ pa fɛ̃ || nu pʁefeʁ°ʁjõ nø pa mãʒe tu dø sɥit ||]

**1584**

EN Would you like to go out tonight? — I'd rather not.

---

FR Aimerais-tu sortir ce soir? — Je ne préférerais pas. > J'aimerais mieux pas.

IPA [ɛm°ʁɛ ty sɔʁtiʁ sø swaʁ || — ʒø nø pʁefeʁ°ʁɛ pa || > ʒ‿ɛm°ʁɛ mjø pa ||]

**1585**

EN Would you rather have milk or juice? — Juice, please.

---

FR Préférerais-tu du lait ou du jus? — Du jus, s'il te plaît.

IPA [pʁefeʁ°ʁɛ ty dy lɛ u dy ʒy || — dy ʒy | s‿il tø plɛ ||]

**1586**

EN Which would you rather do: go to the movies or watch a DVD at home?

FR Que préférerais-tu faire : aller au cinéma ou regarder un DVD à la maison?

IPA [kø pʁefeʁˀʁɛ ty fɛʁ | ale o sinema u ʁˀgaʁde ʁ‿œ̃ dividi a la mɛzɔ̃ ‖]

**1587**

EN I'd rather stand than sit.

FR Je préférerais rester debout plutôt que de m'asseoir.

IPA [ʒø pʁefeʁˀʁɛ ʁeste dˀbu plyto kø dø m‿aswaʁ ‖]

**1588**

EN Jessica would rather not go out.

FR Jessica préférerait ne pas sortir.

IPA [(...) pʁefeʁˀʁɛ nø pa sɔʁtiʁ ‖]

**1589**

EN I'd prefer to sit than stand.

FR Je préférerais m'asseoir plutôt que de rester debout.

IPA [ʒø pʁefeʁˀʁɛ m‿aswaʁ plyto kø dø ʁeste dˀbu ‖]

**1590**

EN I'd prefer to sit rather than stand.

---

FR Je préférerais m'asseoir plutôt que de rester debout.
IPA [ʒø pʁefeʁ°ʁɛ m‿aswaʁ plyto kø dø ʁeste d°bu ‖]

**1591**

EN Zhirong would prefer not to go out.

---

FR Zhirong préférerait ne pas sortir.
IPA [(...) pʁefeʁ°ʁɛ nø pa sɔʁtiʁ ‖]

**1592**

EN I'd rather go out than stay home.

---

FR Je préférerais sortir plutôt que de rester à la maison.
IPA [ʒø pʁefeʁ°ʁɛ sɔʁtiʁ plyto kø dø ʁeste a la mɛzɔ̃ ‖]

**1593**

EN I'd rather have a dog than a cat.

---

FR Je préférerais avoir un chien plutôt qu'un chat.
IPA [ʒø pʁefeʁ°ʁɛ avwa ʁ‿œ̃ ʃjɛ̃ plyto k‿œ̃ ʃa ‖]

**1594**

EN We'd rather go to the movies than watch a DVD at home.

FR Nous préférerions aller au cinéma plutôt que de regarder un DVD à la maison.

IPA [nu pʁefeʁˀʁjɔ̃ ale o sinema plyto kø dø ʁˀɡaʁde ʁ‿œ̃ dividi a la mɛzɔ̃ ‖]

**1595**

EN I'd rather be at home right now than here.

FR Je préférerais être à la maison en ce moment plutôt qu'être ici.

IPA [ʒø pʁefeʁˀʁɛ ɛtʁ a la mɛzɔ̃ ɑ̃ sø momɑ̃ plyto k‿ɛtʁ isi ‖]

**1596**

EN Don't you want to watch TV? — No, I'd rather read my novel.

FR N'as-tu pas envie de regarder la télé? — Non, je préférerais lire un roman.

IPA [n‿a ty pa z‿ɑ̃vi dø ʁˀɡaʁde la tele ‖ — nɔ̃ | ʒø pʁefeʁˀʁɛ liʁ œ̃ ʁomɑ̃ ‖]

**1597**

EN Would you like some tea? — Well, I'd rather have coffee if you have some.

FR Voudrais-tu du thé? — En fait, je préférerais du café si tu en as.

IPA [vudʁɛ ty dy te ‖ — ɑ̃ fɛ | ʒø pʁefeʁ°ʁɛ dy kafe si ty ɑ̃ n̺a ‖]

**1598**

EN Should we go out now? — I'd rather wait until it stops raining.

FR Devrions-nous sortir maintenant? > Devrait-on sortir maintenant? — Je préférerais attendre qu'il cesse de pleuvoir.

IPA [d°vʁijɔ̃ nu sɔʁtiʁ mɛ̃t°nɑ̃ ‖ > d°vʁɛ t̺ɔ̃ sɔʁtiʁ mɛ̃t°nɑ̃ ‖ — ʒø pʁefeʁ°ʁɛ atɑ̃dʁ k̺il sɛs dø pløvwaʁ ‖]

**1599**

EN Should we have dinner now, or wait until later?

FR Devrait-on dîner maintenant, ou attendre encore un peu?

IPA [d°vʁɛ t̺ɔ̃ dine mɛ̃t°nɑ̃ | u atɑ̃dʁ ɑ̃kɔʁ œ̃ pø ‖]

**1600**

EN Would you like a glass of juice, or some water?

FR Voudrais-tu un verre de jus ou de l'eau?

IPA [vudʁɛ ty œ̃ vɛʁ dø ʒy u dø l̺o ‖]

# GMS #1601 - 1700

**1601**

**EN** Do you want to go to the movies, or just watch TV?

---

**FR** Veux-tu aller au cinéma ou simplement regarder la télé?

**IPA** [vø ty ale o sinema u sɛ̃plᵊmɑ̃ ʁᵊgaʁde la tele ‖]

**1602**

**EN** Should we call your brother tonight, or would you rather wait until tomorrow morning?

---

**FR** Devrait-on appeler ton frère ce soir ou préférerais-tu attendre à demain matin?

**IPA** [dᵊvʁɛ t‿ɔ̃ apᵊle tɔ̃ fʁɛʁ sø swaʁ u pʁefeʁᵊʁɛ ty atɑ̃dʁ a dᵊmɛ̃ matɛ̃ ‖]

**1603**

**EN** I'd rather stay home tonight. I'd prefer not to go out.

---

**FR** Je préférerais rester à la maison ce soir. Je préférerais ne pas sortir.

**IPA** [ʒø pʁefeʁᵊʁɛ ʁɛste a la mɛzɔ̃ sø swaʁ ‖ ʒø pʁefeʁᵊʁɛ nø pa sɔʁtiʁ ‖]

**1604**

EN Should we walk home, or would you rather take a taxi?

---

FR Devrions-nous rentrer à pied ou préférerais-tu prendre un taxi?

IPA [dᵊvʁijɔ̃ nu ʁɑ̃tʁe a pje u pʁefeʁᵊʁɛ ty pʁɑ̃dʁ œ̃ taksi ||]

**1605**

EN Do you want me to come with you, or would you prefer to go alone?

---

FR Veux-tu que je t'accompagne ou préférerais-tu y aller seul (♀ seule)?

IPA [vø ty kø ʒø t‿akɔ̃paɲ u pʁefeʁᵊʁɛ ty i ale sœl (♀ sœl) ||]

**1606**

EN Yiting doesn't want to go to college. She'd rather get a job.

---

FR Yiting ne veut pas aller à l'université. Elle préférerait se trouver un emploi.

IPA [(...) nø vø pa z‿ale a l‿ynivɛʁsite || ɛl pʁefeʁᵊʁɛ sø tʁuve ʁ‿œ̃ n‿ɑ̃plwa ||]

**1607**

EN Can I help you with your suitcase? — No, thank you.
I'd rather do it myself.

FR Puis-je t'aider avec ta valise? — Non, merci. Je
préférerais le faire moi-même.

IPA [pɥi ʒø t̪ede avɛk ta valiz || — nɔ̃ | mɛʁsi || ʒø
pʁefeʁˀʁɛ lø fɛʁ mwamɛm ||]

**1608**

EN I'd rather not call him. I'd prefer to write him an
email.

FR Je préférerais ne pas l'appeler. Je préférerais lui
envoyer un courriel.

IPA [ʒø pʁefeʁˀʁɛ nø pa l̪apˀle || ʒø pʁefeʁˀʁɛ lɥi
ɑ̃vwaje ʁ‿œ̃ kuʁjɛl ||]

**1609**

EN Which would you prefer to be: a bus driver or an
airplane pilot?

FR Que préférerais-tu être : un chauffeur d'autobus ou un
pilote d'avion?

IPA [kø pʁefeʁˀʁɛ ty ɛtʁ | œ̃ ʃofœʁ d̪‿otobys u œ̃ pilɔt
d̪‿avjɔ̃ ||]

**1610**

EN I'd rather be an airplane pilot than a bus driver.

FR Je préférerais être un pilote d'avion plutôt qu'un chauffeur d'autobus.

IPA [ʒø pʁefeʁ°ʁɛ etʁ œ̃ pilɔt d‿avjɔ̃ plyto k‿œ̃ ʃofœʁ d‿otobys ‖]

**1611**

EN Which would you prefer to be: a journalist or a school teacher?

FR Que préférerais-tu être : un journaliste ou un enseignant?

IPA [kø pʁefeʁ°ʁɛ ty etʁ | œ̃ ʒuʁnalist u œ̃ n‿ɑ̃sɛɲɑ̃ ‖]

**1612**

EN I'd rather be a journalist than a school teacher.

FR Je préférerais être un journaliste plutôt qu'un enseignant.

IPA [ʒø pʁefeʁ°ʁɛ etʁ œ̃ ʒuʁnalist plyto k‿œ̃ ɑ̃sɛɲɑ̃ ‖]

**1613**

EN Where would you prefer to live: in a big city or a small town?

FR Où préférerais-tu vivre : dans une grande ville ou un petit village?

IPA [u pʁefeʁ°ʁɛ ty vivʁ | dɑ̃ z‿yn gʁɑ̃d vil u œ̃ p°ti vilaʒ ‖]

**1614**

EN   I'd rather live in a big city than a small town.

FR   Je préférerais vivre dans une grande ville plutôt que dans un petit village.

IPA   [ʒø pʁefeʁˀʁɛ vivʁ dã z‿yn gʁãd vil plyto kø dã z‿œ̃ pˀti vilaʒ ‖]

**1615**

EN   Which would you prefer to have: a small house or a big one?

FR   Que préférerais-tu avoir : une petite ou une grande maison?

IPA   [kø pʁefeʁˀʁɛ ty avwaʁ | yn pˀtit u yn gʁãd mɛzõ ‖]

**1616**

EN   I'd rather have a big house than a small one.

FR   Je préférerais avoir une grande maison plutôt qu'une petite maison.

IPA   [ʒø pʁefeʁˀʁɛ avwa ʁ‿yn gʁãd mɛzõ plyto k‿yn pˀtit mɛzõ ‖]

**1617**

EN   Which would you prefer to study: electronics or philosophy?

FR   Que préférerais-tu étudier : l'électronique ou la philosophie?

IPA   [kø pʁefeʁˀʁɛ ty etydje | l‿elɛktʁonik u la filozofi ‖]

**1618**

EN I'd rather study philosophy than electronics.

FR Je préférerais étudier la philosophie plutôt que l'électronique.

IPA [ʒø pʁefeʁˤʁɛ etydje la filozofi plyto kø l‿elɛktʁonik ||]

**1619**

EN Which would you prefer to watch: a football game or a movie?

FR Que préférerais-tu regarder : un match de football ou un film?

IPA [kø pʁefeʁˤʁɛ ty ʁˤgaʁde | œ̃ matʃ dø futbɔl u œ̃ film ||]

**1620**

EN I'd rather watch a movie than a football game.

FR Je préférerais regarder un film plutôt qu'un match de football.

IPA [ʒø pʁefeʁˤʁɛ ʁˤgaʁde ʁ‿œ̃ film plyto k‿œ̃ matʃ dø futbɔl ||]

**1621**

EN Come here and look at this. — What is it?

FR Viens ici et regarde ça. — Qu'est-ce que c'est?

IPA [vjɛ̃ isi e ʁˤgaʁd sa || — kɛsˤ kø sɛ ||]

---

**1622**

EN   I don't want to talk to you. Go away!

FR   Je ne veux pas te parler. Va-t'en!
IPA  [ʒø nø vø pa tø paʁle ‖ va t'en ‖‖]

---

**1623**

EN   I'm not ready yet. Please wait for me.

FR   Je ne suis pas encore prêt (♀prête). Attends-moi s'il
     te plaît.
IPA  [ʒø nø sɥi pa z‿ɑ̃kɔʁ pʁɛ (♀pʁɛt) ‖ atɑ̃ mwa s‿il tø
     plɛ ‖‖]

---

**1624**

EN   Please be quiet. I'm trying to concentrate.

FR   Silence, s'il vous plaît. J'essaie de me concentrer.
IPA  [silɑ̃s | s‿il vu plɛ ‖ ʒ‿esɛ dø mø kõsɑ̃tʁe ‖‖]

---

**1625**

EN   Have a good trip. Have a nice time. Have a good
     flight. Have fun!

FR   Bon voyage. Passe du bon temps. Bon vol. Amuse-toi
     bien!
IPA  [bõ vwajaʒ ‖ pas dy bõ tɑ̃ ‖ bõ vɔl ‖ amyz twa bjɛ̃
     ‖‖]

**1626**

EN Here, have some candy.

FR Tiens, prend une friandise.
IPA [tjɛ̃ | pʁɑ̃ d̯yn fʁijɑ̃diz |||]

**1627**

EN Be careful! Don't fall!

FR Attention! Ne tombe pas!
IPA [atɑ̃sjɔ̃ || nø tɔ̃b pa |||]

**1628**

EN Please don't go. Stay here with me.

FR Ne t'en va pas. Reste ici avec moi.
IPA [nø t̯ɑ̃ va pa || ʁɛst isi avɛk mwa |||]

**1629**

EN Be here on time. Don't be late.

FR Arrive à l'heure. Ne sois pas en retard.
IPA [aʁiv a l̯œʁ || nø swa pa z̯ɑ̃ ʁ°taʁ |||]

**1630**

EN It's a nice day. Let's go out.

FR C'est une belle journée. Allons dehors.
IPA [sɛ t̯yn bɛl ʒuʁne || alɔ̃ døɔʁ |||]

**1631**

EN Come on! Let's dance.

FR Allez! Dansons.
IPA [ale || dãsɔ̃ |||]

**1632**

EN Are you ready? Let's go.

FR Es-tu prêt (♀prête)? Allons-y.
IPA [ɛ ty pʁɛ (♀pʁɛt) || alɔ̃ z‿i |||]

**1633**

EN Let's have fish for dinner tonight.

FR Mangeons du poisson pour dîner ce soir.
IPA [mãʒɔ̃ dy pwasɔ̃ puʁ dine sø swaʁ |||]

**1634**

EN Should we go out tonight? — No, I'm tired. Let's stay home.

FR On sort ce soir? — Non, je suis fatigué (♀fatiguée). Restons à la maison.
IPA [ɔ̃ sɔʁ sø swaʁ || — nɔ̃ | ʒø sɥi fatige (♀fatige) || ʁestɔ̃ a la mɛzɔ̃ |||]

---

**1635**

EN   It's cold. Let's not go out. Let's stay home.

---

FR   Il fait froid. Ne sortons pas. Restons à la maison.
IPA  [il fɛ fʁwa || nø sɔʁtɔ̃ pa || ʁɛstɔ̃ a la mɛzɔ̃ |||]

---

**1636**

EN   Let's not have fish for dinner tonight. Let's have chicken.

---

FR   Ne mangeons pas de poisson ce soir. Mangeons du poulet!
IPA  [nø mɑ̃ʒɔ̃ pa dø pwasɔ̃ sø swaʁ || mɑ̃ʒɔ̃ dy pulɛ |||]

---

**1637**

EN   I'm tired of arguing. Let's not do it any more.

---

FR   J'en ai assez qu'on se dispute. Ne le faisons plus.
IPA  [ʒ‿ɑ̃ ɛ ase k‿ɔ̃ sø dispyt || nø lø fᵊzɔ̃ plys |||]

---

**1638**

EN   Would you like to play tennis? — No, let's go for a swim.

---

FR   Aimerais-tu jouer au tennis? — Non, allons nager.
IPA  [ɛmᵊʁɛ ty ʒwe o tenis || — nɔ̃ | alɔ̃ naʒe |||]

1639

EN Do you want to walk home? — No, let's take the bus.

FR Veux-tu rentrer à pied? — Non, prenons l'autobus.
IPA [vø ty ʁɑ̃tʁe a pje || — nɔ̃ | pʁ°nɔ̃ l̩otobys ||]

1640

EN Shall I put some music on? — No, let's watch a movie.

FR Devrais-je mettre de la musique? — Non, écoutons un film.
IPA [d°vʁɛ ʒø mɛtʁ dø la myzik || — nɔ̃ | ekutɔ̃ z‿œ̃ film ||]

1641

EN Should we have dinner at home? — No, let's go to a restaurant.

FR On dîne à la maison? — Non, allons au restaurant.
IPA [ɔ̃ din a la mɛzɔ̃ || — nɔ̃ | alɔ̃ o ʁɛstoʁɑ̃ ||]

1642

EN Would you like to go now? — No, let's wait a while.

FR Voudrais-tu y aller maintenant? — Non, attendons un peu.
IPA [vudʁɛ ty i ale mɛ̃t°nɑ̃ || — nɔ̃ | atɑ̃dɔ̃ z‿œ̃ pø ||]

---

**1643**

**EN** Shall I wait for you? — No, don't wait for me.

---

**FR** Devrais-je t'attendre? — Non, ne m'attends pas.

**IPA** [dᵊvʁɛ ʒø t‿atɑ̃dʁ || — nɔ̃ | nø m‿atɑ̃ pa ||]

---

**1644**

**EN** Should we go home now? — No, let's not go home yet.

---

**FR** Devrait-on rentrer à la maison maintenant? — Non, ne rentrons pas tout de suite.

**IPA** [dᵊvʁɛ t‿ɔ̃ ʁɑ̃tʁe a la mɛzɔ̃ mɛ̃t°nɑ̃ || — nɔ̃ | nø ʁɑ̃tʁɔ̃ pa tu dø sɥit ||]

---

**1645**

**EN** Shall we go out? — No, let's not go out.

---

**FR** On sort? — Non, ne sortons pas.

**IPA** [ɔ̃ sɔʁ || — nɔ̃ | nø sɔʁtɔ̃ pa ||]

---

**1646**

**EN** Do you want me to close the window? — No, leave the window open.

---

**FR** Veux-tu que je ferme la fenêtre? — Non, laisse la fenêtre ouverte.

**IPA** [vø ty kø ʒø fɛʁm la f°nɛtʁ || — nɔ̃ | lɛs la f°nɛtʁ uvɛʁt ||]

**1647**

EN Should I call you tonight? — No, call me in the morning.

FR Devrais-je t'appeler ce soir? — Non, appelle-moi demain matin.

IPA [dᵊvʁɛ ʒø t‿apᵊle sø swaʁ ‖ — nɔ̃ | apɛl mwa dᵊmɛ̃ matɛ̃ ‖]

**1648**

EN Do you think we should wait for Howard? — No, let's not wait for him.

FR Penses-tu qu'on devrait attendre Howard? — Non, ne l'attendons pas.

IPA [pɑ̃s ty k‿ɔ̃ dᵊvʁɛ atɑ̃dʁ (...) ‖ — nɔ̃ | nø l‿atɑ̃dɔ̃ pa ‖]

**1649**

EN Do you want me to turn on the light? — No, leave the light off.

FR Veux-tu que j'allume? — Non, laisse la lumière éteinte.

IPA [vø ty kø ʒ‿alym ‖ — nɔ̃ | lɛs la lymjɛʁ etɛ̃t ‖]

**1650**

EN Should we take a taxi? — No, let's take a bus.

FR On prend un taxi? — Non, prenons l'autobus.

IPA [ɔ̃ pʁɑ̃ d‿œ̃ taksi ‖ — nɔ̃ | pʁᵊnɔ̃ l‿otobys ‖]

**1651**

EN There's a man on the roof.

FR Il y a un homme sur le toit.
IPA [i l̯i a œ̃ n̯ɔm syʁ lø twa ‖]

**1652**

EN There's a train coming at ten thirty (10:30).

FR Il y a un train qui arrive à dix heures trente (10 h 30).
IPA [i l̯i a œ̃ tʁɛ̃ ki aʁiv a di z̯œʁ tʁɑ̃t (10 h 30) ‖]

**1653**

EN There are seven (7) days in a week.

FR Il y a sept jours dans une semaine.
IPA [i l̯i a sɛt ʒuʁ dɑ̃ z̯yn s̯mɛn ‖]

**1654**

EN There's a big tree in the yard.

FR Il y a un gros arbre dans le jardin.
IPA [i l̯i a œ̃ gʁo z̯aʁbʁ dɑ̃ lø ʒaʁdɛ̃ ‖]

**1655**

EN There's nothing on TV tonight.

FR Il n'y a rien à la télé ce soir.
IPA [il n̯i a ʁjɛ̃ a la tele sø swaʁ ‖]

**1656**

EN  Do you have any money? — Yes, there's some in my wallet.

FR  As-tu de l'argent? — Oui, j'en ai dans mon portefeuille.

IPA [a ty dø l̩aʁʒɑ̃ || — wi | ʒ̩ɑ̃ ɛ dɑ̃ mɔ̃ pɔʁt°fœj ||]

**1657**

EN  Excuse me, is there a hotel near here? — Yes, there is. > No, there isn't.

FR  Excusez-moi, y a-t-il un hôtel près d'ici? — Oui, il y en a un. Non, il n'y en a pas.

IPA [ɛkskyze mwa | i a t̩il œ̃ n̩otɛl pʁɛ d̩isi || — wi | i l̩i ɑ̃ n̩a œ̃ || nɔ̃ | il n̩i ɑ̃ n̩a pa ||]

**1658**

EN  We can't go skiing. There isn't any snow.

FR  On ne peut pas aller skier. Il n'y a pas de neige.

IPA [ɔ̃ nø pø pa z̩ale skje || il n̩i a pa dø nɛʒ ||]

**1659**

EN  There are some big trees in the yard.

FR  Il y a de gros arbres dans le jardin.

IPA [i l̩i a dø gʁo z̩aʁbʁ dɑ̃ lø ʒaʁdɛ̃ |||]

**1660**

EN There are a lot of accidents on this road.

---

FR Il y a beaucoup d'accidents sur cette route.

IPA [i l̩ i a boku d̪aksidɑ̃ syʁ sɛt ʁut ‖]

**1661**

EN Are there any restaurants near here? — Yes, there are. > No, there aren't.

---

FR Y a-t-il des restaurants près d'ici? > Est-ce qu'il y a des restaurants près d'ici? — Oui, il y en a. Non, il n'y en a pas.

IPA [i a t il de ʁɛstoʁɑ̃ pʁɛ d̪isi ‖ > ɛsˀ k il i a de ʁɛstoʁɑ̃ pʁɛ d̪isi ‖ — wi | i l̩i ɑ̃ n̩a ‖ nɔ̃ | il n̩i ɑ̃ n̩a pa ‖]

**1662**

EN This restaurant is very quiet. There aren't many people here.

---

FR Ce restaurant est très silencieux. Il n'y a pas beaucoup de gens ici.

IPA [sø ʁɛstoʁɑ̃ e tʁɛ silɑ̃sjø ‖ il n̩i a pa boku dø ʒɑ̃ isi ‖]

**1663**

EN How many players are there on a football team?

---

FR Combien de joueurs y a-t-il dans une équipe de football?

IPA [kɔ̃bjɛ̃ dø ʒwœ ʁ i a t il dɑ̃ z yn ekip dø futbɔl ‖]

---

**1664**

EN There are eleven (11) players on a football team.

FR Il y a onze joueurs dans une équipe de football.
IPA [i l̡ i a ɔ̃z ʒwœʁ dɑ̃ z̡ yn ekip dø futbɔl ‖]

---

**1665**

EN There's a book on the table.

FR Il y a un livre sur la table.
IPA [i l̡ i a œ̃ livʁ syʁ la tabl ‖]

---

**1666**

EN There's a train at ten thirty (10:30). It's an express train.

FR Il y a un train à dix heures trente (10 h 30). C'est un train express.
IPA [i l̡ i a œ̃ tʁɛ̃ a di z̡ œʁ tʁɑ̃t (10 h 30) ‖ sɛ t̡ œ̃ tʁɛ̃ ɛkspʁɛs ‖]

---

**1667**

EN There's a lot of salt in this soup.

FR Il y a beaucoup de sel dans cette soupe.
IPA [i l̡ i a boku dø sɛl dɑ̃ sɛt sup ‖]

**1668**

EN  I don't like this soup. It's too salty.

---

FR  Je n'aime pas cette soupe. Elle est trop salée.
IPA  [ʒø nˌɛm pa sɛt sup ‖ ɛ lˌe tʁo sale ‖]

**1669**

EN  Bedford isn't an old town. There aren't any old buildings.

---

FR  Bedford n'est pas un vieux village. Il n'y a pas de vieux bâtiments.
IPA  [(...) nˌe pa z ˌœ̃ vjø vilaʒ ‖ il nˌi a pa dø vjø batimɑ̃ ‖]

**1670**

EN  Look! There's a photo of your brother in the newspaper!

---

FR  Regarde! Il y a une photo de ton frère dans le journal.
IPA  [ʁ°gaʁd ‖ i lˌi a yn foto dø tɔ̃ fʁɛʁ dɑ̃ lø ʒuʁnal ‖]

**1671**

EN  Excuse me, is there a bank near here? — Yes, at the end of the block.

---

FR  Excuse-moi, y a-t-il une banque près d'ici? — Oui, au bout de ce pâté de maisons.
IPA  [ɛkskyz mwa | i a tˌil yn bɑ̃k pʁɛ dˌisi ‖ — wi | o bu dø sø pate dø mɛzɔ̃ ‖]

1672

**EN** There are five (5) people in my family: my parents, my two (2) sisters, and me.

**FR** Il y a cinq personnes dans ma famille : mes parents, mes deux sœurs et moi.

**IPA** [i l‿i a sɛ̃k pɛʁsɔn dɑ̃ ma famij | me paʁɑ̃ | me dø sœʁ e mwa ‖]

1673

**EN** How many students are there in the class? — Twenty.

**FR** Combien d'étudiants y a-t-il dans la classe? — Vingt.

**IPA** [kɔ̃bjɛ̃ d‿etydjɑ̃ i a t‿il dɑ̃ la klas ‖ — vɛ̃ ‖]

1674

**EN** The road is usually very quiet. There isn't much traffic.

**FR** La route est généralement très tranquille. Il n'y a pas beaucoup de circulation.

**IPA** [la ʁut e ʒeneʁalᵊmɑ̃ tʁɛ tʁɑ̃kil ‖ il n‿i a pa boku dø siʁkylasjɔ̃ ‖]

1675

EN Is there a bus from downtown to the airport? — Yes, every twenty (20) minutes.

FR Y a-t-il un autobus du centre-ville à l'aéroport? — Oui, à toutes les vingt minutes.

IPA [i a t̪il œ n̪otobys dy sãtʁ°vil a l̪aeʁopɔʁ || — wi | a tut le vɛ̃ minyt ||]

1676

EN Are there any problems? — No, everything is okay.

FR Y a-t-il un problème? — Non, tout va bien.

IPA [i a t̪il œ pʁoblɛm || — nɔ̃ | tu va bjɛ̃ ||]

1677

EN There's nowhere to sit down. There aren't any chairs.

FR Il n'y a nulle part où s'asseoir. Il n'y a pas de chaise.

IPA [il n̪i a nyl pa ʁu s̪aswaʁ || il n̪i a pa dø ʃez ||]

1678

EN There are eight (8) planets in the solar system.

FR Il y a huit planètes dans le système solaire.

IPA [i l̪i a ɥit planɛt dã lø sistɛm solɛʁ ||]

**1679**

**EN** There are twenty-six (26) letters in the English alphabet.

**FR** Il y a vingt-six (26) lettres dans l'alphabet anglais.
**IPA** [i l̪i a vɛ̃tsis (26) lɛtʁ dã l̪alfabɛ ãglɛ ||]

**1680**

**EN** There are thirty (30) days in September.

**FR** Il y a trente jours en septembre.
**IPA** [i l̪i a tʁãt ʒuʁ ã sɛptãbʁ ||]

**1681**

**EN** There are fifty (50) states in the United States.

**FR** Il y a cinquante états aux États-Unis.
**IPA** [i l̪i a sɛ̃kãt eta o z̪etazuni |||]

**1682**

**EN** There are five (5) players on a basketball team.

**FR** Il y a cinq joueurs dans une équipe de basketball.
**IPA** [i l̪i a sɛ̃k ʒwœʁ dã z̪yn ekip dø (...) |||]

**1683**

EN There's a flight at ten thirty (10:30). — Is it a non-stop flight?

---

FR Il y a un vol à dix heures trente (10 h 30). — Est-ce un vol direct?

IPA [i l̬i a œ̃ vɔl a di z‿œʁ tʁɑ̃t (10 h 30) || — ɛsº œ̃ vɔl diʁɛkt ||]

**1684**

EN I'm not going to buy this shirt. It's too expensive.

---

FR Je ne vais pas acheter cette chemise. Elle est trop chère.

IPA [ʒø nø vɛ pa z‿aʃºte sɛt ʃºmiz || ɛ l̬e tʁo ʃɛʁ ||]

**1685**

EN What's wrong? — There's something in my eye.

---

FR Qu'y a-t-il? — J'ai quelque chose dans l'œil.

IPA [k̬i a t̬il || — ʒ̬ɛ kɛlk ʃoz dɑ̃ l̬œj ||]

**1686**

EN There's a red car outside your house. Is it yours?

---

FR Il y a une voiture rouge en face de ta maison. Est-ce la tienne?

IPA [i l̬i a yn vwatyʁ ʁuʒ ɑ̃ fas dø ta mɛzɔ̃ || ɛsº la tjɛn ||]

**1687**

**EN** Is there anything good on TV tonight? — Yes, there's a movie at eight [o'clock] (8:00).

**FR** Est-ce qu'il y a quelque chose de bon à la télé ce soir? — Oui, il y a un film à vingt heures (20 h).

**IPA** [ɛsᵊ k i̯l i a kɛlk ʃoz dø bɔ̃ a la tele sø swaʁ || — wi | i l̯i a œ̃ film a vɛ̃ t œʁ (20 h) ||]

**1688**

**EN** What's that building? — It's a school.

**FR** Qu'est-ce que cet édifice? — C'est une école.

**IPA** [kɛsᵊ kø sɛ t edifis || — sɛ t yn ekɔl ||]

**1689**

**EN** Is there a restaurant in this hotel? — No, I'm afraid not.

**FR** Y a-t-il un restaurant dans cet hôtel? — J'ai bien peur que non.

**IPA** [i a t̯il œ̃ ʁɛstoʁɑ̃ dɑ̃ sɛ t otɛl || — ʒ ɛ bjɛ̃ pøʁ kø nɔ̃ ||]

**1690**

**EN** There's a train every hour.

**FR** Il y a un train toutes les heures.

**IPA** [i l̯i a œ̃ tʁɛ̃ tut le z œʁ ||]

---

**1691**

EN  The time now is eleven fifteen (11:15) . There was a train at eleven [o'clock] (11:00).

---

FR  Il est maintenant onze heures quinze (11 h 15). Il y avait un train à onze heures (11 h).

IPA  [i l e mɛ̃t°nɑ̃ t͜ɔ̃z œʁ kɛ̃z (11 h 15) || i l i avɛ t͜œ tʁɛ̃ a ɔ̃z œʁ (11 h) ||]

---

**1692**

EN  There's a good nature program on TV tonight.

---

FR  Il y a une bonne émission de nature à la télé ce soir.

IPA  [i l i a yn bɔn emisjɔ̃ dø natyʁ a la tele sø swaʁ ||]

---

**1693**

EN  There was a good nature program on TV last night.

---

FR  Il y avait une bonne émission de nature hier soir.

IPA  [i l i avɛ t͜ yn bɔn emisjɔ̃ dø natyʁ jɛʁ swaʁ ||]

---

**1694**

EN  We're staying at a very big hotel. There are one thousand two hundred fifty (1,250) rooms.

---

FR  Nous séjournons dans un très grand hôtel. Il y a mille deux cents cinquante (1250) chambres.

IPA  [nu seʒuʁnɔ̃ dɑ̃ z͜œ tʁe gʁɑ̃ d otɛl || i l i a mil dø sɑ̃ sɛ̃kɑ̃t (1250) ʃɑ̃bʁ ||]

**1695**

EN We stayed at a very big hotel. There were one thousand two hundred fifty (1,250) rooms.

FR Nous avons séjourné dans un très grand hôtel. Il y avait mille deux cents cinquante (1250) chambres.

IPA [nu z‿avɔ̃ seʒuʁne dɑ̃ z‿œ̃ tʁɛ gʁɑ̃ d‿otɛl || i l‿i avɛ mil dø sɑ̃ sɛ̃kɑ̃t (1250) ʃɑ̃bʁ ||]

**1696**

EN Are there any phone messages for me this morning?

FR Y a-t-il des messages téléphoniques pour moi ce matin?

IPA [i a t‿il de mesaʒ telefonik puʁ mwa sø matɛ̃ ||]

**1697**

EN Were there any phone messages for me yesterday?

FR Y avait-il des messages téléphoniques pour moi hier?

IPA [i avɛ t‿il de mesaʒ telefonik puʁ mwa jɛʁ ||]

**1698**

EN I'm hungry, but there isn't anything to eat.

FR J'ai faim, mais il n'y a rien à manger.

IPA [ʒ‿ɛ fɛ̃ | mɛ il n‿i a ʁjɛ̃ a mɑ̃ʒe ||]

**1699**

EN  I was hungry when I got home, but there wasn't anything to eat.

FR  J'avais faim quand je suis arrivé (♀arrivée) à la maison, mais il n'y avait rien à manger.

IPA  [ʒ‿avɛ fɛ̃ kɑ̃ ʒə sɥi aʁive (♀aʁive) a la mɛzɔ̃ | mɛ il n‿i avɛ ʁjɛ̃ a mɑ̃ʒe ‖]

**1700**

EN  Look! There's been an accident.

FR  Regarde! Il y a eu un accident.

IPA  [ʁəgaʁd ‖ i l‿i a y œ̃ n‿aksidɑ̃ ‖]

# GMS #1701 - 1800

---

**1701**

**EN** This road is very dangerous. There have been many accidents on it.

---

**FR** Cette route est très dangereuse. Il y a eu beaucoup d'accidents sur cette route.

**IPA** [sɛt ʁut e tʁɛ dãʒˤˈʁøz ‖ i lˌi a y boku dˌaksidã syʁ sɛt ʁut ‖]

---

**1702**

**EN** There was an accident last night.

---

**FR** Il y a eu un accident hier soir.

**IPA** [i lˌi a y œ̃ nˌaksidã jɛʁ swaʁ ‖]

---

**1703**

**EN** Do you think there will be a lot of people at the party on Saturday?

---

**FR** Penses-tu qu'il y aura beaucoup de gens à la fête samedi?

**IPA** [pãs ty kˌil i oʁa boku dø ʒã a la fɛt samˤdi ‖]

**1704**

EN The manager of the company is leaving, so there will be a new manager soon.

FR Le manager de l'entreprise démissionne, alors il y aura bientôt un nouveau manager.

IPA [lø manadʒe dø lˌɑ̃tʁˠpʁiz demisjɔn | alɔ ʁˌi lˌi oʁa bjɛ̃to tˌœ̃ nuvo manadʒe ||]

**1705**

EN I'm going out of town tomorrow. I'm packing my things today because there won't be time tomorrow.

FR Je vais à l'extérieur de la ville demain. Je fais mes valises aujourd'hui, parce que je n'aurai pas le temps demain.

IPA [ʒø vɛ a lˌeksteʁjœʁ dø la vil dˠmɛ̃ || ʒø fɛ me valiz oʒuʁdɥi | paʁs kø ʒø nˌoʁe pa lø tɑ̃ dˠmɛ̃ ||]

**1706**

EN There will be rain tomorrow afternoon.

FR Il y aura de la pluie demain après-midi.

IPA [i lˌi oʁa dø la plɥi dˠmɛ̃ apʁɛ midi ||]

**1707**

EN There will be a typhoon this weekend.

FR Il y aura un typhon ce week-end.

IPA [i lˌi oʁa œ̃ tifɔ̃ sø wikɛnd ||]

---

**1708**

EN  There's already been three (3) hurricanes this
summer.

---

FR   Il y a déjà eu trois ouragans cet été.
IPA  [i l‿i a deʒa y tʁwa z‿uʁagɑ̃ sɛ t‿ete ||]

---

**1709**

EN  There was a clock on the wall near the window.

---

FR   Il y avait une horloge sur le mur près de la fenêtre.
IPA  [i l‿i avɛ t‿yn ɔʁlɔʒ syʁ lø myʁ pʁe dø la fᵊnɛtʁ ||]

---

**1710**

EN  There were some flowers in a vase on the table.

---

FR   Il y avait quelques fleurs dans un vase sur la table.
IPA  [i l‿i avɛ kɛlk flœʁ dɑ̃ z‿œ̃ vaz syʁ la tabl ||]

---

**1711**

EN  There were some books on the shelves.

---

FR   Il y avait quelques livres sur les tablettes.
IPA  [i l‿i avɛ kɛlk livʁ syʁ le tablɛt ||]

---

**1712**

EN  There was an armchair in the corner near the door.

---

FR   Il y avait un fauteuil dans le coin près de la porte.
IPA  [i l‿i avɛ t‿œ̃ fotœj dɑ̃ lø kwɛ̃ pʁe dø la pɔʁt ||]

**1713**

EN    There was a sofa opposite the armchair.

----

FR    Il y avait un sofa à l'opposé du fauteuil.

IPA   [i l͜i avɛ t͜œ̃ sofa a l͜opoze dy fotœj ‖]

**1714**

EN    I opened the envelope, but it was empty. There was nothing in it.

----

FR    J'ai ouvert l'enveloppe, mais elle était vide. Il n'y avait rien à l'intérieur.

IPA   [ʒ͜ɛ uvɛʁ l͜ɑ̃vºlɔp | mɛ ɛ l͜ete vid ‖ il n͜i avɛ ʁjɛ̃ a l͜ɛ̃teʁjœʁ ‖]

**1715**

EN    We stayed at a very nice hotel. — Really? Was there a swimming pool?

----

FR    Nous avons séjourné dans un hôtel très agréable. — Vraiment? Y avait-il une piscine?

IPA   [nu z͜avɔ̃ seʒuʁne dɑ̃ z͜œ̃ n͜otel tʁɛ z͜agʁeabl ‖ — vʁemɑ̃ ‖ i avɛ t͜il yn pisin ‖]

**1716**

EN    Did you buy any cherries? — No, there weren't any at the store.

----

FR    As-tu acheté des cerises? — Non, il n'y en avait pas au magasin.

IPA   [a ty aʃºte de sºʁiz ‖ — nɔ̃ | il n͜i ɑ̃ n͜avɛ pa o magazɛ̃ ‖]

**1717**

EN The wallet was empty. There wasn't any money in it.

FR Le portefeuille était vide. Il n'y avait pas d'argent à l'intérieur.

IPA [lø pɔʁt°fœj etɛ vid || il n̩ i avɛ pa d̩aʁʒɑ̃ a l̩ɛ̃teʁjœʁ ||]

**1718**

EN Were there many people at the meeting? — No, very few.

FR Y avait-il beaucoup de personnes à la réunion? — Non, très peu.

IPA [i avɛ t̩il boku dø pɛʁsɔn a la ʁeynjɔ̃ || — nɔ̃ | tʁɛ pø ||]

**1719**

EN We didn't visit the museum. There wasn't enough time.

FR Nous n'avons pas visité le musée. Il n'y avait pas assez de temps.

IPA [nu n̩avɔ̃ pa vizite lø myze || il n̩ i avɛ pa z̩ase dø tɑ̃ ||]

---

**1720**

**EN** I'm sorry I'm late. There was a lot of traffic.

---

**FR** Je suis désolé d'être en retard. Il y avait beaucoup de circulation.

**IPA** [ʒø sɥi dezole d̪ɛtʁ ɑ̃ ʁ°taʁ ‖ i l̪i avɛ boku dø siʁkylasjɔ̃ ‖]

---

**1721**

**EN** Twenty years ago there weren't many tourists here. Now there are a lot.

---

**FR** Il y a vingt ans, il n'y avait pas beaucoup de touristes ici. Maintenant, il y en a beaucoup.

**IPA** [i l̪i a vɛ̃ t̪ɑ̃ | il n̪i avɛ pa boku dø tuʁist isi ‖ mɛ̃t°nɑ̃ | i l̪i ɑ̃ n̪a boku ‖]

---

**1722**

**EN** There are twenty-four (24) hours in a day.

---

**FR** Il y a vingt-quatre heures dans une journée.

**IPA** [i l̪i a vɛ̃tkatʁ œʁ dɑ̃ z̪yn ʒuʁne ‖]

---

**1723**

**EN** There was a party at work last Friday, but I didn't go.

---

**FR** Il y avait une fête au travail vendredi dernier, mais je n'y suis pas allé (♀ allée).

**IPA** [i l̪i avɛ t̪yn fɛt o tʁavaj vɑ̃dʁ°di dɛʁnje | mɛ ʒø n̪i sɥi pa z̪ale (♀ ale) ‖]

**1724**

EN Where can I buy a bottle of water? — There's a convenience store at the end of the block.

FR Où puis-je acheter une bouteille d'eau? — Il y a une épicerie de quartier au bout du pâté de maisons.

IPA [u pɥi ʒø aʃᵊte ʁ‿yn butɛj d‿o || — i l‿i a yn episᵊʁi dø kaʁtje o bu dy pate dø mɛzɔ̃ ||]

**1725**

EN Why are the police outside the bank? — There was a robbery.

FR Pourquoi la police est-elle en face de la banque? — Il y a eu un cambriolage.

IPA [puʁkwa la polis e t‿ɛl ɑ̃ fas dø la bɑ̃k || — i l‿i a y œ̃ kɑ̃bʁijolaʒ ||]

**1726**

EN When we got to the theater, there was a long line outside.

FR Lorsque nous sommes sortis (♀sorties) du cinéma, il y avait une longue file dehors.

IPA [lɔʁskᵊ nu sɔm sɔʁti (♀sɔʁti) dy sinema | i l‿i avɛ t‿yn lɔ̃g fil døɔʁ ||]

**1727**

EN When you arrive tomorrow, there will be somebody at the airport to meet you.

FR Quand tu arriveras demain, il y aura quelqu'un à l'aéroport pour t'accueillir.

IPA [kɑ̃ ty aʁivˠ°ʁa d°mɛ̃ | i l̪i oʁa kɛlkœ̃ a l̪aeʁopɔʁ puʁ t̪akœjiʁ ||]

**1728**

EN Ten years ago there were five hundred (500) children in the school. Now there are more than a thousand.

FR Il y a dix ans, il y avait cinq cents (500) enfants dans l'école. Maintenant, il y en a plus de mille.

IPA [i l̪i a di z̪ɑ̃ | i l̪i avɛ sɛ̃k sɑ̃ (500) ɑ̃fɑ̃ dɑ̃ l̪ekɔl || mɛ̃t°nɑ̃ | i l̪i ɑ̃ n̪a plys dø mil ||]

**1729**

EN Last week I went back to the town where I was born. It's very different now. There have been a lot of changes.

FR La semaine dernière, je suis retourné dans le village où je suis né. C'est très différent maintenant. Il y a eu beaucoup de changement.

IPA [la s°mɛn dɛʁnjɛʁ | ʒø sɥi ʁ°tuʁne dɑ̃ lø vilaʒ u ʒø sɥi ne || sɛ tʁɛ difeʁɑ̃ mɛ̃t°nɑ̃ || i l̪i a y boku dø ʃɑ̃ʒ°mɑ̃ ||]

1730

EN  I think everything will be okay. I don't think there will be any problems.

FR  Je pense que tout ira bien. Je pense qu'il n'y aura pas de problème.

IPA  [ʒø pɑ̃s kø tu t‿iʁa bjɛ̃ || ʒø pɑ̃s k‿il n‿i oʁa pa dø pʁoblɛm ||]

1731

EN  Is it true that you're moving to Berlin?

FR  Est-ce vrai que tu déménages à Berlin?

IPA  [ɛsᵊ vʁɛ kø ty demenaʒ a (...) ||]

1732

EN  We have to go now. It's very late.

FR  Nous devons partir. Il est tard.

IPA  [nu dᵊvɔ̃ paʁtiʁ || i l‿e taʁ ||]

1733

EN  Is it true that Jirou can fly a helicopter?

FR  Est-ce vrai que Jirou peut piloter un hélicoptère?

IPA  [ɛsᵊ vʁɛ kø (...) pø pilote ʁ‿œ̃ n‿elikɔpteʁ ||]

**1734**

EN What day is it today? Tuesday? — No, today's Wednesday.

---

FR Quel jour sommes-nous? Mardi? — Non, nous sommes mercredi.

IPA [kɛl ʒuʁ sɔm nu || maʁdi || — nɔ̃ | nu sɔm mɛʁkʁ°di ||]

**1735**

EN It's ten (10) kilometers from downtown to the airport.

---

FR Il y a dix (10) kilomètres entre le centre-ville et l'aéroport.

IPA [i l‿i a dis (10) kilomɛtʁ ɑ̃tʁ lø sɑ̃tʁ°vil e l‿aeʁopɔʁ ||]

**1736**

EN Is it okay to call you at the office?

---

FR Est-ce convenable de t'appeler au bureau?

IPA [ɛs° kɔ̃v°nabl dø t‿ap°le o byʁo ||]

**1737**

EN Do you want to walk to the hotel? — I don't know. How far is it?

---

FR Veux-tu marcher à l'hôtel? — Je ne sais pas. À quelle distance est-ce?

IPA [vø ty maʁʃe a l‿otɛl || — ʒø nø sɛ pa || a kɛl distɑ̃s ɛs° ||]

**1738**

EN  It's Kelly's birthday today. She's twenty-seven (27).

---

FR  C'est l'anniversaire de Kelly aujourd'hui. Elle a vingt-sept (27) ans.

IPA  [sɛ l̩aniveʁseʁ dø (...) oʒuʁdɥi ‖ ɛ l̩a vɛ̃tsɛt (27) ɑ̃ ‖]

**1739**

EN  I don't believe it! That's impossible.

---

FR  Je n'y crois pas! C'est impossible.

IPA  [ʒø n̩i kʁwa pa ‖ sɛ t̩ɛ̃posibl ‖]

**1740**

EN  How far is it from here to the train station?

---

FR  À quelle distance d'ici se trouve la gare?

IPA  [a kɛl distɑ̃s d̩isi sø tʁuv la gaʁ ‖]

**1741**

EN  How far is it from the hotel to the beach?

---

FR  À quelle distance de l'hôtel se trouve la plage?

IPA  [a kɛl distɑ̃s dø l̩otɛl sø tʁuv la plaʒ ‖]

**1742**

EN  How far is it from Taipei to Tokyo?

---

FR  À quelle distance de Taipei se trouve Tokyo?

IPA  [a kɛl distɑ̃s dø (...) sø tʁuv (...) ‖]

---

**1743**

EN  How far is it from your house to the airport?

---

FR  À quelle distance de ta maison se trouve l'aéroport?
IPA  [a kɛl distɑ̃s dø ta mɛzɔ̃ sø tʁuv l‿aeʁɔpɔʁ ‖]

---

**1744**

EN  The weather isn't so nice today. It's cloudy.

---

FR  Il ne fait pas très beau aujourd'hui. C'est nuageux.
IPA  [il nø fɛ pa tʁɛ bo oʒuʁdɥi ‖ sɛ nɥaʒø ‖]

---

**1745**

EN  There was strong wind yesterday.

---

FR  Il y avait des vents forts hier.
IPA  [i l‿i avɛ de vɑ̃ fɔʁ jɛʁ ‖]

---

**1746**

EN  It's hot in this room. Open a window.

---

FR  Il fait chaud dans cette pièce. Ouvre une fenêtre.
IPA  [il fɛ ʃo dɑ̃ sɛt pjɛs ‖ uvʁ yn fᵊnɛtʁ ‖]

---

**1747**

EN  It was a nice day yesterday. It was warm and sunny.

---

FR  C'était une belle journée hier. Il faisait chaud et c'était
ensoleillé.
IPA  [se etɛ yn bɛl ʒuʁne jɛʁ ‖ il fᵊzɛ ʃo e se etɛ ɑ̃soleje
‖]

1748

**EN** There was a storm last night. Did you hear it?

**FR** Il y a eu une tempête la nuit dernière. L'as-tu entendue?

**IPA** [i l‿i a y yn tɑ̃pɛt la nɥi dɛʁnjɛʁ || l‿a ty ɑ̃tɑ̃dy ||]

1749

**EN** I was afraid because it was very dark.

**FR** J'avais peur, parce qu'il faisait noir.

**IPA** [ʒ‿avɛ pøʁ | paʁs k‿il fᵊzɛ nwaʁ ||]

1750

**EN** It's often cold here, but there isn't much rain.

**FR** Il fait souvent froid ici, mais il ne pleut pas beaucoup.

**IPA** [il fɛ suvɑ̃ fʁwa isi | mɛ il nø plø pa boku ||]

1751

**EN** It's a long way from here to the nearest gas station.

**FR** La prochaine station-service est loin d'ici.

**IPA** [la pʁoʃen stasjɔ̃sɛʁvis e lwɛ̃ d‿isi ||]

**1752**

EN If you go to bed late, it's difficult to get up early in the morning.

FR Si tu vas au lit tard, il est difficile de se lever tôt le matin.

IPA [si ty va o li taʁ | i l̥e difisil dø sø lᵊve to lø matɛ̃ ||]

**1753**

EN Hello, Junko. It's nice to see you again. How are you?

FR Salut, Junko. C'est bon de te revoir. Comment vas-tu?

IPA [saly | (...) || sɛ bɔ̃ dø tø ʁᵊvwaʁ || komɑ̃ va ty ||]

**1754**

EN It's impossible to work in this office. There's too much noise.

FR C'est impossible de travailler dans ce bureau. Il y a trop de bruit.

IPA [sɛ t̥ɛ̃posibl dø tʁavaje dɑ̃ sø byʁo || i l̥i a tʁo dø bʁɥi ||]

**1755**

EN Everybody's very nice at work. It's easy to make friends.

FR Tout le monde est très gentil au travail. C'est facile de se faire des amis.

IPA [tu lø mɔ̃d e tʁɛ ʒɑ̃ti o tʁavaj || sɛ fasil dø sø fɛʁ de z̥ami ||]

**1756**

EN I like traveling. It's interesting to visit different places.

---

FR J'aime voyager. C'est intéressant de visiter des endroits différents.

IPA [ʒ‿em vwajaʒe ‖ se t‿ɛ̃teʁesɑ̃ dø vizite de z‿ɑ̃dʁwa difeʁɑ̃ ‖]

**1757**

EN Some cities are not safe. It's dangerous at night.

---

FR Certaines villes ne sont pas sûres. C'est dangereux la nuit.

IPA [seʁten vil nø sɔ̃ pa syʁ ‖ se dɑ̃ʒ°ʁø la nɥi ‖]

**1758**

EN She isn't tired, but he is.

---

FR Elle n'est pas fatiguée, mais lui si. > Elle n'est pas fatiguée, mais lui oui.

IPA [el n‿e pa fatige ǀ me lɥi si ‖ > el n‿e pa fatige ǀ me lɥi wi ‖]

**1759**

EN She likes tea, but he doesn't.

---

FR Elle aime le thé, mais pas lui. > Elle aime le thé, mais lui non.

IPA [e l‿em lø te ǀ me pa lɥi ‖ > e l‿em lø te ǀ me lɥi nɔ̃ ‖]

**1760**

EN  I haven't seen the movie, but my sister has.

FR  Je n'ai pas vu le film, mais ma sœur oui.

IPA  [ʒø n̪ɛ pa vy lø film | mɛ ma sœʁ wi ‖]

**1761**

EN  Please help me. — I'm sorry, I can't.

FR  S'il te plaît, aide-moi. — Je suis désolé (♀ désolée),
je ne peux pas.

IPA  [s̪il tø plɛ | ɛd mwa ‖ — ʒø sɥi dezole (♀ dezole) |
ʒø nø pø pa ‖]

**1762**

EN  Are you tired? — I was, but I'm not now.

FR  Es-tu fatigué (♀ fatiguée)? — Je l'étais, mais pas
maintenant.

IPA  [ɛ ty fatige (♀ fatige) ‖ — ʒø l̪ete | mɛ pa mɛ̃tˀnã ‖]

**1763**

EN  Do you think Lucy will call tonight? — She might.

FR  Penses-tu que Lucy va appeler ce soir? — Peut-être.

IPA  [pãs ty kø (...) va apˀle sø swaʁ ‖ — pø ɛtʁ ‖]

**1764**

EN Are you going to study tonight? — I should, but I probably won't.

FR Vas-tu étudier ce soir? — Je devrais, mais je ne vais probablement pas le faire.

IPA [va ty etydje sø swaʁ || — ʒø dᵊvʁɛ | mɛ ʒø nø vɛ pʁobablᵊmã pa lø feʁ ||]

**1765**

EN My sister has seen the movie, but I haven't.

FR Ma sœur a vu le film, mais pas moi. > Ma sœur a vu le film, mais moi non.

IPA [ma sœʁ a vy lø film | mɛ pa mwa || > ma sœʁ a vy lø film | mɛ mwa nõ ||]

**1766**

EN Are you and Jack working tomorrow? — I am, but Jack isn't.

FR Est-ce que Jack et toi travaillez demain? — Moi oui, mais Jack non. > Je travaille, mais pas Jack.

IPA [ɛsᵊ kø (...) e twa tʁavaje dᵊmɛ̃ || — mwa wi | mɛ (...) nõ || > ʒø tʁavaj | mɛ pa (...) ||]

**1767**

EN Are you tired? — Yes, I am. > No, I'm not.

---

FR Es-tu fatigué (♀ fatiguée)? — Oui, je le suis. Non, je ne le suis pas.

IPA [ɛ ty fatige (♀ fatige) || — wi | ʒø lø sɥi || nɔ̃ | ʒø nø lø sɥi pa ||]

**1768**

EN Will Ganesh be here tomorrow? — Yes, he will. > No, he won't.

---

FR Ganesh sera-t-il ici demain? — Oui, il sera ici. Non, il ne sera pas ici.

IPA [(...) sᵊʁa t‿il isi dᵊmɛ̃ || — wi | il sᵊʁa isi || nɔ̃ | il nø sᵊʁa pa z‿isi ||]

**1769**

EN Is there a bus to the airport? — Yes, there is. > No, there isn't.

---

FR Y a-t-il un autobus vers l'aéroport? — Oui, il y en a un. Non, il n'y en a pas.

IPA [i a t‿il œ̃ n‿otobys vɛʁ l‿aeʁopɔʁ || — wi | i l‿i ɑ̃ n‿a œ̃ || nɔ̃ | il n‿i ɑ̃ n‿a pa ||]

**1770**

EN I don't like hot weather, but Lila does.

---

FR Je n'aime pas la chaleur, mais Lila oui.

IPA [ʒø n‿ɛm pa la ʃalœʁ | mɛ (...) wi ||]

**1771**

EN Martin works hard, but I don't.

FR Martin travaille fort, mais pas moi.
IPA [(...) tʁavaj fɔʁ | mɛ pa mwa ||]

**1772**

EN Do you enjoy your work? — Yes, I do.

FR Aimes-tu ton travail? — Oui.
IPA [ɛm ty tɔ̃ tʁavaj || — wi ||]

**1773**

EN Did you and Nicole like the movie? — I did, but Nicole didn't.

FR Est-ce que Nicole et toi avez aimé le film? – Je l'ai aimé, mais pas Nicole.
IPA [ɛs° kø (...) e twa ave ɛme lø film || — ʒø l ̩ɛ ɛme | mɛ pa (...) ||]

**1774**

EN I had a good time. — I did, too.

FR J'ai passé du bon temps. — Moi aussi.
IPA [ʒ ̩ɛ pase dy bɔ̃ tɑ̃ || — mwa osi ||]

**1775**

EN Fatima wasn't hungry, but we were.

FR Fatima n'avait pas faim, mais nous oui.
IPA [(...) n‿avɛ pa fɛ̃ | mɛ nu wi ||]

**1776**

EN I'm not married, but my brother is.

FR Je ne suis pas marié (♀mariée), mais mon frère oui.
IPA [ʒø nø sɥi pa maʁje (♀maʁje) | mɛ mɔ̃ fʁɛʁ wi ||]

**1777**

EN Fahim can't help you, but I can.

FR Fahim ne peut pas t'aider, mais moi oui.
IPA [(...) nø pø pa t‿ede | mɛ mwa wi ||]

**1778**

EN I haven't read the book, but Paul has.

FR Je n'ai pas lu le livre, mais Paul oui.
IPA [ʒø n‿ɛ pa ly lø livʁ | mɛ (...) wi ||]

**1779**

EN Rebecca won't be here, but Antonio will.

FR Rebecca ne sera pas ici, mais Antonio oui.
IPA [(...) nø s°ʁa pa z‿isi | mɛ (...) wi ||]

**1780**

EN You weren't late, but I was.

---

FR Tu n'étais pas en retard, mais moi oui.
IPA [ty n‿etɛ pa z‿ɑ̃ ʁ°taʁ | mɛ mwa wi ‖]

**1781**

EN My sister can play the piano, but I can't.

---

FR Ma sœur peut jouer du piano, mais pas moi.
IPA [ma sœʁ pø ʒwe dy pjano | mɛ pa mwa ‖]

**1782**

EN Anabel's working today, but I'm not.

---

FR Anabel travaille aujourd'hui, mais pas moi.
IPA [(...) tʁavaj oʒuʁdɥi | mɛ pa mwa ‖]

**1783**

EN I was working, but my friends weren't.

---

FR Je travaillais, mais mes amis (♀amies) non.
IPA [ʒø tʁavajɛ | mɛ me z‿ami (♀ami) nɔ̃ ‖]

**1784**

EN Richard has been to China, but I haven't.

---

FR Richard est allé en Chine, mais pas moi.
IPA [(...) e ale ɑ̃ ʃin | mɛ pa mwa ‖]

**1785**

EN I'm ready to go, but Sonia isn't.

FR Je suis prêt (♀ prête), mais Sonia non.
IPA [ʒø sɥi pʁɛ (♀ pʁɛt) | mɛ (...) nɔ̃ ||]

**1786**

EN I've seen the movie, but Enzo hasn't.

FR J'ai vu le film, mais Enzo non.
IPA [ʒ‿ɛ vy lø film | mɛ (...) nɔ̃ ||]

**1787**

EN I don't like hot weather, but Cecilia does.

FR Je n'aime pas la chaleur, mais Cecilia oui.
IPA [ʒø n‿em pa la ʃalœʁ | mɛ (...) wi ||]

**1788**

EN Steve likes hot weather, but I don't.

FR Steve aime la chaleur, mais pas moi. > Steve aime la chaleur, mais moi non.
IPA [(...) em la ʃalœʁ | mɛ pa mwa || > (...) em la ʃalœʁ | mɛ mwa nɔ̃ ||]

**1789**

EN My mother wears glasses, but my father doesn't.

FR Ma mère porte des lunettes, mais pas mon père.
IPA [ma mɛʁ pɔʁt de lynet | mɛ pa mɔ̃ pɛʁ ||]

**1790**

EN  You don't know Vanessa very well, but I do.

FR  Tu ne connais pas Vanessa très bien, mais moi si.
IPA [ty nø konɛ pa (...) tʁɛ bjɛ̃ | mɛ mwa si ||]

**1791**

EN  I didn't enjoy the party, but my friends did.

FR  Je n'ai pas aimé la fête, mais mes amis (♀ amies) si.
IPA [ʒø n‿ɛ pa z‿eme la fɛt | mɛ me z‿ami (♀ ami) si ||]

**1792**

EN  I don't watch TV much, but Erhard does.

FR  Je ne regarde pas la télé, mais Erhard si.
IPA [ʒø nø ʁˀgaʁd pa la tele | mɛ (...) si ||]

**1793**

EN  Hannah lives in Switzerland, but her parents don't.

FR  Hannah vit en Suisse, mais pas ses parents.
IPA [(...) vi t‿ɑ̃ sɥis | mɛ pa se paʁɑ̃ ||]

**1794**

EN  You had breakfast this morning, but I didn't.

FR  Tu as déjeuné ce matin, mais pas moi.
IPA [ty a deʒœne sø matɛ̃ | mɛ pa mwa ||]

**1795**

EN  I didn't go out last night, but my friends did.

FR  Je ne suis pas sorti (♀sortie) hier soir, mais mes amis (♀amies) si.

IPA  [ʒø nø sɥi pa sɔʁti (♀sɔʁti) jɛʁ swaʁ | mɛ me z‿ami (♀ami) si ‖]

**1796**

EN  I like sports, but my sister doesn't.

FR  J'aime le sport, mais ma sœur non.

IPA  [ʒ‿ɛm lø spɔʁ | mɛ ma sœʁ nɔ̃ ‖]

**1797**

EN  I don't eat meat, but Tom does.

FR  Je ne mange pas de viande, mais Tom si.

IPA  [ʒø nø mɑ̃ʒ pa dø vjɑ̃d | mɛ (...) si ‖]

**1798**

EN  I'm Japanese, but my husband isn't.

FR  Je suis Japonaise, mais mon mari ne l'est pas. > Je suis Japonaise, mais pas mon mari.

IPA  [ʒø sɥi ʒaponɛz | mɛ mɔ̃ maʁi nø l‿e pa ‖ > ʒø sɥi ʒaponɛz | mɛ pa mɔ̃ maʁi ‖]

**1799**

EN  I haven't been to Mexico, but Zoe has.

FR  Je ne suis pas allé (♀allée) au Mexique, mais Zoë oui.

IPA  [ʒø nø sɥi pa z‿ale (♀ale) o mexique | mɛ (...) wi ‖]

**1800**

EN  Are you tired? — I was earlier, but I'm not now.

FR  Es-tu fatigué (♀fatiguée)? — Je l'étais plus tôt, mais pas maintenant.

IPA  [ɛ ty fatige (♀fatige) ‖ — ʒø l‿etɛ plys to | mɛ pa mɛ̃t°nɑ̃ ‖]

# GMS #1801 - 1900

---

**1801**

**EN** Fabian's happy today, but he wasn't yesterday.

---

**FR** Fabian est joyeux aujourd'hui, mais il ne l'était pas hier.

**IPA** [(...) e ʒwajø oʒuʁdɥi | mɛ il nø l̪etɛ pa z̪jɛʁ ‖]

---

**1802**

**EN** The stores aren't open yet, but the museum is.

---

**FR** Les boutiques ne sont pas encore ouvertes, mais le musée si.

**IPA** [le butik nø sɔ̃ pa z̪ɑ̃kɔʁ uvɛʁt | mɛ lø myze si ‖]

---

**1803**

**EN** I don't have a telescope, but I know somebody who does.

---

**FR** Je n'ai pas de téléscope, mais je connais quelqu'un qui en a un.

**IPA** [ʒø n̪ɛ pa dø teleskop | mɛ ʒø konɛ kɛlkœ̃ ki ɑ̃ n̪a œ̃ ‖]

**1804**

EN I would like to help you, but I'm sorry I can't.

---

FR J'aimerais t'aider, mais je suis désolé (♀désolée), je ne peux pas.

IPA [ʒ‿ɛmˀʁɛ t‿ede | mɛ ʒø sɥi dezole (♀dezole) | ʒø nø pø pa ||]

**1805**

EN I don't usually drive to work, but I did yesterday.

---

FR Je ne conduis généralement pas pour me rendre au travail, mais je l'ai fait hier.

IPA [ʒø nø kɔ̃dɥi ʒeneʁalˀmɑ̃ pa puʁ mø ʁɑ̃dʁ o tʁavaj | mɛ ʒø l‿ɛ fɛ jɛʁ ||]

**1806**

EN Have you ever been to Peru? — No, but Eveline has. She went there on vacation last year.

---

FR As-tu déjà vu le Pérou? — Non, mais Eveline si. Elle y est allée en vacances l'an dernier.

IPA [a ty deʒa vy lø peʁu || — nɔ̃ | mɛ (...) si || ɛ l‿i e t‿ale ɑ̃ vakɑ̃s l‿ɑ̃ dɛʁnje ||]

**1807**

EN Do you and Fausto watch TV a lot? — I do, but he doesn't.

---

FR Est-ce que Fausto et toi regardez souvent la télé? — Moi si, mais lui non.

IPA [ɛsᵊ kø (...) e twa ʁᵊgaʁde suvɑ̃ la tele || — mwa si | mɛ lɥi nɔ̃ ||]

**1808**

EN I've been invited to Gerhard's wedding, but Evita hasn't.

---

FR J'ai été invité (♀invitée) au mariage de Gerhard, mais pas Evita.

IPA [ʒ‿ɛ ete ɛ̃vite (♀ɛ̃vite) o maʁjaʒ dø (...) | mɛ pa z‿(...) ||]

**1809**

EN Do you think Ingrid will pass her driving test? — Yes, I'm sure she will.

---

FR Penses-tu qu'Ingrid passera son examen de conduite? — Oui, je suis sûr (♀sûre) qu'elle le passera.

IPA [pɑ̃s ty k (...) pasᵊʁa sɔ̃ n‿egzamɛ̃ dø kɔ̃dɥit || — wi | ʒø sɥi syʁ (♀syʁ) k‿ɛl lø pasᵊʁa ||]

**1810**

EN Are you going out tonight? — I might. I don't know for sure.

FR Sors-tu ce soir? — Peut-être. Je n'en suis pas certain (♀certaine).

IPA [sɔʁ ty sø swaʁ || — pø ɛtʁ || ʒø n‿ã sɥi pa sɛʁtɛ̃ (♀sɛʁtɛn) ||]

**1811**

EN Are you Brazilian? — No, I'm not.

FR Es-tu Brésilien (♀Brésilienne)? — Non. > Non, je ne le suis pas.

IPA [ɛ ty bʁeziljɛ̃ (♀bʁeziljɛn) || — nɔ̃ || > nɔ̃ | ʒø nø lø sɥi pa ||]

**1812**

EN Do you have a car? — No, I don't.

FR As-tu une voiture? — Non. > Non, je n'en ai pas.

IPA [a ty yn vwatyʁ || — nɔ̃ || > nɔ̃ | ʒø n‿ã ɛ pa ||]

**1813**

EN Do you feel okay? — Yes, I do.

FR Te sens-tu bien? — Oui. > Oui, je me sens bien.

IPA [tø sãs ty bjɛ̃ || — wi || > wi | ʒø mø sãs bjɛ̃ ||]

---

**1814**

**EN**  Is it snowing? — No, it isn't.

---

**FR**  Neige-t-il? — Non. > Non, il ne neige pas.
**IPA**  [nɛʒ t̪il || — nɔ̃ || > nɔ̃ | il nø nɛʒ pa |||]

---

**1815**

**EN**  Are you hungry? — Yes, I am.

---

**FR**  As-tu faim? — Oui. > Oui, j'ai faim.
**IPA**  [a ty fɛ̃ || — wi || > wi | ʒ̯ɛ fɛ̃ |||]

---

**1816**

**EN**  Do you like classical music? — Yes, I do.

---

**FR**  Aimes-tu la musique classique? — Oui. > Oui,
j'aime la musique classique.
**IPA**  [ɛm ty la myzik klasik || — wi || > wi | ʒ̯ɛm la
myzik klasik |||]

---

**1817**

**EN**  Will you be in Miami tomorrow? — No, I won't.

---

**FR**  Seras-tu à Miami demain? — Non. > Non, je n'y
serai pas.
**IPA**  [sᵊʁa ty a (...) dᵊmɛ̃ || — nɔ̃ || > nɔ̃ | ʒø n̯i sᵊʁɛ pa
|||]

**1818**

EN Have you ever broken your arm? — Yes, I have.

FR T'es-tu déjà cassé le bras? — Oui. > Oui, je me suis déjà cassé le bras.

IPA [t̯ɛ ty deʒa kase lø bʁa || — wi || > wi | ʒø mø sɥi deʒa kase lø bʁa ||]

**1819**

EN Did you buy anything yesterday? — Yes, I did.

FR As-tu acheté quelque chose hier? — Oui. > Oui, j'ai acheté quelque chose.

IPA [a ty aʃ°te kɛlk ʃoz jɛʁ || — wi || > wi | ʒ̯ɛ aʃ°te kɛlk ʃoz ||]

**1820**

EN Were you asleep at three am (3:00)? — Yes, I was.

FR Étais-tu endormi (♀endormie) à trois heures (3 h) du matin? — Oui. > Oui, je l'étais.

IPA [etɛ ty ãdɔʁmi (♀ãdɔʁmi) a tʁwa z̯œʁ (3 h) dy matɛ̃ || — wi || > wi | ʒø l̯etɛ ||]

**1821**

EN You're late. — I am? Sorry.

FR Tu es en retard. — Je suis en retard? Désolé.

IPA [ty ɛ ã ʁ°taʁ || — ʒø sɥi z̯ã ʁ°taʁ || dezole ||]

---

**1822**

**EN** I was sick last week. — You were? I didn't know that.

---

**FR** J'étais malade la semaine dernière. — Ah oui? Je ne savais pas.

**IPA** [ʒ̞ete malad la s°mɛn dɛʁnjɛʁ || — a wi || ʒø nø savɛ pa ||]

---

**1823**

**EN** It's raining again. — It is? It was sunny ten (10) minutes ago.

---

**FR** Il pleut encore. — Encore? C'était ensoleillé il y a dix minutes.

**IPA** [il plø ãkɔʁ || — ãkɔʁ || se ete ãsolɛje i l̞i a dis minyt ||]

---

**1824**

**EN** There's a message for you. — There is? Where is it?

---

**FR** Il y a un message pour toi. — Ah oui? Où ça?

**IPA** [i l̞i a œ̃ mesaʒ puʁ twa || — a wi || u sa ||]

---

**1825**

**EN** Giovanni can't drive. — He can't? I didn't know that.

---

**FR** Giovanni ne sait pas conduire. — Ah non? Je ne savais pas.

**IPA** [(...) nø sɛ pa kɔ̃dɥiʁ || — a nɔ̃ || ʒø nø savɛ pa ||]

**1826**

EN I'm not hungry. — You're not? I am.

FR Je n'ai pas faim. — Ah non? Moi si.
IPA [ʒø n‿ɛ pa fɛ̃ || — a nɔ̃ || mwa si ||]

**1827**

EN Emilia isn't at work today. — She isn't? Is she sick?

FR Emilia n'est pas au travail aujourd'hui. — Ah non?
Est-elle malade?
IPA [(...) n‿e pa o tʁavaj oʒuʁdɥi || — a nɔ̃ || e t‿ɛl malad
||]

**1828**

EN I speak four (4) languages. — You do? Which ones?

FR Je parle quatre langues. — Ah oui? Lesquelles?
IPA [ʒø paʁl katʁ lɑ̃g || — a wi || lɛkɛl ||]

**1829**

EN Luka doesn't eat meat. — He doesn't? Does he eat
fish?

FR Luka ne mange pas de viande. — Ah non? Mange-t-il
du poisson?
IPA [(...) nø mɑ̃ʒ pa dø vjɑ̃d || — a nɔ̃ || mɑ̃ʒ t‿il dy
pwasɔ̃ ||]

---

**1830**

**EN** Nadya got married last week. — She did? Really?

---

**FR** Nadya s'est mariée la semaine dernière. — Ah oui? Vraiment?

**IPA** [(...) s̪e maʁje la s°mɛn dɛʁnjeʁ || — a wi || vʁɛmɑ̃ ||]

---

**1831**

**EN** I've bought a new car. — Oh, you have?

---

**FR** J'ai acheté une nouvelle voiture. — Oh! Ah oui?

**IPA** [ʒ̪ɛ aʃ°te yn nuvɛl vwatyʁ || — o || a wi ||]

---

**1832**

**EN** I'm writing a book. — You are? What about?

---

**FR** J'écris un nouveau livre. — Ah oui? Sur quoi?

**IPA** [ʒ̪ekʁi œ̃ nuvo livʁ || — a wi || syʁ kwa ||]

---

**1833**

**EN** I don't like Dmitry. — You don't? Why not?

---

**FR** Je n'aime pas Dmitry. — Ah non? Pourquoi?

**IPA** [ʒø n̪ɛm pa (...) || — a nɔ̃ || puʁkwa ||]

1834

EN  It's a nice day, isn't it? — Yes, it's perfect.

FR  C'est une belle journée, n'est-ce pas? — Oui, c'est parfait.

IPA  [sɛ t‿yn bɛl ʒuʁne | n‿e sø pa || — wi | sɛ paʁfɛ ||]

1835

EN  Santo lives in Milan, doesn't he? — Yes, that's right.

FR  Santo vit à Milan, n'est-ce pas? — Oui, c'est ça.

IPA  [(...) vi a (...) | n‿e sø pa || — wi | sɛ sa ||]

1836

EN  You closed the window, didn't you? — Yes, I think so.

FR  Tu as fermé la fenêtre, n'est-ce pas? — Oui, je pense que oui.

IPA  [ty a fɛʁme la fᵊnɛtʁ | n‿e sø pa || — wi | ʒø pɑ̃s kø wi ||]

1837

EN  Those shoes are nice, aren't they? — Yes, very nice.

FR  Ces chaussures sont jolies, n'est-ce pas? — Oui, très jolies.

IPA  [se ʃosyʁ sɔ̃ ʒoli | n‿e sø pa || — wi | tʁɛ ʒoli ||]

---

**1838**

**EN** Marta will be here soon, won't she? — Yes, probably.

---

**FR** Marta sera bientôt ici, n'est-ce pas? — Oui, probablement.

**IPA** [(...) sᵊʁa bjẽto t‿isi | n‿e sø pa || — wi | pʁobablᵊmã ||]

---

**1839**

**EN** That isn't your car, is it? — No, it's my mother's.

---

**FR** Ce n'est pas ta voiture, n'est-ce pas? — Non, c'est celle de ma mère.

**IPA** [sø n‿e pa ta vwatyʁ | n‿e sø pa || — nõ | sɛ sɛl dø ma mɛʁ ||]

---

**1840**

**EN** You haven't met my mother, have you? — No, I haven't.

---

**FR** Tu n'as pas rencontré ma mère, n'est-ce pas? — Non. > Non, je ne l'ai pas rencontrée.

**IPA** [ty n‿a pa ʁãkõtʁe ma mɛʁ | n‿e sø pa || — nõ || > nõ | ʒø nø l‿ɛ pa ʁãkõtʁe ||]

**1841**

EN Clara doesn't go out much, does she? — No, she doesn't.

FR Clara ne sort pas beaucoup, n'est-ce pas? — Non. > Non, elle ne sort pas beaucoup.

IPA [(...) nø sɔʁ pa boku | n‿e sø pa || — nɔ̃ || > nɔ̃ | ɛl nø sɔʁ pa boku ||]

**1842**

EN You won't be late, will you? — No, I'm never late.

FR Tu ne seras pas en retard, n'est-ce pas? — Non, je ne suis jamais en retard.

IPA [ty nø sᵊʁa pa z‿ɑ̃ ʁᵊtaʁ | n‿e sø pa || — nɔ̃ | ʒø nø sɥi ʒamɛ z‿ɑ̃ ʁᵊtaʁ ||]

**1843**

EN I work in a bank. — You do? I work in a bank, too.

FR Je travaille dans une banque. — Ah oui? Je travaille dans une banque aussi.

IPA [ʒø tʁavaj dɑ̃ z‿yn bɑ̃k || — a wi || ʒø tʁavaj dɑ̃ z‿yn bɑ̃k osi ||]

**1844**

EN I didn't go to work yesterday. — You didn't? Were you sick?

FR Je ne suis pas allé (♀allée) au travail hier. — Ah non? Étais-tu malade?

IPA [ʒø nø sɥi pa z‿ale (♀ale) o tʁavaj jɛʁ || — a nõ || etɛ ty malad ||]

**1845**

EN Dennis doesn't like me. — He doesn't? Why not?

FR Dennis ne m'aime pas. — Ah non? Pourquoi?

IPA [(...) nø m‿ɛm pa || — a nõ || puʁkwa ||]

**1846**

EN You look tired. — I do? I feel fine.

FR Tu as l'air fatigué (♀fatiguée). — Ah oui? Je me sens bien.

IPA [ty a l‿ɛʁ fatige (♀fatige) || — a wi || ʒø mø sãs bjɛ̃ ||]

**1847**

EN Lara called me last night. — She did? What did she say?

FR Lara m'a appelé (♀appelée) hier soir. — Ah oui? Qu'a-t-elle dit? > Ah oui? Qu'est-ce qu'elle t'a dit?

IPA [(...) m‿a apˀle (♀apˀle) jɛʁ swaʁ || — a wi || k‿a t‿ɛl di || > a wi || kɛsˀ k‿ɛl t‿a di ||]

**1848**

EN  I've bought a new car. — You have? What kind is it?

---

FR  J'ai acheté une nouvelle voiture. — Ah oui? C'est quel genre de voiture?

IPA  [ʒ ɛ aʃºte yn nuvɛl vwatyʁ || — a wi || sɛ kɛl ʒɑ̃ʁ dø vwatyʁ ||]

**1849**

EN  Albert doesn't eat meat. — He doesn't? Does he eat eggs?

---

FR  Albert ne mange pas de viande. — Ah non? Mange-t-il des œufs?

IPA  [(...) nø mɑ̃ʒ pa dø vjɑ̃d || — a nɔ̃ || mɑ̃ʒ t il de z ø ||]

**1850**

EN  I've lost my key. — You have? When did you have it last?

---

FR  J'ai perdu ma clé. — Ah oui? Quand l'avais-tu pour la dernière fois?

IPA  [ʒ ɛ pɛʁdy ma kle || — a wi || kɑ̃ l avɛ ty puʁ la dɛʁnjɛʁ fwa ||]

**1851**

EN  Angela can't drive. — She can't? She should learn.

---

FR  Angela ne sait pas conduire. — Ah non? Elle devrait apprendre.

IPA  [(...) nø sɛ pa kɔ̃dɥiʁ || — a nɔ̃ || ɛl dºvʁɛ apʁɑ̃dʁ ||]

**1852**

EN I was born in Italy. — You were? I didn't know that.

FR Je suis né (♀née) en Italie. — Ah oui? Je ne savais pas.

IPA [ʒø sɥi ne (♀ne) ã italie || — a wi || ʒø nø savɛ pa ||]

**1853**

EN I didn't sleep well last night. — You didn't? Was the bed uncomfortable?

FR Je n'ai pas bien dormi la semaine dernière. — Ah non? Le lit était-il inconfortable?

IPA [ʒø n‿ɛ pa bjɛ̃ dɔʁmi la sᵊmɛn dɛʁnjɛʁ || — a nɔ̃ || lø li etɛ t‿il ɛ̃kɔ̃fɔʁtabl ||]

**1854**

EN There's a football game on TV tonight. — There is? Are you going to watch it?

FR Il y a un match de football à la télé ce soir. — Ah oui? Vas-tu le regarder?

IPA [i l‿i a œ̃ matʃ dø futbɔl a la tele sø swaʁ || — a wi || va ty lø ʁᵊgaʁde ||]

**1855**

EN I'm not happy. — You're not? Why not?

FR Je ne suis pas heureux (♀heureuse). — Ah non? Pourquoi?

IPA [ʒø nø sɥi pa z‿øʁø (♀øʁøz) || — a nɔ̃ || puʁkwa ||]

**1856**

EN I saw Khalid last week. — You did? How is he?

FR J'ai vu Khalid la semaine dernière. — Ah oui? Comment va-t-il?

IPA [ʒ‿ɛ vy (...) la s°mɛn dɛʁnjɛʁ || — a wi || komɑ̃ va t‿il ||]

**1857**

EN Shakira works in a factory. — She does? What kind of factory?

FR Shakira travaille dans une usine. — Ah oui? Quel genre d'usine?

IPA [(...) tʁavaj dɑ̃ z‿yn yzin || — a wi || kɛl ʒɑ̃ʁ d‿yzin ||]

**1858**

EN I won't be here next week. — You won't? Where will you be?

FR Je ne serai pas ici la semaine prochaine. — Ah non? Où seras-tu?

IPA [ʒø nø s°ʁɛ pa z‿isi la s°mɛn pʁoʃɛn || — a nɔ̃ || u s°ʁa ty ||]

**1859**

EN The clock isn't working. — It isn't? It was working yesterday.

FR L'horloge ne fonctionne pas. — Ah non? Elle fonctionnait hier.

IPA [lˌɔʁlɔʒ nø fɔ̃ksjɔn pa || — a nɔ̃ || ɛl fɔ̃ksjɔnɛ jɛʁ ||]

**1860**

EN It's a nice day, isn't it? — Yes, it's beautiful.

FR C'est une belle journée, n'est-ce pas? — Oui, c'est magnifique.

IPA [sɛ tˌyn bɛl ʒuʁne | nˌe sø pa || — wi | sɛ maɲifik ||]

**1861**

EN These flowers are nice, aren't they? — Yes, what kind are they?

FR Ces fleurs sont jolies, n'est-ce pas? — Oui, de quelle sorte sont-elles?

IPA [se flœʁ sɔ̃ ʒoli | nˌe sø pa || — wi | dø kɛl sɔʁt sɔ̃ tˌɛl ||]

**1862**

EN Bernard was at the party, wasn't he? — Yes, but I didn't speak to him.

FR Bernard était à la fête, n'est-ce pas? — Oui, mais je ne lui ai pas parlé.

IPA [(...) ete a la fɛt | nˌe sø pa || — wi | mɛ ʒø nø lɥi ɛ pa paʁle ||]

**1863**

EN You've been to Brazil, haven't you? — Yes, many times.

FR Tu es allé (♀allée) au Brésil, n'est-ce pas? — Oui, plusieurs fois.

IPA [ty ɛ ale (♀ale) o bʁezil | n̪e sø pa || — wi | plyzjœʁ fwa ||]

**1864**

EN You speak Chinese, don't you? — Yes, but not very well.

FR Tu parles chinois, n'est-ce pas? — Oui, mais pas très bien.

IPA [ty paʁl ʃinwa | n̪e sø pa || — wi | mɛ pa tʁɛ bjɛ̃ ||]

**1865**

EN Caroline looks tired, doesn't she? — Yes, she works very hard.

FR Caroline a l'air fatiguée, n'est-ce pas? — Oui, elle travaille beaucoup.

IPA [(...) a l̪ɛʁ fatige | n̪e sø pa || — wi | ɛl tʁavaj boku ||]

**1866**

EN  You'll help me, won't you? — Yes, of course I will.

FR  Tu vas m'aider, n'est-ce pas? — Oui, bien sûr. >
Oui, bien sûr que oui.

IPA  [ty va m‿ede | n‿e sø pa || — wi | bjɛ̃ syʁ || > wi |
bjɛ̃ syʁ kø wi ||]

**1867**

EN  You haven't eaten yet, have you? — No, I'm not
hungry.

FR  Tu n'as pas encore mangé, n'est-ce pas? — Non, je
n'ai pas faim.

IPA  [ty n‿a pa z‿ãkɔʁ mãʒe | n‿e sø pa || — nɔ̃ | ʒø n‿ɛ
pa fɛ̃ ||]

**1868**

EN  You aren't tired, are you? — No, I feel fine.

FR  Tu n'es pas fatigué (♀ fatiguée), n'est-ce pas? — Non,
je vais bien. > Non, je me sens bien.

IPA  [ty n‿ɛ pa fatige (♀ fatige) | n‿e sø pa || — nɔ̃ | ʒø vɛ
bjɛ̃ || > nɔ̃ | ʒø mø sãs bjɛ̃ ||]

**1869**

EN Igor's a very nice person, isn't he? — Yes, everybody likes him.

FR Igor est une gentille personne, n'est-ce pas? — Oui, tout le monde l'aime.

IPA [(...) e t‿yn ʒɑ̃tij pɛʁsɔn | n‿e sø pa || — wi | tu lø mɔ̃d l‿ɛm ||]

**1870**

EN You can play the piano, can't you? — Yes, but I'm not very good.

FR Tu peux jouer du piano, n'est-ce pas? — Oui, mais je ne suis pas très bon (♀ bonne).

IPA [ty pø ʒwe dy pjano | n‿e sø pa || — wi | mɛ ʒø nø sɥi pa tʁɛ bɔ̃ (♀ bɔn) ||]

**1871**

EN You don't know Larisa's sister, do you? — No, I've never met her.

FR Tu ne connais pas la sœur de Larissa, n'est-ce pas? — Non, je ne l'ai jamais rencontrée.

IPA [ty nø kɔnɛ pa la sœʁ dø laʁisa | n‿e sø pa || — nɔ̃ | ʒø nø l‿e ʒamɛ ʁɑ̃kɔ̃tʁe ||]

---

**1872**

**EN** Claude went to college, didn't he? — Yes, he studied psychology.

---

**FR** Claude est allé à l'université, n'est-ce pas? — Oui, il a étudié la psychologie.

**IPA** [(...) e ale a l‿ynivɛʁsite | n‿e sø pa || — wi | i l‿a etydje la psikɔloʒi ||]

---

**1873**

**EN** The movie wasn't very good, was it? — No, it was terrible.

---

**FR** Le film n'était pas très bon, n'est-ce pas? — Non, il était terrible.

**IPA** [lø film n‿ete pa tʁɛ bɔ̃ | n‿e sø pa || — nɔ̃ | i l‿ete tɛʁibl ||]

---

**1874**

**EN** Charlotte lives near you, doesn't she? — Yes, just a few blocks away.

---

**FR** Charlotte vit près de chez toi, n'est-ce pas? — Oui, à seulement quelques pâtés de maisons.

**IPA** [(...) vi pʁɛ dø ʃe twa | n‿e sø pa || — wi | a sœl°mã kɛlk pate dø mɛzɔ̃ ||]

**1875**

EN You won't tell anybody what I said, will you? — No, of course not.

FR Tu ne raconteras pas ce que je t'ai dit à personne, n'est-ce pas? — Non, bien sûr que non.

IPA [ty nø ʁakɔ̃tˢʁa pa sø kø ʒø tˌɛ di a pɛʁsɔn | nˌe sø pa || — nɔ̃ | bjɛ̃ syʁ kø nɔ̃ ||]

**1876**

EN Diane works very hard. It's said that she works sixteen (16) hours a day.

FR Diane travaille beaucoup. On dit qu'elle travaille seize heures par jour.

IPA [(...) tʁavaj boku || ɔ̃ di kˌel tʁavaj sɛz œʁ paʁ ʒuʁ ||]

**1877**

EN The police are looking for a missing boy. It's believed that he was last seen walking home.

FR La police recherche un garçon disparu. On croit qu'il a été vu pour la dernière fois alors qu'il rentrait à la maison.

IPA [la polis ʁˢʃɛʁʃ œ̃ gaʁsɔ̃ dispaʁy || ɔ̃ kʁwa kˌil a ete vy puʁ la dɛʁnjeʁ fwa alɔʁ kˌil ʁɑ̃tʁɛ a la mɛzɔ̃ ||]

**1878**

**EN** The strike started three (3) weeks ago. It's expected that it'll end soon.

**FR** La grève a commencé il y a trois semaines. On s'attend à ce qu'elle finisse bientôt.

**IPA** [la gʁɛv a kɔmãse i l‿i a tʁwa sᵊmɛn || ɔ̃ s‿atã a sø k‿ɛl finis bjẽto ||]

**1879**

**EN** A friend of mine has been arrested. It's alleged that he hit a police officer.

**FR** Un de mes amis a été arrêté. On présume qu'il a frappé un policier.

**IPA** [œ̃ dø me z‿ami z‿a ete aʁete || ɔ̃ pʁezym k‿il a fʁape œ̃ polisje ||]

**1880**

**EN** It's reported that two (2) people were injured in the explosion.

**FR** On rapporte que deux personnes ont été blessées dans l'explosion.

**IPA** [ɔ̃ ʁapɔʁt kø dø pɛʁson ɔ̃ ete blese dã l‿eksplozjɔ̃ ||]

**1881**

**EN** Let's go and see that movie. It's supposed to be good.

**FR** Allons voir ce film. Il est censé être bon.

**IPA** [alɔ̃ vwaʁ sø film || i l‿e sãse ɛtʁ bɔ̃ ||]

**1882**

EN Emil is supposed to have hit a police officer, but I don't believe it.

FR Emil est censé avoir frappé un policier, mais je ne le crois pas.

IPA [(...) e sɑ̃se avwaʁ fʁape œ̃ polisje | mɛ ʒø nø lø kʁwa pa ||]

**1883**

EN The plan is supposed to be a secret, but everybody seems to know about it.

FR Le plan est censé être un secret, mais tout le monde semble le connaître.

IPA [lø plɑ̃ n̩ e sɑ̃se ɛtʁ œ̃ sᵊkʁɛ | mɛ tu lø mɔ̃d sɑ̃bl lø konɛtʁ ||]

**1884**

EN What are you doing at work? You're supposed to be on vacation.

FR Que fais-tu au travail? Tu es censé (♀censée) être en vacances.

IPA [kø fɛ ty o tʁavaj || ty ɛ sɑ̃se (♀sɑ̃se) ɛtʁ ɑ̃ vakɑ̃s ||]

---

**1885**

**EN** Svetlana was supposed to call me last night, but she didn't.

---

**FR** Svetlana était censée m'appeler hier soir, mais elle ne l'a pas fait.

**IPA** [(...) etɛ sɑ̃se m‿apᵊle jɛʁ swaʁ | mɛ ɛl nø l‿a pa fɛ ||]

---

**1886**

**EN** Our guests were supposed to arrive at seven thirty (7:30), but they were late.

---

**FR** Nos invités (♀invitées) étaient censés (♀censées) arriver à sept heures trente (7 h 30), mais ils (♀elles) étaient en retard.

**IPA** [no z‿ɛ̃vite (♀ɛ̃vite) etɛ sɑ̃se (♀sɑ̃se) aʁive a sɛ t‿œʁ tʁɑ̃t (7 h 30) | mɛ il (♀ɛl) etɛ t‿ɑ̃ ʁᵊtaʁ ||]

---

**1887**

**EN** I'd better hurry. I'm supposed to meet Maksim in ten (10) minutes.

---

**FR** Je dois me dépêcher. Je suis censé (♀censée) rencontrer Maksim dans dix minutes.

**IPA** [ʒø dwa mø depeʃe || ʒø sɥi sɑ̃se (♀sɑ̃se) ʁɑ̃kɔ̃tʁe (...) dɑ̃ dis minyt ||]

**1888**

EN You're not supposed to park your car here. It's private parking only.

FR Tu n'es pas censé (♀censée) garer ta voiture ici. C'est un parking privé.

IPA [ty n̩ɛ pa sãse (♀sãse) gaʁe ta vwatyʁ isi || sɛ t̩œ̃ paʁkiŋ pʁive ||]

**1889**

EN Gerard is feeling much better after his operation, but he's still not supposed to do any heavy lifting.

FR Gerard se sent beaucoup mieux depuis son opération, mais il n'est toujours pas censé lever quoi que ce soit de lourd.

IPA [(...) sø sã boku mjø dᵊpɥi sɔ̃ n̩opeʁasjɔ̃ | mɛ il n̩e tuʒuʁ pa sãse lᵊve kwa kø sø swa dø luʁ ||]

**1890**

EN This coat is dirty. You should get it cleaned.

FR Ce manteau est sale. Tu devrais le faire nettoyer.

IPA [sø mãto e sal || ty dᵊvʁɛ lø fɛʁ netwaje ||]

**1891**

EN I think you should get your hair cut really short.

FR Je pense que tu devrais te faire couper les cheveux vraiment courts.

IPA [ʒø pãs kø ty dᵊvʁɛ tø fɛʁ kupe le ʃᵊvø vʁɛmã kuʁ ||]

**1892**

EN How often do you have your car serviced?

FR À quelle fréquence fais-tu entretenir ta voiture?

IPA [a kɛl fʁekɑ̃s fɛ ty ɑ̃tʁ°t°niʁ ta vwatyʁ ‖]

**1893**

EN I don't like having my picture taken.

FR Je n'aime pas qu'on prenne ma photo.

IPA [ʒø n‿ɛm pa k‿ɔ̃ pʁɛn ma foto ‖]

**1894**

EN Our neighbor just got air conditioning installed in their house.

FR Notre voisin (♀voisine) vient de se faire installer l'air climatisé dans sa maison.

IPA [nɔtʁ vwazɛ̃ (♀vwazin) vjɛ̃ dø sø fɛʁ ɛ̃stale l‿ɛʁ klimatize dɑ̃ sa mɛzɔ̃ ‖]

**1895**

EN Casper had his license taken away for driving too fast again.

FR Casper s'est fait retirer son permis de conduire pour avoir encore conduit trop rapidement.

IPA [(...) s‿e fɛ ʁ°tiʁe sɔ̃ pɛʁmi dø kɔ̃dɥiʁ pu ʁ‿avwaʁ ɑ̃kɔʁ kɔ̃dɥi tʁo ʁapid°mɑ̃ ‖]

**1896**

EN Olivia got her passport stolen.

FR Olivia s'est fait voler son passeport.
IPA [(...) s̬e fɛ vole sɔ̃ paspɔʁ ||]

**1897**

EN Have you ever had your flight canceled?

FR A-t-on déjà annulé ton vol?
IPA [a t̬ɔ̃ deʒa anyle tɔ̃ vɔl ||]

**1898**

EN Did I tell you about Luisa? She got her purse stolen last week.

FR T'ai-je parlé de Luisa? Elle s'est fait voler son sac à main la semaine dernière.
IPA [t̬ɛ ʒø paʁle dø (...) || ɛl s̬e fɛ vole sɔ̃ sak a mɛ̃ la sᵊmɛn dɛʁnjɛʁ ||]

**1899**

EN Hubert was in a fight last night. He got his nose broken.

FR Hubert s'est battu hier soir. Il s'est fait casser le nez.
IPA [(...) s̬e baty jɛʁ swaʁ || il s̬e fɛ kase lø ne ||]

**1900**

EN  Olivia said that she was going away for a few days and would call me when she got back.

FR  Olivia a dit qu'elle partait pour quelques jours et qu'elle m'appellerait à son retour.

IPA  [(...) a di k‿ɛl paʁtɛ puʁ kɛlk ʒuʁ e k‿ɛl m‿apɛlˀʁɛ a sɔ̃ ʁˀtuʁ ‖]

# GMS #1901 - 2000

**1901**

**EN** Leonardo's coming to the party tonight. — He is? I thought you said he wasn't coming.

**FR** Leonardo vient à la fête ce soir. – Ah oui? Je pensais que tu avais dit qu'il ne viendrait pas.

**IPA** [(...) vjɛ̃ a la fɛt sø swaʁ || — a wi || ʒø pɑ̃sɛ kø ty avɛ di k̩il nø vjɛ̃dʁɛ pa ||]

**1902**

**EN** I know lots of people. — You do? I thought you said you didn't know anybody.

**FR** Je connais des tas de gens. — Ah oui? Je pensais que tu avais dit que tu ne connaissais personne.

**IPA** [ʒø konɛ de ta dø ʒɑ̃ || — a wi || ʒø pɑ̃sɛ kø ty avɛ di kø ty nø konɛsɛ pɛʁsɔn ||]

**1903**

**EN** Isabelle will be here next week. — She will? But didn't you say she wouldn't be here?

**FR** Isabelle va être ici la semaine prochaine. — Ah oui? N'avais-tu pas dit qu'elle ne serait pas ici?

**IPA** [(...) va ɛtʁ isi la sᵊmɛn pʁoʃɛn || — a wi || n̩avɛ ty pa di k̩ɛl nø sᵊʁɛ pa z̩isi ||]

**1904**

EN I'm going out tonight. — You are? But you said you were staying home.

FR Je sors ce soir. — Ah oui? Mais tu as dit que tu restais à la maison.

IPA [ʒø sɔʁ sø swaʁ || — a wi || mɛ ty a di kø ty ʁɛstɛ a la mɛzɔ̃ ||]

**1905**

EN I can speak a little French. — You can? But earlier you said you couldn't.

FR Je parle un peu français. — Ah oui? Mais tu as dit que tu ne pouvais pas plus tôt.

IPA [ʒø paʁl œ̃ pø fʁɑ̃sɛ || — a wi || mɛ ty a di kø ty nø puvɛ pa plys to ||]

**1906**

EN I haven't been to the movies in ages. — You haven't? I thought you said you had just gone a few days ago.

FR Je ne suis pas allé (♀allée) au cinéma depuis des lunes. — Ah non? Je pensais que tu avais dit que tu y étais allé (♀allée) il y a quelques jours.

IPA [ʒø nø sɥi pa z‿ale (♀ale) o sinema dᵊpɥi de lyn || — a nɔ̃ || ʒø pɑ̃sɛ kø ty avɛ di kø ty i etɛ ale (♀ale) i l‿i a kɛlk ʒuʁ ||]

**1907**

EN Maalik said he had woken up feeling sick, so he hadn't gone to work.

FR Maalik a dit qu'il s'était mal senti à son réveil, alors il n'était pas allé au travail.

IPA [(...) a di k‿il s‿ete mal sãti a sõ ʁevɛj | alɔ ʁ‿il n‿etɛ pa z‿ale o tʁavaj ‖]

**1908**

EN Jasmine said that her new job is pretty interesting. > Jasmine said that her new job was pretty interesting.

FR Jasmine a dit que son nouveau travail est plutôt intéressant. > Jasmine a dit que son nouveau travail était plutôt intéressant.

IPA [(...) a di kø sõ nuvo tʁavaj e plyto t‿ẽteʁesã ‖ > (...) a di kø sõ nuvo tʁavaj etɛ plyto t‿ẽteʁesã ‖]

**1909**

EN She told me that she wants to go to South America next year. > She told me that she wanted to go to South America next year.

FR Elle m'a dit qu'elle veut aller en Amérique du Sud cette année. > Elle m'a dit qu'elle voulait aller en Amérique du Sud cette année.

IPA [ɛl m‿a di k‿ɛl vø ale ʁ‿ã n‿ameʁik dy syd sɛt ane ‖ > ɛl m‿a di k‿ɛl vulɛ ale ʁ‿ã n‿ameʁik dy syd sɛt ane ‖]

**1910**

EN The doctor told me to stay in bed for a few days.

FR Le docteur m'a dit de rester au lit pour quelques jours.

IPA [lø dɔktœʁ m‿a di dø ʁeste o li puʁ kɛlk ʒuʁ ‖]

**1911**

EN I told Lucien not to shout.

FR J'ai dit à Lucien de ne pas crier.

IPA [ʒ‿ɛ di a (...) dø nø pa kʁije ‖]

**1912**

EN Michiko asked me not to tell anybody what had happened.

FR Michiko m'a demandé de ne pas raconter à personne ce qui s'était passé.

IPA [(...) m‿a dᵊmɑ̃de dø nø pa ʁakɔ̃te a pɛʁsɔn sø ki s‿etɛ pase ‖]

**1913**

EN Noboru was taking a long time to get ready, so I told him to hurry up.

FR Noboru tardait trop à se préparer, alors je lui ai dit de se dépêcher.

IPA [(...) taʁdɛ tʁo a sø pʁepaʁe | alɔʁ ʒø lɥi ɛ di dø sø depeʃe ‖]

**1914**

EN Lilianne was nervous about the situation, so I told her to relax and take it easy.

FR Lilianne était nerveuse à propos de la situation, alors je lui ai dit de relaxer et de ne pas s'en faire.

IPA [(...) ete nɛʁvøz a pʁopo dø la sitɥasjɔ̃ | alɔʁ ʒø lɥi ɛ di dø ʁ°lakse e dø nø pa s‿ɑ̃ fɛʁ ‖]

**1915**

EN The customs officer looked at me suspiciously and asked me to open my bag.

FR Le douanier m'a regardé (♀ regardée) d'un air suspicieux et m'a demandé d'ouvrir mon sac.

IPA [lø dwanje m‿a ʁ°gaʁde (♀ ʁ°gaʁde) d‿œ̃ ɛʁ syspisjø e m‿a d°mɑ̃de d‿uvʁiʁ mɔ̃ sak ‖]

**1916**

EN What happened to you last night?

FR Que t'est-il arrivé hier soir?

IPA [kø t‿e t‿il aʁive jɛʁ swaʁ ‖]

**1917**

EN How many people came to the meeting?

FR Combien de gens sont venus à la réunion?

IPA [kɔ̃bjɛ̃ dø ʒɑ̃ sɔ̃ v°ny a la ʁeynjɔ̃ ‖]

---

**1918**

EN Which bus goes downtown?

---

FR Quel autobus va au centre-ville?
IPA [kɛ l‿otobys va o sɑ̃tʁ°vil ‖]

---

**1919**

EN Who do you want to speak to?

---

FR À qui veux-tu parler?
IPA [a ki vø ty paʁle ‖]

---

**1920**

EN What was the weather like yesterday?

---

FR Quel temps faisait-il hier?
IPA [kɛl tɑ̃ fᵊzɛ t‿il jɛʁ ‖]

---

**1921**

EN To whom do you wish to speak?

---

FR À qui souhaites-tu parler?
IPA [a ki swɛt ty paʁle ‖]

---

**1922**

EN Haven't we met somewhere before?

---

FR Ne nous sommes-nous pas déjà rencontrés
(♀rencontrées)?
IPA [nø nu sɔm nu pa deʒa ʁɑ̃kɔ̃tʁe (♀ʁɑ̃kɔ̃tʁe) ‖]

**1923**

EN Don't you want to go to the party? — No, I don't want to go.

FR Ne veux-tu pas aller à la fête? — Non, je ne veux pas y aller.

IPA [nø vø ty pa z‿ale a la fɛt ‖ — nɔ̃ | ʒø nø vø pa z‿i ale ‖|]

**1924**

EN Why don't we go out for a meal tonight?

FR Pourquoi ne sortons-nous pas manger ce soir?

IPA [puʁkwa nø sɔʁtɔ̃ nu pa mɑ̃ʒe sø swaʁ ‖|]

**1925**

EN Why wasn't Nicholas at work yesterday?

FR Pourquoi Nicholas n'était-il pas au travail hier?

IPA [puʁkwa (...) n‿etɛ t‿il pa o tʁavaj jɛʁ ‖|]

**1926**

EN We won't see Miriam tonight. — Why not? Isn't she coming?

FR Nous ne verrons pas Miriam ce soir. — Pourquoi? Ne vient-elle pas?

IPA [nu nø veʁɔ̃ pa (...) sø swaʁ ‖ — puʁkwa ‖ nø vjɛ̃ t‿ɛl pa ‖|]

**1927**

EN I'll have to borrow some money. — Why? Don't you have any?

FR J'aurai besoin d'emprunter de l'argent. — Pourquoi? N'en as-tu pas?

IPA [ʒ‿oʁɛ bøzwɛ̃ d‿ɑ̃pʁœ̃te dø l‿aʁʒɑ̃ ‖ — puʁkwa ‖ n‿ɑ̃ a ty pa ‖|]

**1928**

EN What time is it? > Do you know what time it is?

FR Quelle heure est-il? > Sais-tu quelle heure il est?

IPA [kɛ l‿œʁ e t‿il ‖ > sɛ ty kɛ l‿œʁ i l‿e ‖|]

**1929**

EN Who are those people? — I don't know who those people are.

FR Qui sont ces gens? > Je ne sais pas qui sont ces gens.

IPA [ki sɔ̃ se ʒɑ̃ ‖ > ʒø nø sɛ pa ki sɔ̃ se ʒɑ̃ ‖|]

**1930**

EN Where can I find Oliver? > Can you tell me where I can find Oliver?

FR Où puis-je trouver Oliver? > Peux-tu me dire où je peux trouver Oliver?

IPA [u pɥi ʒø tʁuve (...) ‖ > pø ty mø diʁ u ʒø pø tʁuve (...) ‖|]

1931

EN How much will it cost? > Do you have any idea
how much it'll cost?

---

FR Combien est-ce que ça coûtera? > As-tu une idée de
combien ça coûtera?

IPA [kɔ̃bjɛ̃ n̩ ɛs° kø sa kut°ʁa ‖ > a ty yn ide dø kɔ̃bjɛ̃ sa
kut°ʁa ‖]

1932

EN What time does the movie begin? > Do you know
what time the movie begins?

---

FR À quelle heure le film commence-t-il? > Sais-tu à
quelle heure commence le film?

IPA [a kɛ l̩ œʁ lø film komɑ̃s t̩ il ‖ > sɛ ty a kɛ l̩ œʁ
komɑ̃s lø film ‖]

1933

EN What do you mean? > Please explain what you
mean.

---

FR Que veux-tu dire? > Explique ce que tu veux dire,
s'il te plaît.

IPA [kø vø ty diʁ ‖ > ɛksplik sø kø ty vø diʁ | s̩ il tø plɛ
‖]

**1934**

EN Why did she leave early? > I wonder why she left early.

FR Pourquoi est-elle partie tôt? > Je me demande pourquoi elle est partie tôt.

IPA [puʁkwa e t‿ɛl paʁti to ‖ > ʒø mø d°mãd puʁkwa ɛ l‿e paʁti to ‖]

**1935**

EN How far is it to the airport? > Can you tell me how far it is to the airport?

FR À quelle distance est l'aéroport? > Peux-tu me dire à quelle distance est l'aéroport?

IPA [a kɛl distãs e l‿aeʁopɔʁ ‖ > pø ty mø diʁ a kɛl distãs e l‿aeʁopɔʁ ‖]

**1936**

EN How much does it cost to park here? > Could you tell me how much it costs to park here?

FR Combien est-ce que ça coûte pour se garer ici? > Pourrais-tu me dire combien ça coûte pour se garer ici?

IPA [kɔ̃bjɛ̃ n‿ɛs° kø sa kut puʁ sø gaʁe isi ‖ > puʁe ty mø diʁ kɔ̃bjɛ̃ sa kut puʁ sø gaʁe isi ‖]

**1937**

EN She asked if I was willing to travel.

FR Elle a demandé si j'étais partant pour voyager.

IPA [ε l̪a dᵊmãde si ʒ‿etε paʁtã puʁ vwajaʒe ‖]

**1938**

EN She wanted to know what I did in my spare time.

FR Elle voulait savoir ce que je fais dans mes temps libres.

IPA [εl vulε savwaʁ sø kø ʒø fε dã me tã libʁ ‖]

**1939**

EN She asked how long I had been working at my present job.

FR Elle a demandé depuis combien de temps j'occupais mon emploi actuel.

IPA [ε l̪a dᵊmãde dᵊpɥi kɔ̃bjɛ̃ dø tã ʒ‿okypε mɔ̃ n‿ãplwa aktɥεl ‖]

**1940**

EN She asked why I had applied for the job.

FR Elle a demandé pourquoi je postulais pour cet emploi.

IPA [ε l̪a dᵊmãde puʁkwa ʒø postulais puʁ sε t‿ãplwa ‖]

1941

EN She wanted to know if I could speak another language.

FR Elle voulait savoir si je pouvais parler d'autres langues.

IPA [ɛl vulɛ savwaʁ si ʒø puvɛ paʁle dotʁ lãg ‖]

1942

EN She asked if I had a driver's license.

FR Elle a demandé si j'avais un permis de conduire.

IPA [ɛ l‿a dᵊmãde si ʒ‿avɛ œ̃ pɛʁmi dø kõdɥiʁ ‖]

1943

EN Natalie doesn't have a car, and neither does Oliver.

FR Natalie n'a pas de voiture et Oliver non plus.

IPA [(...) n‿a pa dø vwatyʁ e (...) nõ plys ‖]

1944

EN Is it going to rain? — I hope not.

FR Va-t-il pleuvoir? — J'espère que non.

IPA [va t‿il pløvwaʁ ‖ — ʒ‿ɛspɛʁ kø nõ ‖]

**1945**

EN Do you think Remy will get the job? — I guess so.

FR Penses-tu que Remy va obtenir l'emploi? — Je pense que oui.

IPA [pãs ty kø ʁ°mi va ɔpt°niʁ l‿ãplwa ‖ — ʒø pãs kø wi ‖]

**1946**

EN Is Pauline married? — I don't think she is.

FR Pauline est-elle mariée? — Je ne pense pas qu'elle le soit.

IPA [(...) e t‿ɛl maʁje ‖ — ʒø nø pãs pa k‿ɛl lø swa ‖]

**1947**

EN Do you think you'll get a raise soon? — I hope so.

FR Penses-tu avoir une promotion bientôt? — J'espère que oui.

IPA [pãs ty avwa ʁ‿yn pʁomosjɔ̃ bjɛ̃to ‖ — ʒ‿ɛspɛʁ kø wi ‖]

**1948**

EN Do you have a room for tonight? — I'm afraid not.

FR As-tu une chambre pour ce soir? — J'ai bien peur que non.

IPA [a ty yn ʃãbʁ puʁ sø swaʁ ‖ — ʒ‿ɛ bjɛ̃ pøʁ kø nɔ̃ ‖]

**1949**

EN Do you have to leave already? — I'm afraid so.

FR Dois-tu partir tôt? — J'ai bien peur que oui.
IPA [dwa ty paʁtiʁ to || — ʒ‿ɛ bjɛ̃ pøʁ kø wi ||]

**1950**

EN Do you think John will be at the party? — I hope not.

FR Penses-tu que John sera à la fête? — J'espère que
non.
IPA [pɑ̃s ty kø john s°ʁa a la fɛt || — ʒ‿ɛspeʁ kø nɔ̃ ||]

**1951**

EN Is the concert at seven thirty (7:30)? — I think so.

FR Le concert est-il à dix-neuf heures trente (19 h 30)?
— Je pense que oui.
IPA [lø kɔ̃sɛʁ e t‿il a diznœ v‿œʁ tʁɑ̃t (19 h 30) || — ʒø
pɑ̃s kø wi ||]

**1952**

EN Is Hitomi working tomorrow? — I suppose so.

FR Hitomi travaille-t-il demain? — Je suppose que oui.
IPA [(...) tʁavaj t‿il d°mɛ̃ || — ʒø sypoz kø wi ||]

**1953**

EN You notice the sky is blue and the sun is shining. You say, "It's a beautiful day isn't it?"

FR Tu remarques que le ciel est bleu et que le soleil brille. Tu dis : « C'est une belle journée, n'est-ce pas? »

IPA [ty ʁ°maʁk kø lø sjɛl e blø e kø lø solɛj bʁij ‖ ty di | sɛ t‿yn bɛl ʒuʁne | n‿e sø pa ‖]

**1954**

EN You notice the restaurant prices are very high. You say, "It's pretty expensive, isn't it?"

FR Tu remarques que les prix au restaurant sont très élevés. Tu dis : « C'est plutôt cher, n'est-ce pas? »

IPA [ty ʁ°maʁk kø le pʁi o ʁɛstoʁɑ̃ sõ tʁɛ z‿ɛl°ve ‖ ty di | sɛ plyto ʃɛʁ | n‿e sø pa ‖]

**1955**

EN You really enjoyed your training course. You say, "The course was great, wasn't it?"

FR Tu as vraiment aimé ton cours de formation. Tu dis : « Le cours était génial, n'est-ce pas? »

IPA [ty a vʁɛmɑ̃ t‿eme tõ kuʁ dø fɔʁmasjõ ‖ ty di | lø kuʁ ete ʒenjal | n‿e sø pa ‖]

**1956**

**EN** You notice your friend's hair is much shorter than last time. You say, "You had your hair cut, didn't you?"

---

**FR** Tu remarques que les cheveux de ton ami (♀amie) sont beaucoup plus courts que la dernière fois. Tu dis : « Tu t'es fait couper les cheveux, n'est-ce pas? »

**IPA** [ty ʁ°maʁk kø le ʃ°vø dø tɔ̃ n‿ami (♀ami) sɔ̃ boku plys kuʁ kø la dɛʁnjɛʁ fwa ‖ ty di | ty t‿ɛ fɛ kupe le ʃ°vø | n‿e sø pa ‖]

**1957**

**EN** You notice the woman singing has a nice voice. You say, "She has a good voice, doesn't she?"

---

**FR** Tu remarques que la femme qui chante a une belle voix. Tu dis : « Elle a une belle voix, n'est-ce pas? »

**IPA** [ty ʁ°maʁk kø la fam ki ʃɑ̃t a yn bɛl vwa ‖ ty di | ɛ l‿a yn bɛl vwa | n‿e sø pa ‖]

**1958**

**EN** You're trying on a new jacket and don't like it. You say, "This doesn't look very good on me, does it?"

---

**FR** Tu essaies un veston et tu ne l'aimes pas. Tu dis : « Ça ne me fait pas très bien, n'est-ce pas? »

**IPA** [ty ɛsɛ z‿œ̃ vɛstɔ̃ e ty nø l‿ɛm pa ‖ ty di | sa nø mø fɛ pa tʁɛ bjɛ̃ | n‿e sø pa ‖]

**1959**

EN The cashier is putting your groceries in a plastic bag. You say, "Excuse me, don't you have any paper bags?"

FR Le caissier (♀ la caissière) est en train d'emballer tes achats dans un sac de plastique. Tu dis : « Excusez-moi, n'avez-vous pas de sac de papier? »

IPA [lø kesje (♀ la kesjɛʁ) e t‿ɑ̃ tʁɛ̃ d‿ɑ̃bale te z‿aʃa dɑ̃ z‿œ̃ sak dø plastik || ty di | ɛkskyze mwa | n‿ave vu pa dø sak dø papje ||]

**1960**

EN You're looking for your keys. Maybe Ichirou has seen them. You ask, "You haven't seen my keys, have you?"

FR Tu cherches tes clés. Peut-être qu'Ichirou les a vues. Tu demandes : « Tu n'as pas vu mes clés, n'est-ce pas? »

IPA [ty ʃɛʁʃ te kle || pøtɛtʁ k (...) le z‿a vy || ty d‿mɑ̃d | ty n‿a pa vy me kle | n‿e sø pa ||]

**1961**

EN Serge has a car and you need a ride to the station. You ask, "Could you give me a ride to the station?"

FR Serge a une voiture et tu as besoin qu'on t'emmène à la gare. Tu demandes : « Pourrais-tu m'emmener à la gare? »

IPA [(...) a yn vwatyʁ e ty a bøzwɛ̃ k‿ɔ̃ t‿ɑ̃mɛn a la gaʁ || ty d‿mɑ̃d | puʁɛ ty m‿ɑ̃m‿ne a la gaʁ ||]

**1962**

EN   Would you mind closing the door?

FR   Aurais-tu l'obligeance de fermer la porte?
IPA  [oʁɛ ty l‿obliʒɑ̃s də fɛʁme la pɔʁt ‖]

**1963**

EN   Would you mind turning off the lights?

FR   Aurais-tu l'obligeance d'éteindre les lumières?
IPA  [oʁɛ ty l‿obliʒɑ̃s d‿etɛ̃dʁ le lymjɛʁ ‖]

**1964**

EN   Renee suggested going to the movies.

FR   Renee a suggéré d'aller au cinéma.
IPA  [(...) a sygʒeʁe d‿ale o sinema ‖]

**1965**

EN   Suddenly everybody stopped talking. There was silence.

FR   Tout le monde a soudainement arrêté de parler. C'était silencieux.
IPA  [tu lø mɔ̃d a sudɛnᵊmɑ̃ t‿aʁete də paʁle ‖ se etɛ silɑ̃sjø ‖]

**1966**

EN I'll do the shopping when I've finished cleaning the apartment.

FR Je ferai les courses quand j'aurai fini de nettoyer l'appartement.

IPA [ʒø fʰʁɛ le kuʁs kɑ̃ ʒ‿oʁɛ fini dø netwaje l‿apaʁt°mɑ̃ ‖]

**1967**

EN He tried to avoid answering my question.

FR Il a essayé d'éviter ma question.

IPA [i l‿a esɛje d‿evite ma kɛstjɔ̃ ‖]

**1968**

EN Have you ever considered going to live in another country? — Sure, but I don't know how much it would cost.

FR As-tu déjà songé à vivre dans un autre pays? — Bien sûr, mais je ne sais pas combien ça coûterait.

IPA [a ty deʒa sɔ̃ʒe a vivʁ dɑ̃ z‿œ̃ n‿otʁ pei ‖ — bjɛ̃ syʁ | mɛ ʒø nø sɛ pa kɔ̃bjɛ̃ sa kut°ʁɛ ‖]

**1969**

EN When I'm on vacation, I enjoy not having to get up early.

---

FR Quand je suis en vacances, j'aime ne pas devoir me lever tôt.

IPA [kɑ̃ ʒø sɥi z‿ɑ̃ vakɑ̃s | ʒ‿ɛm nø pa d°vwaʁ mø l°ve to ||]

**1970**

EN Rashmi has given up trying to lose weight.

---

FR Rashmi a laissé tomber ses tentatives de perte de poids.

IPA [(...) a lese tɔ̃be se tɑ̃tativ dø pɛʁt dø pwa ||]

**1971**

EN Niraj doesn't want to retire. He wants to go on working.

---

FR Niraj ne veut pas prendre sa retraite. Il veut continuer de travailler.

IPA [(...) nø vø pa pʁɑ̃dʁ sa ʁ°tʁɛt || il vø kɔ̃tinɥe dø tʁavaje ||]

**1972**

EN You keep interrupting when I'm talking.

---

FR Tu ne cesses de m'interrompre quand je parle.

IPA [ty nø sɛs dø m‿ɛ̃teʁɔ̃pʁ kɑ̃ ʒø paʁl ||]

**1973**

EN I can't imagine Theo riding a motorcycle.

FR Je n'arrive pas à imaginer Theo conduisant une moto.
IPA [ʒø n‿aʁiv pa a imaʒine (...) kɔ̃dɥizɑ̃ t‿yn moto ‖]

**1974**

EN I don't mind being kept waiting.

FR Ça ne me dérange pas qu'on me fasse attendre.
IPA [sa nø mø deʁɑ̃ʒ pa k‿ɔ̃ mø fas atɑ̃dʁ ‖]

**1975**

EN They admitted to having stolen the money.

FR Ils (♀ elles) ont admis avoir volé l'argent.
IPA [il (♀ ɛl) ɔ̃ admi z‿avwaʁ vole l‿aʁʒɑ̃ ‖]

**1976**

EN I now regret saying what I said.

FR Je regrette maintenant ce que j'ai dit.
IPA [ʒø ʁ°gʁɛt mɛ̃t°nɑ̃ sø kø ʒ‿ɛ di ‖]

**1977**

EN She denied that she had stolen the money.

FR Elle a nié avoir volé l'argent.
IPA [ɛ l‿a nje avwaʁ vole l‿aʁʒɑ̃ ‖]

**1978**

EN  Sabine suggested that we go to the movies.

FR  Sabine a suggéré que nous allions au cinéma.

IPA  [(...) a sygʒeʁe kø nu z‿aljɔ̃ o sinema ‖]

**1979**

EN  Should we postpone leaving today until tomorrow?
— No, we should try leaving as soon as possible.

FR  Devrait-on remettre le départ à demain? — Non, on
devrait essayer de partir aussi tôt que possible.

IPA  [dᵊvʁɛ t‿ɔ̃ ʁᵊmɛtʁ lø depaʁ a dᵊmɛ̃ ‖ — nɔ̃ | ɔ̃ dᵊvʁɛ
eseje dø paʁtiʁ osi to kø posibl ‖]

**1980**

EN  My car isn't very reliable. It keeps breaking down.

FR  Ma voiture n'est pas très fiable. Elle ne cesse de
tomber en panne.

IPA  [ma vwatyʁ n‿e pa tʁɛ fjabl ‖ ɛl nø sɛs dø tɔ̃be ʁ‿ɑ̃
pan ‖]

**1981**

EN  It was very funny. I couldn't stop laughing.

FR  C'était très drôle. Je ne pouvais pas arrêter de rire.

IPA  [se ete tʁɛ dʁol ‖ ʒø nø puvɛ pa z‿aʁete dø ʁiʁ ‖]

**1982**

EN It was late, so we decided to take a taxi home.

FR Il était tard, alors nous avons décidé de rentrer en taxi.

IPA [i l̺ete taʁ | alɔʁ nu z̺avɔ̃ deside dø ʁɑ̃tʁe ʁ̺ɑ̃ taksi ||]

**1983**

EN Vincent was in a difficult situation, so I agreed to help him.

FR Vincent était dans une situation difficile, alors j'ai accepté de l'aider.

IPA [(...) etɛ dɑ̃ z̺yn sitɥasjɔ̃ difisil | alɔʁ ʒ̺ɛ aksɛpte dø l̺ede ||]

**1984**

EN How old were you when you learned to drive?

FR Quel âge avais-tu quand tu as appris à conduire?

IPA [kɛ l̺aʒ avɛ ty kɑ̃ ty a apʁi a kɔ̃dɥiʁ ||]

**1985**

EN Valerie failed to make a good impression at the job interview.

FR Valerie n'a pas réussi à donner une bonne impression lors de l'entrevue d'embauche.

IPA [(...) n̺a pa ʁeysi a done ʁ̺yn bɔn ɛ̃pʁesjɔ̃ lɔʁ dø l̺ɑ̃tʁᵊvy d̺ɑ̃boʃ ||]

**1986**

EN  We decided not to go out because of the weather.

FR  Nous avons décidé de ne pas sortir à cause du mauvais temps.

IPA  [nu z‿avɔ̃ deside dø nø pa sɔʁtiʁ a koz dy movɛ tɑ̃ ‖]

**1987**

EN  I promised not to be late.

FR  J'ai promis de ne pas être en retard.

IPA  [ʒ‿ɛ pʁomi dø nø pa z‿etʁ ɑ̃ ʁ°taʁ ‖]

**1988**

EN  Are you thinking of buying a car? — Yeah, but I still haven't made up my mind.

FR  Penses-tu acheter une voiture? — Ouais, mais je ne me suis pas encore décidé (♀décidée).

IPA  [pɑ̃s ty aʃ°te ʁ‿yn vwatyʁ ‖ — wɛ | mɛ ʒø nø mø sɥi pa z‿ɑ̃kɔʁ deside (♀deside) ‖]

**1989**

EN  They seem to have plenty of money.

FR  Ils (♀elles) semblent avoir beaucoup d'argent.

IPA  [il (♀ɛl) sɑ̃bl avwaʁ boku d‿aʁʒɑ̃ ‖]

1990

**EN** I like Victoria, but I think she tends to talk too much.

**FR** J'aime Victoria, mais je pense qu'elle a tendance à trop parler.

**IPA** [ʒ‿ɛm (...) | mɛ ʒø pɑ̃s k‿ɛl a tɑ̃dɑ̃s a tʁo paʁle ||]

1991

**EN** Nikolai pretended not to see me when he passed me on the street.

**FR** Nikolai a prétendu ne pas me voir lorsqu'il est passé à côté de moi dans la rue.

**IPA** [(...) a pʁetɑ̃dy nø pa mø vwaʁ lɔʁsk il e pase a kote dø mwa dɑ̃ la ʁy ||]

1992

**EN** I pretended to be reading the newspaper.

**FR** J'ai prétendu lire le journal.

**IPA** [ʒ‿e pʁetɑ̃dy liʁ lø ʒuʁnal ||]

1993

**EN** You seem to have lost weight.

**FR** Tu sembles avoir perdu du poids.

**IPA** [ty sɑ̃bl avwaʁ pɛʁdy dy pwa ||]

**1994**

EN   Yannick seems to be enjoying his new job.

---

FR   Yannick semble aimer son nouvel emploi.
IPA  [(...) sãbl eme sõ nuvɛ lˌãplwa ‖]

**1995**

EN   I wouldn't dare tell him.

---

FR   Je n'oserais pas lui dire.
IPA  [ʒø nˌoz°ʁɛ pa lɥi diʁ ‖]

**1996**

EN   Can somebody show me how to change the cartridge in this printer? — Sure, I will.

---

FR   Est-ce que quelqu'un pourrait me montrer comment changer la cartouche de cette imprimante? — Bien sûr, je vais te le montrer.
IPA  [ɛs° kø kɛlkœ̃ puʁɛ mø mõtʁe komã ʃãʒe la kaʁtuʃ dø sɛt ɛ̃pʁimãt ‖ — bjɛ̃ syʁ | ʒø vɛ tø lø mõtʁe ‖]

**1997**

EN   Yvonne tends to forget things.

---

FR   Yvonne a tendance à oublier des choses.
IPA  [yvonne a tãdãs a ublije de ʃoz ‖]

**1998**

EN They claim to have solved the problem.

FR Ils prétendent avoir résolu le problème.

IPA [il pʁetɑ̃d avwaʁ ʁezoly lø pʁoblɛm ‖]

**1999**

EN Would you know what to do if there was a fire in the building? — Not really.

FR Saurais-tu quoi faire s'il y avait un incendie dans l'édifice? — Pas vraiment.

IPA [soʁɛ ty kwa fɛʁ s‿il i avɛ t‿œ̃ n‿ɛ̃sɑ̃di dɑ̃ l‿edifis ‖ — pa vʁɛmɑ̃ ‖]

**2000**

EN I was really astonished. I didn't know what to say.

FR J'étais vraiment étonné (♀ étonnée). Je ne savais pas quoi dire.

IPA [ʒ‿etɛ vʁɛmɑ̃ t‿etone (♀ etone) ‖ ʒø nø savɛ pa kwa diʁ ‖]

# French Index

américaine [ameʁikɛn]: 1051
amérique [n̩ ameʁik]: 1109, 1909
ami [n̩ ami]: 1026, 1050, 1956
amie [ami]: 1026, 1185, 1956
amies [ami]: 1204, 1338, 1783, 1791, 1795
amis [k ami]: 1229, 1249, 1305, 1338
amis [z ami]: 1204, 1222, 1415, 1755, 1783, 1791, 1795, 1879
amuse-toi [amyz twa]: 1625
anglais [ɑ̃glɛ]: 1679
anna [anna]: 1056
année [ane]: 1909
années [z ane]: 1414
annulé [anyle]: 1897
ans [ɑ̃]: 1167, 1182, 1183, 1288, 1422, 1442, 1738
ans [k ɑ̃]: 1004
ans [t ɑ̃]: 1016, 1017, 1721
ans [z ɑ̃]: 1107, 1147, 1282, 1728
appelé [ap°le]: 1324, 1847
appelée [ap°le]: 1847
appeler [ap°le]: 1347, 1352, 1353, 1602, 1763
appeler [z ap°le]: 1301
appelle-moi [apɛl mwa]: 1647
appelle-t-on [apɛl t ɔ̃]: 1094
apporter [apɔʁte]: 1153
apprendre [apʁɑ̃dʁ]: 1483, 1494, 1851
appris [apʁi]: 1183, 1984
après [apʁɛ]: 1005, 1231, 1519
après-midi [apʁɛ midi]: 1090, 1234, 1267, 1281, 1347, 1373, 1706
arbre [z aʁbʁ]: 1654
arbres [z aʁbʁ]: 1085, 1085, 1659
arrêté [aʁete]: 1879
arrêté [t aʁete]: 1965
arrêter [z aʁete]: 1981
arrive [aʁiv]: 1210, 1629, 1652
arrivé [aʁive]: 1143, 1699, 1916
arrivé [t aʁive]: 1509
arrivée [aʁive]: 1699
arrivée [t aʁive]: 1101
arriver [aʁive]: 1886

arriveras [aʁiv°ʁa]: 1727
as [a]: 1413, 1441, 1562, 1794, 1836, 1846, 1904, 1905, 1955, 1961, 1984
as [n̩ a]: 1564, 1597
assez [ase]: 1637
assez [z ase]: 1455, 1719
assidûment [s asidymɑ̃]: 1455
assurément [asyʁemɑ̃]: 1379
as-tu [a ty]: 1001, 1008, 1039, 1050, 1148, 1155, 1187, 1188, 1193, 1196, 1324, 1405, 1656, 1716, 1806, 1812, 1815, 1819, 1927, 1931... +2
a-t-elle [a t ɛl]: 1046, 1070, 1106
a-t-il [a t il]: 1018, 1036, 1041, 1525, 1657, 1661, 1663, 1671, 1673, 1675, 1676, 1685, 1689, 1696, 1769
a-t-on [a t ɔ̃]: 1106, 1897
attend [atɑ̃]: 1532
attendons [atɑ̃dɔ̃]: 1642
attendre [atɑ̃dʁ]: 1391, 1450, 1525, 1578, 1579, 1598, 1599, 1602, 1648, 1974
attends-moi [atɑ̃ mwa]: 1623
attention [atɑ̃sjɔ̃]: 1627
au [o]: 1013, 1029, 1052, 1061, 1165, 1181, 1189, 1191, 1199, 1200, 1216, 1217, 1224, 1233, 1240, 1243, 1255... +72
au-dessus [od°sy]: 1516
aujourd'hui [n̩ oʒuʁdɥi]: 1492
aujourd'hui [oʒuʁdɥi]: 1125, 1259, 1327, 1329, 1363, 1413, 1705, 1738, 1744, 1782, 1801, 1827
auparavant [opaʁavɑ̃]: 1094
aura [l oʁa]: 1288
aura [oʁa]: 1703, 1704, 1706, 1707, 1727, 1730
aurais-tu [oʁɛ ty]: 1962, 1963
aussi [osi]: 1229, 1381, 1560, 1774, 1843, 1979
autant [otɑ̃]: 1461, 1465, 1478, 1479, 1480, 1534, 1534
autant [z otɑ̃]: 1303
autobus [l otobys]: 1918
autobus [n̩ otobys]: 1232, 1675, 1769

brille-t-il  [bʁij t il]: 1123

brisées  [bʁize]: 1038

britanniques  [bʁitanik]: 1051

bruit  [bʁɥi]: 1037, 1754

bureau  [byʁo]: 1010, 1011, 1029, 1063, 1064, 1079, 1087, 1105, 1736, 1754

bureaux  [byʁo]: 1104

bus  [bys]: 1232, 1371

ça  [sa]: 1005, 1126, 1156, 1225, 1289, 1303, 1323, 1430, 1536, 1621, 1824, 1835, 1931, 1936, 1958, 1968... +1

cadeau  [kado]: 1251, 1294

café  [kafe]: 1111, 1150, 1171, 1265, 1542, 1544, 1597

caissier  [kesje]: 1959

caissière  [kesjɛʁ]: 1959

cambriolage  [kãbʁijolaʒ]: 1725

caméra  [kameʁa]: 1326, 1331

canada  [kanada]: 1013

carte  [kaʁt]: 1321, 1448

cartouche  [kaʁtuʃ]: 1996

cassé  [kase]: 1081, 1106, 1818

cassée  [kase]: 1081, 1106

casser  [kase]: 1899

cause  [koz]: 1986

ce  [sø]: 1030, 1032, 1036, 1053, 1087, 1093, 1099, 1100, 1129, 1130, 1147, 1162, 1182, 1189, 1197, 1204, 1206, 1207, 1208... +94

ceinture  [sɛ̃tyʁ]: 1444, 1476

celle  [sɛl]: 1839

censé  [sãse]: 1881, 1882, 1883, 1884, 1887, 1888, 1889

censée  [sãse]: 1884, 1885, 1887, 1888

censées  [sãse]: 1886

censés  [sãse]: 1886

cent  [sã]: 1016, 1017

centre  [sãtʁ]: 1182

centre-ville  [sãtʁ°vil]: 1520, 1675, 1735, 1918

cents  [sã]: 1022, 1024, 1053, 1694, 1695, 1728

cerises  [s°ʁiz]: 1716

certain  [sɛʁtɛ̃]: 1810

certaine  [sɛʁtɛn]: 1810

certaines  [sɛʁtɛn]: 1757

ces  [se]: 1014, 1017, 1026, 1027, 1038, 1092, 1094, 1104, 1142, 1168, 1451, 1837, 1861, 1929

cesse  [sɛs]: 1598, 1980

cesses  [sɛs]: 1972

c'est  [sɛ]: 1151, 1226, 1248, 1251, 1288, 1309, 1316, 1319, 1340, 1427, 1428, 1456, 1475, 1477, 1621, 1630, 1666, 1688, 1729, 1738... +17

cet  [sɛ]: 1369, 1443, 1688, 1689, 1708, 1940

cet  [sɛt]: 1267, 1347

c'était  [se ete]: 1747, 1823, 1965, 1981

cette  [sɛt]: 1016, 1050, 1070, 1107, 1131, 1149, 1163, 1172, 1173, 1174, 1314, 1322, 1326, 1331, 1336, 1340, 1403, 1421... +11

chaise  [ʃɛz]: 1323, 1575, 1677

chaleur  [ʃalœʁ]: 1770, 1787, 1788

chambre  [ʃãbʁ]: 1071, 1072, 1161, 1164, 1166, 1403, 1948

chambres  [ʃãbʁ]: 1027, 1049, 1168, 1694, 1695

chanceux  [ʃãsø]: 1349

changement  [ʃãʒ°mã]: 1489, 1729

changer  [ʃãʒe]: 1520, 1996

chante  [ʃãt]: 1957

chapeau  [ʃapo]: 1330, 1467

chaque  [ʃak]: 1149, 1255, 1440, 1537, 1538

chat  [ʃa]: 1593

chaud  [ʃo]: 1314, 1746, 1747

chauffeur  [ʃofœʁ]: 1609, 1610

chaussures  [ʃosyʁ]: 1136, 1837

chemise  [ʃ°miz]: 1070, 1684

chemises  [ʃ°miz]: 1080

cher  [ʃɛʁ]: 1195, 1493, 1527, 1954

cherches  [ʃɛʁʃ]: 1960

chère  [ʃɛʁ]: 1331, 1684

cheval  [ʃ°val]: 1108, 1184, 1401

cheveux  [ʃ°vø]: 1891, 1956

chez  [ʃe]: 1121, 1202, 1305, 1415, 1498, 1502, 1504, 1874

deux [dø]: 1021, 1047, 1049, 1282, 1672, 1694, 1695, 1880

devaient [dᵊvɛ]: 1423, 1512

devais [dᵊvɛ]: 1502, 1519

devions [dᵊvjɔ̃]: 1424, 1521

d'éviter [d_evite]: 1967

devoir [dᵊvwaʁ]: 1969

devons [dᵊvɔ̃]: 1448, 1486, 1732

devraient [dᵊvʁɛ]: 1490, 1496

devrais [dᵊvʁɛ]: 1456, 1457, 1461, 1463, 1464, 1465, 1467, 1469, 1471, 1473, 1474, 1475, 1476, 1477, 1480, 1481, 1482, 1483, 1484, 1485... +7

devrais-je [dᵊvʁɛ ʒø]: 1318, 1458, 1464, 1640, 1643, 1647

devrait [dᵊvʁɛ]: 1455, 1460, 1462, 1472, 1478, 1479, 1486, 1489, 1492, 1494, 1495, 1648, 1851, 1979

devrait-on [dᵊvʁɛ t ɔ̃]: 1343, 1459, 1598, 1599, 1602, 1644, 1979

devrions [dᵊvʁijɔ̃]: 1466, 1468, 1486, 1493

devrions-nous [dᵊvʁijɔ̃ nu]: 1578, 1598, 1604

d'hôtel [d_otɛl]: 1403

d'ici [d_isi]: 1279, 1282, 1657, 1661, 1671, 1740, 1751

différent [difeʁɑ̃]: 1729

différentes [difeʁɑ̃t]: 1194

différents [difeʁɑ̃]: 1003, 1756

difficile [difisil]: 1268, 1752, 1983

diffusées [difyze]: 1051

dimanche [dimɑ̃ʃ]: 1189, 1546, 1547

dîne [din]: 1641

dîner [dine]: 1317, 1320, 1370, 1408, 1458, 1459, 1539, 1546, 1547, 1569, 1599, 1633

dînions [dinjɔ̃]: 1198

dire [diʁ]: 1126, 1162, 1372, 1536, 1930, 1933, 1935, 1936, 1995, 2000

direct [diʁɛkt]: 1683

dis [di]: 1953, 1954, 1955, 1956, 1957, 1958, 1959

discours [diskuʁ]: 1253

disparu [dispaʁy]: 1877

dispute [dispyt]: 1637

distance [distɑ̃s]: 1737, 1740, 1741, 1742, 1743, 1935, 1935

dit [di]: 1252, 1335, 1536, 1847, 1847, 1875, 1876, 1900, 1902, 1903, 1904, 1905, 1906, 1907, 1908, 1908, 1909, 1909, 1910, 1911... +3

dix [di]: 1107, 1138, 1147, 1413, 1652, 1666, 1683, 1728

dix [dis]: 1398, 1521, 1735, 1823, 1887

dix-huit [dizɥit]: 1422

dix-neuf [diznœ]: 1213, 1951

docteur [dɔktœʁ]: 1910

dois [dwa]: 1413, 1414, 1416, 1420, 1426, 1427, 1429, 1436, 1439, 1441, 1443, 1449, 1451, 1470, 1498, 1500, 1501, 1507, 1511, 1514... +9

dois-tu [dwa ty]: 1504, 1524, 1528, 1949

doit [dwa]: 1411, 1417, 1418, 1422, 1428, 1430, 1432, 1435, 1437, 1438, 1439, 1440, 1442, 1447, 1448, 1453, 1486, 1499, 1513, 1515... +2

doit-elle [dwa t ɛl]: 1505, 1526

doit-il [dwa t il]: 1530

doivent [dwav]: 1415, 1419, 1421, 1425, 1431, 1433, 1444, 1445, 1446, 1452, 1510, 1523

donnée [done]: 1050

donne-la-moi [dɔn la mwa]: 1326

donner [done]: 1336, 1384, 1985

d'orange [d_oʁɑ̃ʒ]: 1554, 1555

dormi [dɔʁmi]: 1176, 1853

dormir [dɔʁmiʁ]: 1388, 1407

dormiras [dɔʁmiʁa]: 1265

douanier [dwanje]: 1915

doucement [dusᵊmɑ̃]: 1404

d'ouvrir [d_uvʁiʁ]: 1915

drôle [dʁol]: 1981

du [dy]: 1040, 1062, 1109, 1150, 1171, 1253, 1380, 1381, 1512, 1516, 1523, 1528, 1542, 1544, 1585... +18

dû [dy]: 1450, 1454, 1503, 1506, 1517, 1525, 1527, 1529, 1539, 1540, 1541

d'un [d‿œ̃]: 1915
d'une [d‿yn]: 1444
durant [dyʁɑ̃]: 1107, 1167, 1435
d'usine [d‿yzin]: 1857
échecs [z‿eʃɛk]: 1397
école [ekɔl]: 1688
économiser [ekonomize]: 1497
écoute [ekut]: 1225
écoute [l‿ekut]: 1161
écoutons [ekutɔ̃]: 1640
édifice [t‿edifis]: 1688
effraction [ʁ‿efʁaksjɔ̃]: 1045
élevés [z‿ɛl°ve]: 1954
elle [ɛ]: 1003, 1004, 1005, 1009, 1054,
    1071, 1089, 1151, 1159, 1255,
    1257, 1259, 1272, 1274, 1276,
    1277, 1412, 1435, 1668, 1684...
    +12
elle [ɛl]: 1050, 1061, 1133, 1158, 1236,
    1252, 1258, 1259, 1273, 1275,
    1278, 1365, 1382, 1387, 1417,
    1432, 1435, 1439... +21
elle [ʁ‿ɛl]: 1499
elles [ɛl]: 1086, 1119, 1299, 1423,
    1506, 1529, 1536, 1886, 1975, 1989
elles [ʁ‿ɛl]: 1431
émission [emisjɔ̃]: 1312, 1692, 1693
émissions [ʁ‿emisjɔ̃]: 1051
emploi [l‿ɑ̃plwa]: 1282, 1484, 1571,
    1994
emploi [n‿ɑ̃plwa]: 1435, 1606, 1939
emploi [t‿ɑ̃plwa]: 1443, 1940
emprunter [ɑ̃pʁœ̃te]: 1565
en [ɑ̃]: 1022, 1024, 1044, 1053, 1087,
    1093, 1109, 1150, 1198, 1223,
    1231, 1246, 1276, 1281, 1289,
    1303, 1344, 1364, 1367... +33
en [ʁ‿ɑ̃]: 1232, 1489, 1538, 1909,
    1980, 1982
en [t‿ɑ̃]: 1063, 1089, 1131, 1226, 1793,
    1886, 1959
en [z‿ɑ̃]: 1099, 1178, 1364, 1629, 1780,
    1821, 1842, 1969
encore [ɑ̃kɔʁ]: 1491, 1578, 1579, 1599,
    1823, 1895

encore [z‿ɑ̃kɔʁ]: 1096, 1097, 1283,
    1332, 1372, 1623, 1802, 1867, 1988
endommagé [ɑ̃domaʒe]: 1083, 1096
endommagée [ɑ̃domaʒe]: 1083
endommagée [t‿ɑ̃domaʒe]: 1157
endommagées [ɑ̃domaʒe]: 1049
endormi [ɑ̃dɔʁmi]: 1280, 1820
endormie [ɑ̃dɔʁmi]: 1820
endroit [n‿ɑ̃dʁwa]: 1042, 1091, 1451
endroits [z‿ɑ̃dʁwa]: 1442, 1756
enfants [ɑ̃fɑ̃]: 1728
enfants [z‿ɑ̃fɑ̃]: 1433, 1434
enseignant [ɑ̃sɛɲɑ̃]: 1612
enseignant [n‿ɑ̃sɛɲɑ̃]: 1611
ensoleillé [ɑ̃solɛje]: 1747, 1823
entendre [z‿ɑ̃tɑ̃dʁ]: 1439
entendu [ɑ̃tɑ̃dy]: 1372
entendue [ɑ̃tɑ̃dy]: 1748
entre [ɑ̃tʁ]: 1735
entré [ɑ̃tʁe]: 1045, 1198
entreprise [n‿ɑ̃tʁ°pʁiz]: 1414
entretenir [ɑ̃tʁ°t°niʁ]: 1892
envie [t‿ɑ̃vi]: 1577
envie [z‿ɑ̃vi]: 1596
environ [ɑ̃viʁɔ̃]: 1182
envoyé [ɑ̃vwaje]: 1041
envoyer [ɑ̃vwaje]: 1608
épicerie [epis°ʁi]: 1724
équipe [ekip]: 1663, 1664, 1682
es [ɛ]: 1473, 1491, 1821, 1863, 1884
espagnol [ɛspaɲɔl]: 1382
essaies [ɛsɛ]: 1482, 1958
essayé [eseje]: 1967
essayer [eseje]: 1979
est [e]: 1010, 1012, 1028, 1040, 1042,
    1048, 1055, 1056, 1059, 1061,
    1063, 1064, 1091, 1096, 1101,
    1140, 1149, 1161, 1185... +30
est [l‿e]: 1009, 1089, 1131, 1159, 1246,
    1256, 1259, 1276, 1360, 1361,
    1362, 1363, 1364, 1365, 1366,
    1420, 1435, 1463, 1466, 1473...
    +10
est [n‿e]: 1045, 1883
est [t‿e]: 1156

est-ce [ɛsˀ]: 1020, 1027, 1052, 1070, 1093, 1114, 1140, 1532, 1661, 1683, 1686, 1687, 1731, 1733, 1736, 1737, 1766, 1773, 1807, 1996

est-ce [n‿ɛsˀ]: 1931, 1936

est-elle [e t‿ɛl]: 1139, 1725, 1827, 1934, 1946

est-il [e t‿il]: 1031, 1032, 1140, 1141, 1143, 1162, 1928, 1951

es-tu [ɛ ty]: 1023, 1043, 1137, 1144, 1154, 1283, 1632, 1762, 1767, 1800, 1811

et [e]: 1052, 1096, 1110, 1117, 1186, 1192, 1199, 1220, 1246, 1326, 1382, 1385, 1389, 1417, 1427, 1433, 1441, 1443, 1474... +17

et [ʁ‿e]: 1473

et [t‿e]: 1287, 1287

étaient [etɛ]: 1175, 1423, 1886

étais [etɛ]: 1906

étais-tu [etɛ ty]: 1450, 1820, 1844

était [etɛ]: 1089, 1717, 1862, 1885, 1908, 1914, 1955, 1983

était [l‿etɛ]: 1004, 1257, 1272, 1274, 1277, 1412, 1714, 1873, 1982

était-il [etɛ t‿il]: 1853

états [eta]: 1681

états-unis [z‿etazuni]: 1065, 1387, 1422, 1442, 1681

été [ete]: 1011, 1016, 1017, 1018, 1020, 1021, 1024, 1025, 1026, 1033, 1034, 1035, 1036, 1038, 1039, 1041, 1045, 1046, 1047, 1049... +37

été [t‿ete]: 1369, 1708

été [z‿ete]: 1019, 1037, 1069

éteindre [etɛ̃dʁ]: 1134

éteinte [etɛ̃t]: 1649

étions [z‿etjɔ̃]: 1178

étonné [t‿etone]: 2000

étonnée [etone]: 2000

étrangères [etʁɑ̃ʒɛʁ]: 1133

être [ɛtʁ]: 1246, 1364, 1413, 1420, 1423, 1428, 1429, 1430, 1431, 1447, 1580, 1595, 1609, 1610, 1611, 1612, 1881, 1883, 1884, 1903

être [s‿etʁ]: 1426

être [z‿etʁ]: 1417, 1580, 1987

étudiants [z‿etydjɑ̃]: 1512

étudie [etydi]: 1513

étudié [etydje]: 1165, 1872

étudier [etydje]: 1455, 1469, 1470, 1471, 1617, 1618, 1764

eu [y]: 1003, 1049, 1406, 1429, 1700, 1701, 1702, 1708, 1725, 1729, 1748

eu [z‿y]: 1509

euro [n‿øʁo]: 1392, 1392

exactement [ɛgzaktˀmɑ̃]: 1528

examen [n‿ɛgzamɛ̃]: 1266, 1271, 1290, 1291, 1500, 1501, 1512, 1521, 1809

excité [ɛksite]: 1429

excitée [ɛksite]: 1429

excuse-moi [ɛkskyz mwa]: 1671

excusez-moi [ɛkskyze mwa]: 1657, 1959

explique [ɛksplik]: 1933

express [ɛkspʁɛs]: 1666

fabrique [fabʁik]: 1091

fabriqué [fabʁike]: 1048

fabriquées [fabʁike]: 1136

face [fas]: 1686, 1725

facile [fasil]: 1508, 1755

faim [fɛ̃]: 1239, 1250, 1322, 1328, 1408, 1427, 1583, 1698, 1699, 1775, 1815, 1826, 1867

faire [fɛʁ]: 1150, 1254, 1334, 1368, 1380, 1409, 1459, 1512, 1528, 1548, 1556, 1557, 1586, 1607, 1755, 1764, 1890, 1891, 1894... +2

fais [fɛ]: 1337, 1385, 1705, 1938

faisais-tu [fˀzɛ ty]: 1103, 1138

faisait [fˀzɛ]: 1090, 1747, 1749

faisait-il [fˀzɛ t‿il]: 1920

faisons [fˀzɔ̃]: 1203, 1637

fais-tu [fɛ ty]: 1100, 1113, 1205, 1234, 1298, 1313, 1337, 1368, 1884, 1892

fait [fɛ]: 1012, 1028, 1061, 1075, 1076, 1078, 1079, 1082, 1170, 1171, 1314, 1327, 1332, 1389, 1508, 1521, 1597, 1635, 1744, 1746... +9

famille [famij]: 1539, 1672

fasse [fas]: 1974

fatigué [fatige]: 1129, 1130, 1154, 1181, 1308, 1329, 1388, 1407, 1413, 1473, 1551, 1572, 1581, 1582, 1634, 1762, 1767, 1800, 1846... +1

fatiguée [fatige]: 1129, 1130, 1154, 1181, 1252, 1278, 1329, 1388, 1407, 1413, 1473, 1551, 1572, 1581, 1634, 1758, 1758, 1762, 1767... +4

fauteuil [fotœj]: 1712, 1713

femme [fam]: 1190, 1957

fenêtre [fᵊnɛtʁ]: 1081, 1106, 1163, 1172, 1173, 1174, 1198, 1314, 1403, 1646, 1709, 1746, 1836

fenêtres [fᵊnɛtʁ]: 1038, 1077, 1077

fera [fʁa]: 1254

ferai [fʁɛ]: 1332, 1966

feras-tu [fʁa ty]: 1372

ferme [fɛʁm]: 1005, 1646

fermé [fɛʁme]: 1096, 1836

fermée [fɛʁme]: 1446

ferment-ils [fɛʁmã t‿il]: 1124

fermer [fɛʁme]: 1962

fête [fɛt]: 1009, 1019, 1039, 1069, 1086, 1088, 1135, 1203, 1209, 1220, 1228, 1231, 1242, 1247, 1343, 1355, 1357, 1385... +11

fêtes [fɛt]: 1015

fiable [fjabl]: 1980

fièvre [fjɛvʁ]: 1441

file [fil]: 1726

filet [filɛ]: 1516

film [film]: 1053, 1177, 1193, 1211, 1233, 1296, 1456, 1619, 1620, 1640, 1687, 1760, 1765, 1773, 1786, 1873, 1881, 1932... +1

fin [fɛ̃]: 1278, 1512

fini [fini]: 1966

finisse [finis]: 1878

finit-il [fini t‿il]: 1211

fleurs [flœʁ]: 1094, 1710, 1861

fois [fwa]: 1007, 1160, 1417, 1850, 1863, 1877, 1956

fonctionnait [fɔ̃ksjonɛ]: 1859

fonctionne [fɔ̃ksjon]: 1859

font [fɔ̃]: 1077, 1084, 1085, 1168

football [futbɔl]: 1040, 1065, 1619, 1620, 1663, 1664, 1854

formation [fɔʁmasjɔ̃]: 1955

fort [fɔʁ]: 1508, 1771

forte [fɔʁt]: 1191

forts [fɔʁ]: 1745

fracassé [fʁakase]: 1172, 1173

fracassée [fʁakase]: 1174

français [fʁɑ̃sɛ]: 1382, 1905

francfort [fʁɑ̃kfɔʁ]: 1259

frappé [fʁape]: 1879, 1882

frapper [fʁape]: 1516

fréquence [fʁekɑ̃s]: 1014, 1892

frère [fʁɛʁ]: 1187, 1381, 1414, 1523, 1602, 1670, 1776

friandise [fʁijɑ̃diz]: 1543, 1626

froid [fʁwa]: 1327, 1635, 1750

fruits [fʁɥi]: 1474

fumer [fyme]: 1496

fumés [fyme]: 1095

gagné [gaɲe]: 1189, 1372

gagner [gaɲe]: 1292

garage [gaʁaʒ]: 1042, 1061

garçon [gaʁsɔ̃]: 1877

garde [gaʁd]: 1451

gare [gaʁ]: 1740, 1961

garer [gaʁe]: 1031, 1888, 1936

gâteau [gato]: 1170

généralement [ʒeneʁalᵊmã]: 1065, 1113, 1132, 1454, 1674, 1805

génial [ʒenjal]: 1955

genre [ʒɑ̃ʁ]: 1574, 1848, 1857

gens [ʒɑ̃]: 1496, 1662, 1703, 1902, 1917, 1929

gentil [ʒɑ̃ti]: 1755

gentille [ʒɑ̃tij]: 1869

grand [gʁɑ̃]: 1487, 1694, 1695

grande [gʁɑ̃d]: 1433, 1613, 1614, 1615, 1616

grand-père [gʁɑ̃pɛʁ]: 1540

gravement [gʁavᵊmã]: 1157

grève [gʁɛv]: 1878

gros [gʁo]: 1654, 1659

j'aille  [ʒ‿aj]: 1360

j'aime  [ʒ‿ɛm]: 1111, 1330, 1333, 1403, 1555, 1568, 1756, 1796, 1816, 1969, 1990

j'aimerais  [ʒ‿ɛm°ʁɛ]: 1549, 1550, 1551, 1554, 1572, 1579, 1584, 1804

j'allume  [ʒ‿alym]: 1340, 1649

jamais  [ʒamɛ]: 1007, 1015, 1094, 1108, 1109, 1184, 1190, 1438, 1842, 1871

jambe  [ʒãb]: 1186

japonaise  [ʒaponɛz]: 1798

jardin  [ʒaʁdɛ̃]: 1261, 1654, 1659

j'aurai  [ʒ‿oʁɛ]: 1282, 1927, 1966

j'avais  [ʒ‿avɛ]: 1699, 1749, 1942

je  [ʒø]: 1007, 1009, 1015, 1022, 1037, 1058, 1069, 1073, 1087, 1094, 1098, 1101, 1111, 1115, 1129, 1130... +360

j'écris  [ʒ‿ekʁi]: 1832

j'en  [ʒ‿ã]: 1637, 1656

j'espère  [ʒ‿ɛspɛʁ]: 1944, 1947, 1950

j'essaie  [ʒ‿ɛsɛ]: 1624

j'étais  [ʒ‿ete]: 1181, 1386, 1388, 1407, 1502, 1541, 1822, 1937, 2000

jeune  [ʒœn]: 1386, 1541

jeunes  [ʒœn]: 1490

j'irai  [ʒ‿iʁɛ]: 1344, 1344, 1367, 1368

j'occupais  [ʒ‿okypɛ]: 1939

john  [john]: 1950

joins-tu  [ʒwɛ̃ ty]: 1229

jolies  [ʒoli]: 1837, 1861

joue  [ʒu]: 1200, 1216, 1243, 1351, 1373

joué  [ʒwe]: 1189

jouent  [ʒu]: 1199

jouer  [ʒwe]: 1329, 1351, 1381, 1397, 1447, 1560, 1561, 1638, 1781, 1870

jouera  [ʒuʁa]: 1560

joues  [ʒu]: 1457

joueur  [ʒwœʁ]: 1447

joueurs  [ʒwœ]: 1663

joueurs  [ʒwœʁ]: 1664, 1682

jour  [ʒuʁ]: 1149, 1255, 1440, 1537, 1538, 1734, 1876

journal  [ʒuʁnal]: 1670, 1992

journaliste  [ʒuʁnalist]: 1611, 1612

journée  [ʒuʁne]: 1248, 1309, 1316, 1319, 1427, 1435, 1630, 1722, 1747, 1834, 1860, 1953

jours  [ʒuʁ]: 1010, 1025, 1027, 1034, 1064, 1104, 1159, 1168, 1277, 1284, 1432, 1653, 1680, 1900, 1906, 1910

joyeux  [ʒwajø]: 1801

jus  [ʒy]: 1554, 1555, 1585, 1600

jusqu'au  [ʒysko]: 1520

jusque  [ʒysk]: 1192

kilomètres  [kilomɛtʁ]: 1398, 1537, 1735

l'a  [l‿a]: 1096, 1097, 1335, 1885

la  [la]: 1006, 1009, 1019, 1033, 1039, 1040, 1041, 1046, 1049, 1051, 1054, 1055, 1060, 1061, 1066... +210

là  [la]: 1417

l'accident  [l‿aksidã]: 1020, 1035, 1157

l'acheter  [l‿aʃ°te]: 1330, 1331, 1487

l'aéroport  [l‿aeʁopɔʁ]: 1675, 1727, 1735, 1743, 1769, 1935, 1935

l'ai  [l‿ɛ]: 1007, 1009, 1193, 1773, 1805, 1840, 1871

l'aider  [l‿ede]: 1983

l'aime  [l‿em]: 1869

l'aimes  [l‿em]: 1958

l'air  [l‿ɛʁ]: 1846, 1865, 1894

laisse  [lɛs]: 1261, 1646, 1649

laissé  [lese]: 1970

lait  [lɛ]: 1012, 1434, 1585

l'allemand  [l‿al°mã]: 1443

l'alphabet  [l‿alfabɛ]: 1679

l'an  [l‿ã]: 1187, 1806

langue  [lãg]: 1494

langues  [lãg]: 1044, 1133, 1194, 1406, 1828, 1941

l'anniversaire  [l‿anivɛʁsɛʁ]: 1251, 1288, 1738

l'appartement  [l‿apaʁt°mã]: 1966

l'appeler  [l‿ap°le]: 1324, 1608

l'après-midi  [l‿apʁɛ midi]: 1379

l'argent  [l‿aʁʒã]: 1372, 1656, 1927, 1975, 1977

larissa [laʁisa]: 1871
l'as-tu [l_a ty]: 1179, 1748
l'attendons [l_atɑ̃dɔ̃]: 1648
l'autobus [l_otobys]: 1248, 1418, 1450, 1509, 1639, 1650
l'autre [l_otʁ]: 1192
l'avais-tu [l_avɛ ty]: 1850
lavé [lave]: 1070, 1175
lavée [lave]: 1070
laver [lave]: 1089, 1090, 1241
l'avion [l_avjɔ̃]: 1210
le [lø]: 1010, 1011, 1012, 1018, 1024, 1028, 1033, 1037, 1040, 1041, 1048, 1054, 1063, 1064, 1065, 1079... +130
l'eau [l_o]: 1600
l'école [l_ekɔl]: 1254, 1426, 1728
l'édifice [l_edifis]: 1999
légumes [legym]: 1474
l'électronique [l_elɛktʁonik]: 1617, 1618
l'emploi [l_ɑ̃plwa]: 1406, 1429, 1945
lendemain [lɑ̃d°mɛ̃]: 1054
lentement [lɑ̃t°mɑ̃]: 1514
l'entreprise [l_ɑ̃tʁ°pʁiz]: 1704
l'entrevue [l_ɑ̃tʁ°vy]: 1985
l'enveloppe [l_ɑ̃v°lɔp]: 1714
leopold [leopold]: 1460
les [le]: 1010, 1013, 1027, 1029, 1042, 1064, 1065, 1077, 1080, 1084, 1085, 1086, 1094, 1104, 1113... +46
l'espagnol [l_espaɲɔl]: 1443
lesquelles [lɛkɛl]: 1828
l'est [l_e]: 1798
l'étais [l_etɛ]: 1762, 1800, 1820
l'était [l_etɛ]: 1801
lettre [lɛtʁ]: 1336
lettres [lɛtʁ]: 1679
leur [lœʁ]: 1299
levé [l°ve]: 1533
levée [l°ve]: 1533
lever [l°ve]: 1375, 1486, 1499, 1507, 1522, 1524, 1533, 1752, 1889, 1969
l'examen [l_egzamɛ̃]: 1268

l'exercice [l_egzɛʁsis]: 1334
l'expliquer [l_eksplike]: 1160
l'explosion [l_eksplozjɔ̃]: 1880
l'extérieur [l_eksteʁjœʁ]: 1284, 1705
l'herbe [l_ɛʁb]: 1078, 1078
l'heure [l_œʁ]: 1580, 1629
l'hôpital [l_opital]: 1021, 1047, 1540
l'horloge [l_ɔʁlɔʒ]: 1859
l'hôtel [l_otɛl]: 1049, 1493, 1737, 1741
libre [libʁ]: 1298
libres [libʁ]: 1938
lieu [ljø]: 1065
l'information [l_ɛ̃fɔʁmasjɔ̃]: 1550
l'ingénierie [l_ɛ̃ʒeniʁi]: 1165
l'intérieur [l_ɛ̃teʁjœʁ]: 1714, 1717
lire [liʁ]: 1477, 1513, 1596, 1992
lit [li]: 1181, 1265, 1287, 1308, 1460, 1473, 1522, 1572, 1752, 1853, 1910
litres [litʁ]: 1434
littérature [liteʁatyʁ]: 1513
livre [livʁ]: 1477, 1665, 1778, 1832
livres [livʁ]: 1237, 1513, 1711
l'obligeance [l_obliʒɑ̃s]: 1962, 1963
l'œil [l_œj]: 1685
loin [lwɛ̃]: 1751
londres [lɔ̃dʁ°]: 1058
longtemps [lɔ̃tɑ̃]: 1151, 1185, 1509, 1525
longue [lɔ̃g]: 1726
l'opposé [l_opoze]: 1713
l'ordinateur [l_ɔʁdinatœʁ]: 1093
lors [lɔʁ]: 1020, 1157, 1985
lorsque [lɔʁsk°]: 1424, 1476, 1726
lorsqu'elle [lɔʁsk ɛl]: 1101
lorsqu'il [lɔʁsk il]: 1254, 1991
lorsqu'on [lɔʁsk ɔ̃]: 1453
loterie [lɔt°ʁi]: 1349
lourd [luʁ]: 1889
lourde [luʁd]: 1306
lu [ly]: 1778
lui [lɥi]: 1005, 1007, 1008, 1251, 1336, 1514, 1608, 1758, 1759, 1807, 1862, 1913, 1914, 1995
lumière [lymjɛʁ]: 1649

lumières [lymjɛʁ]: 1453, 1963
lundi [lœdi]: 1224, 1288
lunes [lyn]: 1906
lunettes [lynɛt]: 1421, 1424, 1511, 1789
l'université [l_ynivɛʁsite]: 1606, 1872
l'usine [l_yzin]: 1424
l'utilise [l_ytiliz]: 1093
lycéens [liseɛ̃]: 1445
m'a [m_a]: 1050, 1067, 1068, 1069, 1095, 1847, 1909, 1910, 1912, 1915
ma [ma]: 1054, 1059, 1061, 1067, 1157, 1164, 1166, 1169, 1306, 1405, 1539, 1672, 1760, 1765, 1781, 1789... +7
machine [maʃin]: 1089, 1090, 1421
madame [madam]: 1434, 1435
magasin [magazɛ̃]: 1434, 1716
magasins [magazɛ̃]: 1124
magnifique [maɲifik]: 1860
m'aider [m_ede]: 1866
m'aime [m_ɛm]: 1845
main [mɛ̃]: 1898
mains [mɛ̃]: 1175, 1241
maintenant [mɛ̃t°nã]: 1089, 1256, 1324, 1387, 1463, 1486, 1486, 1518, 1535, 1572, 1578, 1579, 1598, 1599, 1642, 1644, 1691... +6
mais [mɛ]: 1003, 1005, 1007, 1045, 1054, 1065, 1111, 1133, 1135, 1157, 1158, 1189, 1190, 1228, 1346, 1380, 1382, 1383, 1385... +80
maison [mɛzɔ̃]: 1016, 1033, 1045, 1107, 1132, 1140, 1140, 1144, 1159, 1206, 1207, 1230, 1230, 1231, 1260, 1263, 1284, 1371, 1377, 1416... +27
maisons [mɛzɔ̃]: 1017, 1062, 1084, 1092, 1142, 1671, 1724, 1874
mal [mal]: 1441, 1907
malade [malad]: 1412, 1491, 1822, 1827, 1844
manager [manadʒe]: 1704
mange [mãʒ]: 1568, 1797, 1829, 1849
mangé [mãʒe]: 1427, 1867

mangeons [mãʒɔ̃]: 1633, 1636
manger [mãʒe]: 1250, 1261, 1317, 1320, 1328, 1370, 1437, 1474, 1479, 1570, 1583, 1698, 1699, 1924
mangeras-tu [mãʒ°ʁa ty]: 1370
mangés [mãʒe]: 1155
mange-t-il [mãʒ t_il]: 1829, 1849
manteau [mãto]: 1300, 1464, 1487, 1890
m'appeler [m_ap°le]: 1260, 1885
m'appellerait [m_apɛl°ʁɛ]: 1900
marathon [maʁatɔ̃]: 1187
marcher [maʁʃe]: 1248, 1334, 1737
mardi [maʁdi]: 1734
mari [maʁi]: 1798
mariage [maʁjaʒ]: 1052, 1240, 1808
marie [maʁi]: 1225
marié [maʁje]: 1776
mariée [maʁje]: 1776, 1830, 1946
marier [maʁje]: 1295, 1490
marieront [maʁiʁɔ̃]: 1295
mariés [maʁje]: 1145
m'asseoir [m_aswaʁ]: 1309, 1323, 1359, 1576, 1587, 1589, 1590
match [matʃ]: 1189, 1619, 1620, 1854
matin [matɛ̃]: 1210, 1239, 1287, 1289, 1299, 1377, 1438, 1602, 1647, 1696, 1752, 1794, 1820
m'attends [m_atã]: 1643
mauvais [movɛ]: 1416, 1436, 1986
mauvaise [movɛz]: 1041
me [mø]: 1120, 1163, 1175, 1176, 1186, 1241, 1286, 1329, 1335, 1384, 1449, 1484, 1507, 1522, 1524, 1536, 1537, 1551... +20
médecin [medsɛ̃]: 1492
même [mɛm]: 1415
mêmes [mɛm]: 1440, 1452
m'emmener [m_ãm°ne]: 1961
merci [mɛʁsi]: 1607
mercredi [mɛʁkʁ°di]: 1734
mère [mɛʁ]: 1059, 1139, 1789, 1839, 1840
mes [me]: 1068, 1073, 1074, 1095, 1132, 1226, 1415, 1431, 1511,

1672, 1705, 1783, 1791, 1795, 1879, 1938, 1960

message [mesaʒ]: 1824

messages [mesaʒ]: 1696, 1697

métro [metʁo]: 1538

mets [mɛ]: 1370

mets-tu [mɛ ty]: 1300

mettre [mɛtʁ]: 1640

mexique [mexique]: 1799

mieux [mjø]: 1287, 1584, 1889

milieu [miljø]: 1191

militaire [militɛʁ]: 1510

mille [mil]: 1022, 1024, 1053, 1694, 1695, 1728

milles [mil]: 1537

mince [mɛ̃s]: 1437

m'interrompre [m ɛ̃tɛʁɔ̃pʁ]: 1972

minuit [minɥi]: 1232, 1280

minute [minyt]: 1391, 1391

minutes [minyt]: 1283, 1509, 1675, 1823, 1887

moi [mwa]: 1325, 1341, 1430, 1559, 1561, 1563, 1628, 1672, 1696, 1697, 1765, 1766, 1771, 1774, 1777, 1780, 1781, 1782, 1784... +7

moi-même [mwamɛm]: 1607

moins [mwɛ̃]: 1442

mois [mwa]: 1033, 1225

moment [momɑ̃]: 1087, 1093, 1099, 1276, 1595

mon [mɔ̃]: 1034, 1087, 1179, 1187, 1381, 1408, 1414, 1438, 1540, 1565, 1656, 1776, 1789, 1798, 1915, 1939

monde [mɔ̃d]: 1040, 1494, 1495, 1755, 1869, 1883, 1965

monnaie [monɛ]: 1384, 1392

montagnes [mɔ̃taɲ]: 1403

monté [mɔ̃te]: 1108, 1184

monter [mɔ̃te]: 1401

m'ont-ils [m ɔ̃ t il]: 1536

montrer [mɔ̃tʁe]: 1163, 1996

montrerai [mɔ̃tʁ°ʁɛ]: 1326

mordu [mɔʁdy]: 1025

mordue [mɔʁdy]: 1025

moscou [moscou]: 1530

mot [mo]: 1030, 1032, 1162

moto [moto]: 1400, 1973

mur [myʁ]: 1709

musée [myze]: 1475, 1719, 1802

musique [myzik]: 1161, 1191, 1574, 1640, 1816

n'a [n a]: 1019, 1045, 1097, 1116, 1189, 1417, 1508, 1532, 1534, 1564, 1943, 1985

nagé [naʒe]: 1192

nager [naʒe]: 1383, 1395, 1638

nageur [naʒœʁ]: 1383

nageuse [naʒøz]: 1383

n'ai [n ɛ]: 1037, 1069, 1094, 1115, 1190, 1239, 1332, 1372, 1408, 1410, 1577, 1760, 1778, 1791, 1803, 1826, 1853, 1867

n'aie [n ɛ]: 1366

n'aime [n em]: 1111, 1575, 1580, 1668, 1770, 1787, 1833, 1893

n'aimeras [n em°ʁa]: 1296

n'aimes [n em]: 1484

n'arrive [n aʁiv]: 1409, 1973

n'arrivera [n aʁiv°ʁa]: 1289

n'as [n a]: 1285, 1427, 1488, 1531, 1840, 1867, 1960

n'as-tu [n a ty]: 1596

nature [natyʁ]: 1692, 1693

n'aurai [n oʁɛ]: 1705

n'avaient [n avɛ]: 1536

n'avais [n avɛ]: 1408, 1533

n'avais-tu [n avɛ ty]: 1903

n'avait [n avɛ]: 1775

n'avez-vous [n ave vu]: 1959

n'avions [n avjɔ̃]: 1102

n'avons [n avɔ̃]: 1189, 1509, 1535, 1583, 1719

né [ne]: 1022, 1023, 1043, 1055, 1058, 1729, 1852

ne [nø]: 1005, 1007, 1015, 1069, 1073, 1087, 1088, 1096, 1097, 1099, 1102, 1104, 1112, 1128, 1129, 1130, 1131, 1132, 1133... +203

née [ne]: 1022, 1023, 1043, 1056, 1058, 1059, 1139, 1852

neige  [neʒ]: 1363, 1658, 1814

neiger  [neʒe]: 1363

neige-t-il  [neʒ t il]: 1814

n'en  [n ɑ̃]: 1568, 1810, 1812, 1927

nerveuse  [nɛʁvøz]: 1914

n'es  [n ɛ]: 1868, 1888

nés  [ne]: 1057

n'est  [n e]: 1030, 1071, 1108, 1109, 1159, 1380, 1416, 1430, 1436, 1515, 1669, 1758, 1827, 1839, 1889, 1980

n'est-ce  [n e sø]: 1834, 1835, 1836, 1837, 1838, 1839, 1840, 1841, 1842, 1860, 1861, 1862, 1863, 1864, 1865, 1866, 1867, 1868, 1869, 1870... +12

n'étaient  [n ete]: 1052

n'étais  [n ete]: 1780

n'était  [n ete]: 1873, 1907

n'était-il  [n ete t il]: 1925

n'étions  [n etjɔ̃]: 1088

nettoie  [netwa]: 1010, 1063, 1077, 1079

nettoyé  [netwaje]: 1010, 1011, 1063, 1064, 1105, 1164, 1166

nettoyée  [netwaje]: 1071, 1072

nettoyées  [netwaje]: 1014, 1027, 1149, 1168

nettoyer  [netwaje]: 1077, 1079, 1168, 1890, 1966

nettoyés  [netwaje]: 1104

n'étudie  [n etydi]: 1455

neuf  [nœ]: 1246

neuf  [nœf]: 1022, 1053

new  [nuw]: 1210

nez  [ne]: 1899

nié  [nje]: 1977

noir  [nwaʁ]: 1749

nombreux  [nɔ̃bʁø]: 1541

non  [nɔ̃]: 1052, 1323, 1324, 1325, 1341, 1342, 1384, 1578, 1596, 1607, 1634, 1638, 1639, 1640, 1641, 1642, 1643, 1644, 1645, 1646... +65

nos  [no]: 1195, 1886

n'oserais  [n ozᵊʁɛ]: 1995

notes  [nɔt]: 1445

notre  [nɔtʁ]: 1045, 1894

nourriture  [nuʁityʁ]: 1428, 1519

nous  [nu]: 1088, 1102, 1135, 1177, 1178, 1189, 1191, 1195, 1198, 1203, 1229, 1230, 1251, 1262... +44

nouveau  [nuvo]: 1156, 1188, 1704, 1832, 1908, 1908

nouveaux  [nuvo]: 1462, 1472

nouvel  [nuvɛ]: 1282, 1484, 1571, 1994

nouvelle  [nuvɛl]: 1152, 1335, 1831, 1848

nouvelles  [nuvɛl]: 1062

nuageux  [nɥaʒø]: 1744

nuit  [nɥi]: 1118, 1128, 1172, 1174, 1176, 1191, 1388, 1748, 1757

nulle  [nyl]: 1677

numéro  [nymeʁo]: 1416, 1436

n'y  [n i]: 1065, 1135, 1228, 1503, 1517, 1655, 1657, 1658, 1661, 1662, 1669, 1674, 1677, 1698, 1699, 1714, 1716, 1717, 1719... +6

obtenir  [ɔptᵊniʁ]: 1500, 1501, 1945

obtenir  [ʁ ɔptᵊni]: 1442

œufs  [z ø]: 1849

œuvres  [z œvʁ]: 1002

offrirons  [ofʁiʁɔ̃]: 1251

oh  [o]: 1324, 1831

oignons  [z ɔɲɔ̃]: 1568

oiseau  [n wazo]: 1198

oiseaux  [z wazo]: 1261

on  [ɔ̃]: 1019, 1042, 1060, 1061, 1062, 1063, 1067, 1068, 1075, 1076, 1077, 1078, 1079, 1080, 1081, 1082, 1083, 1084, 1085, 1086... +32

ont  [ɔ̃]: 1017, 1021, 1035, 1047, 1049, 1065, 1068, 1073, 1074, 1080, 1086, 1092, 1195, 1197, 1415, 1433, 1529, 1880, 1975

ont  [l ɔ̃]: 1026

ont-elles  [ɔ̃ t ɛl]: 1038, 1092, 1136, 1142

ont-ils  [ɔ̃ t il]: 1506, 1529

onze  [ɔ̃z]: 1257, 1258, 1664, 1691

pays [pei]: 1040, 1495, 1510, 1968
peint [pɛ̃]: 1060, 1066
peinte [pɛ̃t]: 1033, 1066
peints [pɛ̃]: 1026
peinture [pɛ̃tyʁ]: 1087
pendant [pɑ̃dɑ̃]: 1178, 1414
pensais [pɑ̃sɛ]: 1901, 1902, 1906
pense [pɑ̃s]: 1267, 1291, 1292, 1293,
    1295, 1296, 1308, 1309, 1310,
    1325, 1327, 1328, 1329, 1330,
    1331, 1334, 1462, 1463... +25
penses-tu [pɑ̃s ty]: 1268, 1301, 1467,
    1468, 1482, 1483, 1484, 1485,
    1648, 1703, 1763, 1809, 1945,
    1947, 1950, 1988
perdre [pɛʁdʁ]: 1451
perdu [pɛʁdy]: 1146, 1179, 1850, 1993
père [pɛʁ]: 1789
permis [pɛʁmi]: 1031, 1442, 1500,
    1501, 1895, 1942
pérou [peʁu]: 1806
personne [pɛʁsɔn]: 1069, 1869, 1875,
    1902, 1912
personnes [pɛʁsɔn]: 1021, 1035, 1047,
    1672, 1718, 1880
perte [pɛʁt]: 1970
petit [pˀti]: 1239, 1523, 1613, 1614
petite [pˀtit]: 1615, 1616
peu [pø]: 1578, 1579, 1599, 1642,
    1718, 1905
peur [pøʁ]: 1689, 1749, 1948, 1949
peut [pø]: 1302, 1381, 1382, 1403,
    1406, 1411, 1658, 1733, 1777, 1781
peut-être [pø ɛtʁ]: 1350, 1763, 1810
peut-être [pøtɛtʁ]: 1344, 1346, 1347,
    1348, 1349, 1351, 1353, 1354,
    1355, 1356, 1357, 1360, 1361,
    1362, 1363, 1364, 1365, 1366,
    1367, 1368... +13
peuvent [pœv]: 1385, 1523
peux [pø]: 1087, 1134, 1232, 1260,
    1339, 1358, 1359, 1381, 1384,
    1470, 1761, 1804, 1870, 1930
peux-tu [pø ty]: 1160, 1163, 1383,
    1384, 1390, 1391, 1395, 1396,
    1397, 1398, 1399, 1400, 1401,
    1930, 1935

philippines [filipin]: 1194
philosophie [filozofi]: 1617, 1618
photo [foto]: 1050, 1151, 1670, 1893
piano [pjano]: 1381, 1781, 1870
pièce [pjɛs]: 1314, 1340, 1746
pièces [pjɛs]: 1014
pied [pje]: 1503, 1517, 1604, 1639
pilote [pilɔt]: 1609, 1610
piloter [pilote]: 1733
piscine [pisin]: 1715
plage [plaʒ]: 1095, 1741
plaisait [plɛzɛ]: 1005
plaît [plɛ]: 1098, 1156, 1390, 1391,
    1392, 1394, 1550, 1554, 1573,
    1585, 1623, 1624, 1761, 1933
plan [plɑ̃]: 1883
planètes [planet]: 1678
plans [plɑ̃]: 1304
plastique [plastik]: 1959
pleut [plø]: 1099, 1153, 1310, 1564,
    1750, 1823
pleuvait [pløvɛ]: 1102
pleuvoir [pløvwaʁ]: 1245, 1267, 1345,
    1348, 1598, 1944
pleuvra [pløvʁa]: 1285
plu [ply]: 1116, 1178
pluie [plɥi]: 1706
plupart [plypaʁ]: 1040, 1442
plus [ply]: 1426, 1455
plus [plys]: 1071, 1287, 1289, 1332,
    1352, 1353, 1428, 1497, 1637,
    1728, 1800, 1905, 1943, 1956
plusieurs [plyzjœ]: 1051
plusieurs [plyzjœʁ]: 1194, 1510, 1863
plutôt [plyto]: 1303, 1587, 1589, 1590,
    1592, 1593, 1594, 1595, 1610,
    1612, 1614, 1616, 1618, 1620,
    1908, 1954
poids [pwa]: 1970, 1993
poisson [pwasɔ̃]: 1633, 1636, 1829
police [polis]: 1054, 1725, 1877
policier [polisje]: 1879, 1882
pont [pɔ̃]: 1036, 1076, 1096, 1147
populaire [popylɛʁ]: 1428

porte [pɔʁt]: 1060, 1066, 1390, 1432, 1440, 1712, 1789, 1962

portefeuille [pɔʁtᵊfœj]: 1656, 1717

porter [pɔʁte]: 1247, 1421, 1424, 1444, 1476, 1511

porteras-tu [pɔʁtᵊʁa ty]: 1240

poser [poze]: 1358

possible [posibl]: 1360, 1361, 1362, 1363, 1364, 1365, 1366, 1979

postal [pɔstal]: 1415

postale [pɔstal]: 1321

poste [pɔst]: 1029

postulais [postulais]: 1940

poulet [pulɛ]: 1636

pour [pu]: 1252, 1384, 1392, 1418, 1442, 1538, 1895

pour [puʁ]: 1159, 1197, 1284, 1306, 1317, 1320, 1336, 1367, 1370, 1414, 1422, 1430, 1438, 1443, 1447, 1450, 1458, 1459, 1487... +20

pourquoi [puʁkwa]: 1041, 1120, 1144, 1154, 1229, 1300, 1450, 1506, 1529, 1531, 1532, 1533, 1534, 1535, 1536, 1725, 1833, 1845, 1855... +7

pourrais-je [puʁɛ ʒø]: 1392, 1393, 1394

pourrais-tu [puʁɛ ty]: 1390, 1391, 1936, 1961

pourrait [puʁɛ]: 1317, 1320, 1996

pouvaient [puvɛ]: 1389

pouvais [puvɛ]: 1386, 1388, 1407, 1905, 1941, 1981

pouvait [puvɛ]: 1387, 1412

pouvoir [puvwaʁ]: 1500, 1501

pouvons [puvɔ̃]: 1402

pratiqué [pʁatike]: 1040

préfère [pʁefɛʁ]: 1580

préférerais [pʁefeʁᵊʁɛ]: 1576, 1577, 1578, 1581, 1584, 1587, 1589, 1590, 1592, 1593, 1595, 1596, 1597, 1598, 1603, 1603, 1607, 1608, 1610... +5

préférerais-tu [pʁefeʁᵊʁɛ ty]: 1544, 1585, 1586, 1602, 1604, 1605, 1609, 1611, 1613, 1615, 1617, 1619

préférerait [pʁefeʁᵊʁɛ]: 1579, 1582, 1588, 1591, 1606

préférerions [pʁefeʁᵊʁjɔ̃]: 1583, 1594

prend [pʁɑ̃]: 1418, 1626, 1650

prendra [pʁɑ̃dʁa]: 1303

prendre [pʁɑ̃dʁ]: 1239, 1248, 1285, 1322, 1371, 1446, 1538, 1604, 1971

prends [pʁɑ̃]: 1348

prenne [pʁɛn]: 1893

prenons [pʁᵊnɔ̃]: 1639, 1650

préparer [pʁepaʁe]: 1913

près [pʁɛ]: 1121, 1415, 1657, 1661, 1671, 1709, 1712, 1874

présentement [pʁezɑ̃tᵊmɑ̃]: 1063

président [pʁezidɑ̃]: 1253

présume [pʁezym]: 1879

prêt [pʁɛ]: 1246, 1283, 1623, 1632, 1785

prête [pʁɛt]: 1246, 1623, 1632, 1785

prétendent [pʁetɑ̃d]: 1998

prétendu [pʁetɑ̃dy]: 1991, 1992

prise [pʁiz]: 1151

privé [pʁive]: 1888

prix [pʁi]: 1954

probablement [pʁobablᵊmɑ̃]: 1262, 1764, 1838

problème [pʁoblɛm]: 1160, 1676, 1730, 1998

prochain [pʁoʃɛ̃]: 1065, 1203, 1225, 1288, 1402, 1411, 1556

prochaine [pʁoʃɛn]: 1135, 1201, 1209, 1221, 1226, 1240, 1249, 1251, 1259, 1275, 1365, 1385, 1520, 1562, 1563, 1751, 1858, 1903

professionnellement [pʁofɛsjonɛlᵊmɑ̃]: 1447

profite [pʁofit]: 1321

promener [pʁomne]: 1316, 1319, 1545, 1567

promis [pʁomi]: 1987

promotion [pʁomosjɔ̃]: 1947

prononcé [pʁonɔ̃se]: 1032, 1162

propos [pʁopo]: 1550, 1914

propre [pʁopʁ]: 1149

prudent [pʁydɑ̃]: 1420

prudente [pʁydɑ̃t]: 1420
prudentes [pʁydɑ̃t]: 1423
prudents [pʁydɑ̃]: 1423
psychologie [psikoloʒi]: 1872
pu [py]: 1408
puis-je [pɥi ʒø]: 1314, 1359, 1392,
  1393, 1394, 1554, 1607, 1724, 1930
qu'aimerais-tu [k‿ɛmˀʁɛ ty]: 1548,
  1556, 1566
qu'aimes-tu [k‿ɛm ty]: 1557
qu'aleksey [k (...)]: 1052
quand [kɑ̃]: 1018, 1036, 1046, 1092,
  1142, 1145, 1223, 1347, 1369,
  1386, 1439, 1457, 1530, 1541,
  1699, 1727, 1850, 1966, 1969,
  1972... +1
quarante [kaʁɑ̃t]: 1299
quartier [kaʁtje]: 1724
qu'a-t-elle [k‿a t‿ɛl]: 1847
quatre [katʁ]: 1828
quatre-vingt-neuf [katʁˀvɛ̃nœf]: 1022
quatre-vingts [katʁˀvɛ̃]: 1537
qu'ayman [k (...)]: 1266
que [kø]: 1020, 1027, 1070, 1093,
  1100, 1103, 1113, 1114, 1126,
  1138, 1140, 1178, 1181, 1195,
  1198, 1205, 1234, 1240, 1247...
  +125
quel [kɛ]: 1053, 1092, 1918, 1984
quel [kɛl]: 1574, 1734, 1848, 1857,
  1920
qu'elle [k‿ɛl]: 1252, 1406, 1489, 1809,
  1847, 1876, 1878, 1900, 1903,
  1909, 1946, 1990
quelle [kɛ]: 1117, 1124, 1141, 1211,
  1214, 1215, 1222, 1233, 1468,
  1504, 1524, 1569, 1928, 1928,
  1932, 1932
quelle [kɛl]: 1014, 1737, 1740, 1741,
  1742, 1743, 1861, 1892, 1935
qu'elles [k‿ɛl]: 1073, 1175
quelque [kɛlk]: 1244, 1328, 1337,
  1432, 1459, 1526, 1536, 1549,
  1570, 1685, 1687, 1819
quelques [kɛl]: 1229, 1249, 1305, 1338

quelques [kɛlk]: 1007, 1025, 1034,
  1159, 1237, 1284, 1509, 1573,
  1710, 1711, 1874, 1900, 1906, 1910
quelques-unes [kɛlkˀzyn]: 1002
quelques-uns [kɛlkˀzœ̃]: 1001
quelqu'un [kɛlkœ̃]: 1010, 1011, 1020,
  1045, 1060, 1066, 1067, 1068,
  1070, 1093, 1172, 1173, 1727,
  1803, 1996
quels [kɛl]: 1304
qu'emily [k (...)]: 1558
qu'en [k‿ɑ̃]: 1303, 1372
qu'est-ce [kɛsˀ]: 1126, 1254, 1317,
  1320, 1621, 1688, 1847
question [kɛstjɔ̃]: 1358, 1967
questions [kɛstjɔ̃]: 1521
qu'être [k‿ɛtʁ]: 1595
qu'euna [k (...)]: 1290
qu'hakim [k (...)]: 1362
qu'helen [k (...)]: 1562
qui [ki]: 1343, 1445, 1652, 1803, 1912,
  1919, 1921, 1929, 1957
qu'ichirou [k (...)]: 1960
qu'il [k‿il]: 1267, 1345, 1363, 1492,
  1598, 1661, 1687, 1703, 1730,
  1749, 1877, 1879, 1901, 1907
qu'ils [k‿il]: 1295, 1490
qu'ingrid [k (...)]: 1809
quinze [kɛ̃z]: 1281, 1691
qu'iris [k (...)]: 1294
quoi [kwa]: 1409, 1832, 1889, 1999,
  2000
qu'on [k‿ɔ̃]: 1317, 1320, 1486, 1637,
  1648, 1893, 1961, 1974
qu'un [k‿œ̃]: 1593, 1610, 1612, 1620
qu'une [k‿yn]: 1616
qu'y [k‿i]: 1685
raconter [ʁakɔ̃te]: 1912
raconteras [ʁakɔ̃tˀʁa]: 1875
randonnée [ʁɑ̃done]: 1368
rapide [ʁapid]: 1196
rapidement [ʁapidˀmɑ̃]: 1197, 1895
rapporte [ʁapɔʁt]: 1880
réalisé [ʁealize]: 1053
recherche [ʁˀʃɛʁʃ]: 1877

refait [ʀ°fɛ]: 1087

regarde [ʀ°gaʀd]: 1134, 1245, 1333, 1621, 1670, 1700, 1792

regardé [ʀ°gaʀde]: 1115, 1915

regardée [ʀ°gaʀde]: 1915

regarder [ʀ°gaʀde]: 1235, 1236, 1253, 1312, 1457, 1461, 1478, 1586, 1594, 1596, 1601, 1619, 1620, 1854

regardera [ʀ°gaʀd°ʀa]: 1378

regardes [ʀ°gaʀd]: 1120, 1461

regardes-tu [ʀ°gaʀd ty]: 1120

regardez [ʀ°gaʀde]: 1807

règles [ʀɛgl]: 1452

regrette [ʀ°gʀɛt]: 1976

relaxer [ʀ°lakse]: 1914

remarques [ʀ°maʀk]: 1953, 1954, 1956, 1957

remettre [ʀ°mɛtʀ]: 1979

remy [ʀ°mi]: 1945

rencontre [ʀãkɔ̃tʀ]: 1218, 1230

rencontré [ʀãkɔ̃tʀe]: 1190, 1840

rencontrée [ʀãkɔ̃tʀe]: 1009, 1840, 1871

rencontrées [ʀãkɔ̃tʀe]: 1922

rencontrer [ʀãkɔ̃tʀe]: 1302, 1887

rencontrés [ʀãkɔ̃tʀe]: 1922

rencontres-tu [ʀãkɔ̃tʀ ty]: 1204

rencontrons [ʀãkɔ̃tʀɔ̃]: 1230

rend [ʀã]: 1520

rendre [ʀãdʀ]: 1537, 1805

rentrait [ʀãtʀɛ]: 1877

rentré [ʀãtʀe]: 1140, 1144

rentrée [ʀãtʀe]: 1144

rentrer [ʀãtʀe]: 1232, 1468, 1486, 1503, 1517, 1604, 1639, 1644, 1982

rentreras-tu [ʀãtʀ°ʀa ty]: 1371

rentres-tu [ʀãtʀ ty]: 1231

rentrons [ʀãtʀɔ̃]: 1644

répare [ʀepaʀ]: 1042, 1061, 1075, 1082

réparé [ʀepaʀe]: 1096, 1097

réparée [ʀepaʀe]: 1089, 1169

réparer [ʀepaʀe]: 1061, 1075, 1082, 1090

repassé [ʀ°pase]: 1080

repassées [ʀ°pase]: 1080

répéter [ʀepete]: 1439

répondre [ʀepɔ̃dʀ]: 1521

répondu [ʀepɔ̃dy]: 1417

résolu [ʀezoly]: 1998

restais [ʀɛste]: 1904

restaurant [ʀɛstoʀã]: 1004, 1372, 1428, 1641, 1662, 1689, 1954

restaurants [ʀɛstoʀã]: 1661

reste [ʀɛst]: 1206, 1207, 1325, 1628

rester [ʀɛste]: 1551, 1577, 1587, 1589, 1590, 1592, 1603, 1910

restons [ʀɛstɔ̃]: 1634, 1635

retard [ʀ°taʀ]: 1246, 1289, 1364, 1426, 1449, 1450, 1498, 1502, 1580, 1629, 1720, 1780, 1821, 1842, 1886, 1987

retirer [ʀ°tiʀe]: 1895

retour [ʀ°tuʀ]: 1900

retourné [ʀ°tuʀne]: 1729

retraite [ʀ°tʀɛt]: 1971

retrouvée [ʀ°tʀuve]: 1054

réunion [ʀeynjɔ̃]: 1412, 1718, 1917

réussi [ʀeysi]: 1410, 1985

réveil [ʀevɛj]: 1907

réveillé [ʀeveje]: 1037

réveillée [ʀeveje]: 1037

réveillés [ʀeveje]: 1191

reverras-tu [ʀ°vɛʀa ty]: 1369

revoir [ʀ°vwaʀ]: 1753

rhume [ʀym]: 1441

rien [ʀjɛ̃]: 1045, 1298, 1427, 1655, 1698, 1699, 1714

rire [ʀiʀ]: 1981

rivière [ʀivjɛʀ]: 1192

roman [ʀomã]: 1596

rouge [ʀuʒ]: 1686

rouler [ʀule]: 1425

route [ʀut]: 1446, 1660, 1674, 1701

rue [ʀy]: 1991

rues [ʀy]: 1149

sa [sa]: 1135, 1161, 1190, 1238, 1523, 1894, 1971

sable [sabl]: 1028

sac [sak]: 1179, 1898, 1915, 1959

s'acheter [s̩ aʃ°te]: 1335

sinon [sinɔ̃]: 1265, 1449

situation [sitɥasjɔ̃]: 1423, 1914, 1983

six [si]: 1433, 1499

six [sis]: 1521

skier [skje]: 1396, 1658

s'occuper [s̬okype]: 1523

sœur [sœʁ]: 1006, 1760, 1765, 1781, 1796, 1871

sœurs [sœʁ]: 1672

sofa [sofa]: 1713

soif [swaf]: 1549

soir [swaʁ]: 1100, 1129, 1130, 1137, 1154, 1204, 1205, 1206, 1207, 1208, 1211, 1228, 1229, 1233, 1235, 1236, 1247, 1253, 1260, 1262... +62

sois [swa]: 1364, 1629

soit [swa]: 1365, 1889, 1946

soixante-cinq [swasãtsɛ̃k]: 1053

soixante-seize [swasãtsɛz]: 1024

solaire [solɛʁ]: 1678

soleil [solɛj]: 1123, 1953

sombre [sɔ̃bʁ]: 1340

sommes [sɔm]: 1088, 1726, 1734

sommes-nous [sɔm nu]: 1734, 1922

son [sɔ̃]: 1146, 1266, 1278, 1290, 1291, 1294, 1515, 1809, 1889, 1895, 1896, 1898, 1900, 1907, 1908, 1994

songé [sɔ̃ʒe]: 1968

sonne [sɔn]: 1430

sonné [sone]: 1417

sont [sɔ̃]: 1013, 1027, 1029, 1051, 1052, 1057, 1062, 1104, 1110, 1132, 1149, 1155, 1168, 1194, 1199, 1304, 1419, 1431, 1490, 1511... +9

sont-elles [sɔ̃ t̬el]: 1014, 1861

sont-ils [sɔ̃ t̬il]: 1052, 1117, 1145

sors [sɔʁ]: 1130, 1206, 1229, 1300, 1338, 1904

sors-tu [sɔʁ ty]: 1208, 1350, 1531, 1810

sort [sɔʁ]: 1112, 1564, 1634, 1645, 1841

sorte [sɔʁt]: 1861

sortent [sɔʁt]: 1132

sorti [sɔʁti]: 1137, 1795

sortie [sɔʁti]: 1137, 1795

sorties [sɔʁti]: 1726

sortir [sɔʁtiʁ]: 1129, 1262, 1310, 1327, 1339, 1366, 1366, 1374, 1531, 1577, 1581, 1582, 1584, 1588, 1591, 1592, 1598, 1603, 1986

sortira [sɔʁtiʁa]: 1379

sortis [sɔʁti]: 1117, 1726

sortons [sɔʁtɔ̃]: 1635, 1645

sortons-nous [sɔʁtɔ̃ nu]: 1924

soudainement [sudɛnᵊmã]: 1965

souhaites-tu [swɛt ty]: 1921

soupe [sup]: 1667, 1668

souvent [suvã]: 1030, 1112, 1132, 1158, 1515, 1553, 1568, 1750, 1807

spécial [spesjal]: 1459

sport [spɔʁ]: 1333, 1796

sports [spɔʁ]: 1333

station [stasjɔ̃]: 1520

station-service [stasjɔ̃sɛʁvis]: 1751

sud [syd]: 1109, 1909

suggéré [sygʒeʁe]: 1964, 1978

suis [sɥi]: 1015, 1022, 1058, 1129, 1130, 1175, 1181, 1184, 1186, 1246, 1289, 1298, 1308, 1344, 1346, 1367, 1369, 1371, 1383... +36

suisse [sɥis]: 1044, 1793

suit [sɥi]: 1227

suite [sɥit]: 1466, 1578, 1583, 1644

suivre [sɥivʁ]: 1452, 1541

supplémentaire [syplemãtɛʁ]: 1562

suppose [sypoz]: 1952

sur [sy]: 1005, 1575

sur [syʁ]: 1051, 1425, 1521, 1651, 1660, 1665, 1701, 1709, 1710, 1711, 1832

sûr [syʁ]: 1233, 1344, 1346, 1359, 1367, 1369, 1371, 1380, 1451, 1809, 1866, 1875, 1968, 1996

sûre [syʁ]: 1346, 1367, 1369, 1371, 1809

sûres [syʁ]: 1757

suspicieux [syspisjø]: 1915

sympa [sɛ̃pa]: 1009

système [sistɛm]: 1678
t'a [t‿a]: 1847
ta [ta]: 1139, 1242, 1402, 1488, 1607, 1686, 1743, 1839, 1888, 1892
table [tabl]: 1665, 1710
tableaux [tablo]: 1001, 1026
tablettes [tablɛt]: 1711
t'accompagne [t‿akɔ̃paɲ]: 1605
t'accueillir [t‿akœjiʁ]: 1727
t'ai [t‿ɛ]: 1875
t'aider [t‿ede]: 1607, 1777, 1804
t'ai-je [t‿ɛ ʒø]: 1898
t'appeler [t‿ap°le]: 1307, 1318, 1647, 1736
t'appelle [t‿apɛl]: 1315
t'appellera-t-il [t‿apɛl°ʁa t‿il]: 1347
tard [ta]: 1154, 1473
tard [taʁ]: 1332, 1352, 1353, 1460, 1463, 1518, 1732, 1752, 1982
tardait [taʁdɛ]: 1913
tas [ta]: 1003, 1902
t'attendre [t‿atɑ̃dʁ]: 1643
t'attends [t‿atɑ̃]: 1341
taxi [taksi]: 1231, 1604, 1650, 1982
te [tø]: 1127, 1156, 1229, 1287, 1287, 1326, 1361, 1390, 1391, 1441, 1524, 1533, 1545, 1567, 1585, 1622... +7
télé [tele]: 1115, 1134, 1235, 1236, 1253, 1312, 1333, 1461, 1478, 1596, 1601, 1655, 1687, 1692, 1792, 1807, 1854
téléphone [telefɔn]: 1018, 1024, 1034, 1417, 1430
téléphoniques [telefonik]: 1696, 1697
téléscope [teleskop]: 1803
télévision [televizjɔ̃]: 1051, 1378
t'emmène [t‿ɑ̃mɛn]: 1961
tempête [tɑ̃pɛt]: 1748
t'emprunter [t‿ɑ̃pʁœ̃te]: 1393, 1393
temps [tɑ̃]: 1303, 1366, 1461, 1475, 1525, 1625, 1705, 1719, 1774, 1920, 1938, 1939, 1986
t'en [t‿ɑ̃]: 1628
tendance [tɑ̃dɑ̃s]: 1990, 1997

tennis [tenis]: 1199, 1200, 1216, 1243, 1329, 1351, 1373, 1447, 1457, 1516, 1560, 1561, 1638
tentatives [tɑ̃tativ]: 1970
t'entends [t‿ɑ̃tɑ̃]: 1404
t'enverrai [t‿ɑ̃vɛʁɛ]: 1321
termine [tɛʁmin]: 1227
terminé [tɛʁmine]: 1148
terminer [tɛʁmine]: 1408
terminera [tɛʁmin°ʁa]: 1254
terre [tɛʁ]: 1323, 1575, 1576
terrible [tɛʁibl]: 1873
terriblement [tɛʁibl°mɑ̃]: 1441
t'es [t‿ɛ]: 1956
tes [te]: 1136, 1204, 1222, 1304, 1321, 1367, 1959, 1960
t'est-il [t‿e t‿il]: 1916
t'es-tu [t‿ɛ ty]: 1154, 1533, 1818
thé [te]: 1111, 1544, 1597, 1759
théâtre [teatʁ]: 1297
tienne [tjɛn]: 1686
tiens [tjɛ̃]: 1626
timbres [tɛ̃bʁ]: 1029
toi [twa]: 1121, 1306, 1339, 1415, 1430, 1441, 1487, 1558, 1766, 1773, 1807, 1824, 1874
toit [twa]: 1082, 1651
tombe [tɔ̃b]: 1627
tombé [tɔ̃be]: 1186
tombée [tɔ̃be]: 1186
tomber [tɔ̃be]: 1970, 1980
ton [tɔ̃]: 1148, 1156, 1188, 1215, 1271, 1300, 1393, 1414, 1484, 1500, 1501, 1571, 1602, 1670, 1772, 1897, 1955, 1956
tôt [to]: 1144, 1181, 1287, 1308, 1375, 1438, 1466, 1486, 1506, 1507, 1522, 1524, 1529, 1529, 1533, 1752, 1800... +6
toujours [tuʒuʁ]: 1149, 1255, 1419, 1435, 1439, 1457, 1889
touristes [tuʁist]: 1721
tous [tu]: 1010, 1027, 1064, 1104, 1155, 1168, 1197, 1432, 1512

tout [tu]: 1387, 1461, 1466, 1494, 1578, 1583, 1644, 1676, 1730, 1755, 1869, 1883, 1965

toutes [tut]: 1675, 1690

train [tʁɛ̃]: 1063, 1281, 1299, 1520, 1652, 1666, 1690, 1691, 1959

tranquille [tʁɑ̃kil]: 1674

transportées [tʁɑ̃spɔʁte]: 1021

transporter [tʁɑ̃spɔʁte]: 1306

travail [tʁavaj]: 1148, 1156, 1188, 1255, 1256, 1257, 1258, 1438, 1484, 1491, 1498, 1502, 1508, 1515, 1519, 1528, 1537, 1723, 1755... +9

travaillais [tʁavajɛ]: 1101, 1783

travaille [tʁavaj]: 1003, 1098, 1128, 1131, 1201, 1234, 1270, 1302, 1311, 1339, 1454, 1507, 1766, 1771, 1782, 1843, 1857, 1865, 1876... +1

travaillé [tʁavaje]: 1005, 1413, 1414

travailler [tʁavaje]: 1281, 1354, 1411, 1419, 1435, 1454, 1465, 1480, 1499, 1505, 1508, 1534, 1754, 1971

travaillera [tʁavajˀʁa]: 1376

travailles-tu [tʁavaj ty]: 1118, 1221

travaille-t-il [tʁavaj t il]: 1125, 1534, 1952

travaillez [tʁavaje]: 1766

treize [tʁɛz]: 1167

trente [tʁɑ̃t]: 1138, 1210, 1213, 1255, 1652, 1666, 1680, 1683, 1886, 1951

très [tʁɛ]: 1009, 1030, 1129, 1130, 1132, 1151, 1158, 1176, 1177, 1189, 1195, 1196, 1197, 1252, 1278, 1286, 1306, 1308, 1314... +36

trois [tʁwa]: 1035, 1103, 1277, 1433, 1434, 1708, 1820, 1878

trop [tʁo]: 1331, 1466, 1487, 1490, 1493, 1668, 1684, 1754, 1895, 1913, 1990

trottoir [tʁotwaʁ]: 1425

trouve [tʁuv]: 1073, 1405, 1740, 1741, 1742, 1743

trouvé [tʁuve]: 1050, 1193

trouver [tʁuve]: 1410, 1484, 1606, 1930

tu [ty]: 1120, 1127, 1134, 1150, 1260, 1265, 1285, 1287, 1296, 1337, 1372, 1404, 1413, 1414, 1420, 1426, 1427... +98

typhon [tifɔ̃]: 1707

un [d ɶ̃]: 1650

un [ɶ̃]: 1042, 1047, 1049, 1076, 1177, 1187, 1198, 1212, 1282, 1349, 1435, 1447, 1508, 1512, 1543, 1554, 1563, 1578, 1579, 1596... +43

un [ʁ ɶ̃]: 1025, 1026, 1050, 1153, 1250, 1372, 1384, 1392, 1442, 1484, 1492, 1495, 1500, 1501, 1554, 1586, 1593, 1594, 1606... +3

un [t ɶ̃]: 1042, 1076, 1091, 1170, 1227, 1456, 1477, 1521, 1666, 1691, 1704, 1712, 1713, 1888, 1999

un [z ɶ̃]: 1004, 1195, 1251, 1348, 1383, 1441, 1451, 1482, 1562, 1564, 1614, 1640, 1642, 1669, 1694, 1695, 1710, 1715, 1958, 1959... +1

une [d yn]: 1626

une [ʁ yn]: 1005, 1252, 1314, 1358, 1433, 1444, 1476, 1575, 1616, 1724, 1947, 1985, 1988

une [t yn]: 1151, 1185, 1196, 1248, 1309, 1316, 1319, 1389, 1630, 1688, 1693, 1709, 1723, 1726, 1834, 1860, 1869, 1953, 1973

une [yn]: 1009, 1026, 1091, 1152, 1158, 1160, 1220, 1228, 1279, 1312, 1321, 1323, 1335, 1343, 1383, 1391, 1399, 1400, 1446... +24

une [z yn]: 1003, 1198, 1203, 1385, 1423, 1485, 1613, 1614, 1653, 1663, 1664, 1682, 1722, 1843, 1843, 1857, 1983

usine [yzin]: 1003, 1091, 1857

utilise [n ytiliz]: 1093

utilisé [z ytilize]: 1030

utiliser [z ytilize]: 1087

utilises-tu [ytiliz ty]: 1326